NO CONFIDENCE

THE BREXIT VOTE AND ECONOMICS

DAVID E BLAND

This Edition 2016, First Edition (as *Sinking Britain*) 2013

Copyright, Dr David Bland

Published as an e-book, All rights reserved

Except by direct download on one occasion in each case by a bona fide direct purchaser, no part of this publication may be reproduced, stored in a retrieval system, or transmitted, in any form or by any means, electronic, mechanical, photocopying, recording or otherwise without the prior permission of the copyright owner.

Contents

Chapter One
The Context 1

Chapter Two
First Principles of a New Microeconomics. 23

Chapter Three
More About Keyns 55

Chapter Four
Quons, Brand, and Price. 105

Chapter Five
Productiveness and Productivity 131

Chapter Six
Consumers and Compromise 163

Chapter Seven
Past and Future. 189

Glossary 239

Chapter One

The Context

Rarely does a whole nation have the opportunity democratically to demand a fundamental change in policy and society. For the British, one such decision was to move quickly from the celebrations of Victory-in-Europe Day, in 1945, to the landslide election victory of the then-radical Labour Party. Another such event came on June 24, 2016, when the nation awoke to the recognition that the entire future prospect for the country could change.

The great majority of members of parliament had not wanted to be given the responsibility for deciding the direction that the nation should take, but an undeniable majority of the nation had voted thus. Aside from the pusillanimity of the political class, the most salient feature of the debate leading up to the referendum on June 23 was the dependency of the politicians who led the 'Remain' campaign on the near-unanimous opinion of Economists that quitting the European Union would be a catastrophe for the country.

On June 24, the media revelled in the fact that the 'political class' were the object of contempt by a majority of the active electorate, including many who had voted to remain in the EU, and that Economists were seen as the claque whose advice and admonition to successive governments had led most of the country to lose its traditional industries and all sense of economic optimism. Journalists finally acknowledged a widespread complaint that immigrants were perceived to be privileged above natives in the allocation of scare social housing and of benefits. In constantly batting aside this concern, the political class had produced statistics that ignored the estimated one million illegals, in an attempt to demonstrate that immigrants (origin unspecified) contributed more to the economy in taxes than they received in benefits.

On slightly more solid ground, they drew attention to the dependency of the National Health Service on immigrants; only after the succession of Mrs May to the premiership did they note the fact that a high proportion of British medical graduates, who had been funded by taxpayers, left the country to join better-financed health systems in the USA and the 'white commonwealth'. A significant majority of native British nurses had left the profession altogether because of low pay and overwork in a health service that was characterised by insensitive and arrogant management. The majority of the inhabitants of the relatively 'deprived' majority of the British landmass were well aware that successive governments – and especially the then-current government – had restricted the budget for the health service and reduced real-terms spending on most of the other services that make life tolerable for the sick and the disabled.

London voted in favour of remaining in the EU, which was no surprise. The standard of living is higher than in the rest of the UK for the vast majority of Londoners, even though lower earners have recently found the metropolitan housing market closed to them. The state subsidises London transport, police and other facilities that enable the city to run smoothly to a much higher level (*per capita* of population) than in the rest of the country. Similarly, Scotland voted pro-EU, with the English voters wryly conscious that the average Scot receives an annual 'subsidy' from the English estimated at £1,700. Although Caledonian nationalists lost their own referendum on independence in 2015, they regard the Scots as a distinct European Nation, a notion that many Scottish Conservatives also find appealing. Northern Ireland, the other pro-EU component of the UK in the referendum, had been heavily subsidised by the rest of the UK and very openly subject to the disbursement of massive EU funds. Also of vital importance is the fact that the two separate political entities in Ireland have become largely reconciled, and have welcomed a completely open border which might disappear if Northern Ireland leaves the European Union. It is conceivable that a narrow majority of the Ulster population would vote for a united Ireland, in which case the example and precedent of German reunification would be decisive; the EU did not require the former DDR for one microsecond to stand at the back of the queue of countries wanting accession, a member country simply expanded. Such a decision by the Irish would be a great relief for UK taxpayers and security services.

The new Prime Minister promised a new version of 'one-nation conservatism', reduced the privately-educated proportion of the cabinet, and took a strongly unionist line with Scotland. The stage is now set for society and the political system to liberate themselves from a powerful myth, the presentation of Economics as a scientific method for understanding a vital area of human activity and as the oracle from which policies may be received that purport to improve the lot of the species as a whole. In fact, Economics is built upon a series of pseudo-scientific 'models', intellectual structures which deploy mathematical formularies that ape Physical Science without being able to draw on a mass of experimental verification for their propositions.

Since 2011, first in Manchester, then in London and Cambridge, then almost worldwide, a small proportion of Economics students have had the effrontery to challenge their teachers as to whether what they teach even begins to explain the real world. The fulcrum on which this challenge was based is the utter failure of the professors to predict the economic crash of 2008; or even adequately to explain their failure several years after it happened.

Nevertheless, a broad consensus of their self-styled profession cockily called down doom and disaster on the concept of a sovereign Britain. No explanation of the past, and no credible forecast of the future, is possible within the scope of contemporary Economics. The subject is not sufficiently rational to cope with the world of flesh and blood and human behaviour. This disaster has been a long time brewing, but it is now clearly exposed, and the majority of the population is not conned by it.

Economics as the universities perpetrate it was developed in France, Germany, Switzerland, and Britain, and it was codified in Cambridge in 1890. This chapter summarises how the hegemony of the proponents of the subject became absolute in their surreal world. More than any other country, Britain has followed policies advocated by successive generations of Economists and has been more comprehensively damaged by such policies than any other country. Critics of that last sentence could point to the disastrous deployment of economic advice in Chile, after the fall of the Allende regime, and in Russia in the nineteen-nineties, but in both of those cases the damage was pretty quickly recognised, though recovery has been slow, patchy and incomplete. Millions who voted to 'Leave' the EU sensed that the British economy is in a desperately bad condition, and it is getting worse, despite the patronising platitudes to the contrary from politicians and Economists. Depressing evidence appeared daily in the media, the worst-ever peacetime balance-of-payments statistics were released, and as the referendum campaign dragged on, the government seemed helpless to resolve a potentially terminal crisis of the steel industry.

The slowly-evolving tragedy of the British economy is a cautionary tale, of which most British citizens are very well aware, but they understand little about how it came to be. From the start of 2014, the people were assured that the economy was experiencing a 'recovery' from the recession that followed the 2008 crash, with the official statistics showing strong 'economic growth' which exceeded the norm for the European Union and the United States.

The official statistics also showed that more people were in employment in the UK than ever before, but Middle England knew that an increasing proportion of the workforce received just the minimum wage per hour worked, and the imposition of even that modest level of remuneration put many smaller employers out of business. Various minorities among the workforce, including the young, 'illegals', and some self-employed contract workers, received less than the minimum wage, and some 903,000 employees had 'zero-hours' contracts under which they had no assurance as to how many hours in any week they might be asked to perform their tasks. The headlined economic growth and employment figures were regularly hailed as good news, so people were justified in asking what benefit they derived personally from this 'success'.

British government debt had not ceased to expand, it merely increased at a lesser rate as the government slashed spending, partially by reducing or abolishing services that made life pleasant for some people and tolerable for many more. Spending by households – on credit – remained the main driver of the growth in demand that sucked in material imports. Month by month there was more use of betting machines, and traders reported increased consumer demand for body ornamentation from hairdressers, nail shops, cosmetics and perfume specialists, tanning centres and tattoo parlours. Television and mobile-media fostered the obesity epidemic by promoting an expanding range of fast food outlets, with an increasing trend to deliver the food to the home and thus eliminate even a short walk by the customer. Supermarkets have been more or less successful according to their slickness in bringing the goods to housebound coach-potatoes. Meanwhile, industrial exports have not increased significantly, though under-recognised invisible exports of intellectual property have remained strong throughout the recession.

The growth of private debt – including credit card balances, student loans, and mortgages – set against the rundown of savings that has taken place in recent years, shows that the typical Briton lives an essentially hand-to-mouth existence, with most households having less than £1,000 of reserves to meet contingencies. Individuals' weekly spending of cash and credit, after the deduction of inescapable costs like mortgage servicing, council tax, motor insurance and hire-purchase on the car and on domestic appliances, is dominated by import-dependent consumption.

The presentation of the Gross National Product (the guesstimated total turnover of the economy), by official statisticians and by Economics think-tanks, conceals a dangerous trend; an economy like that of the British, that is 'growing' largely by increasing the number of transactions that distribute imported goods, purchased with the help of increasing consumer borrowing, is not an economy in a benign situation.

George Osborne's supposed achievement, as Chancellor of the Exchequer, in securing 'inward investment' did not contribute significantly to the balanced growth of the economy. Such 'investment' largely took the form of foreigners buying British businesses, complete with their intellectual property, which could then be exploited as and where the new owners saw fit. It was superficially more beneficial to the economy when foreign firms planted their brand-dependant outlets in the UK, but in those cases the alien owner could charge heavily for the use of their brands in the UK and alienate the resulting cash flow. Other alien institutions became owners of both old and projected infrastructure assets in the UK. All such investment ensured that the profits derived from those assets and activities could be alienated and thus not be allocable by native decision-takers. British employees of alien-owned firms face the prospect of increasingly being compelled to accept only internationally-competitive wages, while as consumers they will have to pay prices set by alien brand-owners. Such a pattern of relationships between controllers of capital, workers and consumers exacerbates both the systemic problems in the economy and the fissures in social structures, potentially leading to an even deeper sense of depression in future years.

Thus, in the twenty-tens, Britain's historically unprecedented peacetime balance-of-payments deficit with the rest of the world has been accompanied by the transfer of ever-increasing numbers of investment decisions to foreign interests. The Cameron government blatantly bribed aliens who were potentially investors in electric power supply and in the vanity railway project called HS2, with promises of returns that far exceeded realistic predictions of the construction costs and the potential revenues that would be derived from providing those utilities in a competitive context. A supine parliament and a superficially sensationalist press provided no effective resistance against such folly, which would require progressively impoverished British consumers and taxpayers to honour these contracts over many decades.

From the earliest history of humanity, people have understood that the passage of time does not simply mark a pattern of continual universal improvement of the human condition. Natural disasters, including diseases, can completely overturn the most careful economic plans and the most perfectly-balanced social structures. Armed conflicts tear apart social bonds as they destroy historical monuments and essential investments, and dissipate the resources that should be used to maintain and expand productive capacity. Non-violent disruption, such as was practiced by communist-influenced trade unions and their political affiliates in the West during the 'Cold War' of 1950-90 can significantly influence the performance of an economy, never for the better, though the impact of moderate socialism in the development of the welfare state and of the mixed economy was almost wholly benign.

In the calm of a seminar room it is easy for any group of decently-educated adults to agree that the future of the economy depends upon achieving a balance between consumption, material investment, and the recognition, development, and protection of intellectual property; yet the alienation of the profit from ventures that are located in a country inescapably influences the future pattern and prosperity of the economy. Between 1500 and 1950, massive expropriation of resources was experienced in the areas of the world that were incorporated in colonial empires, as well as in countries which retained a nominal independence while becoming 'economic colonies' of alien capitalism, epitomised in the 'banana republics' of Central America. Almost completely out of sight of the 'Economics profession' for more than a generation, Britain has been blundering into a new version of this subjugation. Even after the recent tweaking of the system of GDP accounting, reported 'investment' within the economy (very little of it creating industrial plant or major infrastructure outside London) is recorded as being some 14% of GDP, while China's investment has declined to some 40% of GDP and the world average is around 23%.

Any pretence that an economy can sensibly be understood independently of the role and actions of government is simply absurd. Those countries that have shaped their policies to reduce fossil fuel use, while the rest of the world continued to increase emissions, have condemned themselves to make massive investments in expensive 'green' technologies, and to make users pay far more for energy than do their competitors in highly polluting countries. Some of the countries that have taken the decision to 'go green' also have among the highest rates of growth of the elderly proportion of the population. The double-whammy of diverting investment into windmills and consequently making firms and families pay more for scarcer electricity, in addition to carrying the costs of supporting more aged citizens – many of whom have multiple health problems – means that countries that have taken those options have their economic growth rates reduced far below the potential optimum, and growth may become negative even before any drain of payments to foreign investors exacerbates the position. Such an outcome diminishes the future ability of the economy to sustain even the most desired social policies.

Old people constitute a greater proportion of the electorate than is indicated by their numbers, because they are more likely than younger people to vote. Grandparents may recognise that yet-unborn generations of their descendants will carry the only future that is available to their genes, but they vote and petition for policies that enable them to retain their accrued pension rights and entitlement to benefits for their natural lifetime. The length and enjoyment of that life-span depends heavily on the availability of medication and of procedures that owe everything to the continuing inventiveness of well-funded clinical science being implemented by investment in new products and facilities. Public awareness of these issues has been increased as a result of the EU membership referendum, where the older generation tended to vote Leave and the young to Remain; this has exacerbated the awareness of the young of their relative disadvantages in having student loan debts to carry as they confront an 'unaffordable' housing market.

Meanwhile, the irrefutable observation that the world is experiencing more extreme weather events, with greater frequency, makes damage from wind, rain, frost, and extreme heat costlier for the economy and more ruinous to people's lives and health. The more investment has been located in coastal cities, or in flood-prone inland locations, or in geologically-active areas, the greater is the risk from storms and surges and earthquakes. The repair and restoration of assets after such incidents is entirely unproductive; the expenditure of effort and materials to effect the repairs reduces the proportion of the national output which is available to raise general living standards and for potential investment in production, research, housing, schools, and the health service. Increasing migration of people, driven both by economic ambition and by the negative forces that create refugees, diminishes historic patterns of social conformity, disrupts the distribution of incomes (especially for the increasing majority of low-income earners), and increases the range of medical conditions that demand costly responses, quite separately from the costs of facing each global epidemic threat.

Differing responses to climate change and to developments in human demography show clearly the extent to which politics dominates the economy at different times in different countries. Beginning in the early seventeenth century, a succession of writers attempted to produce guidance for governments on how best to steer the economy to greater productiveness in ways that would increase wealth with the mutually beneficial impact that general living standards could be maintained, or even made to rise, while the capacity of the country to maintain armed forces and a magnificent monarchy was enhanced. Such texts became increasingly systematic and well-informed over time, and subject-matter gained the description of Political Economy. Nobody could claim that either commentators or the governments they sought to influence were entirely accurate in their proposals and their policies, but there was a broad consensus throughout Europe that political systems and circumstances were always influential, and often decisive, in setting the context for economic activity to be more or less successful than in other times and under other regimes.

Then, in 1776, a Scots professor of natural philosophy published a contrarian book in which his immediate objective was to refute the recent authoritative text on Political Economy by Sir James Stuart 'without once mentioning him'.

Adam Smith took up the extreme position that no economic policy could be perfect, so he railed against any government regulation of, or interference in, trade and industry. Thus he challenged the then prevailing protectionist policies that were broadly supported by reference to the established laws of Political Economy. He wanted the whole concept of Political Economy to be buried, as he argued that the economy would grow most effectively and rapidly if government was withdrawn as far as possible from all control of economic activities. He declared that there were natural laws operative in the economy as there were in the physical universe, and just as Newton had elaborated the laws of gravity that explained the movement of planets, of the tides and of apples falling from the tree, so he would explain economic activity. The universal force that he discerned in economic life was human self-interest; he asserted that if people were allowed to pursue their own interests in conditions of natural liberty, without legal constraint, they would maximise their personal wealth. They would trade with each other to maximise their advantages, this would work reciprocally throughout the system, and thus the aggregate wealth of their society would be maximised. But this would not be a dog-eat-dog society in which the relatively successful ground down the poor, the weak, the aged and the inadequate, because a successful economic system would encourage human beings to apply benevolence and public spirit in their dealings.

Smith's publication coincided with the US Declaration of Independence. The rebellious colonists defended themselves against British attempts to restore control from London. Louis XVI recognised an opportunity to weaken the old enemy and sent French forces to stiffen the colonists' campaign. The war spread into Europe and onto the high seas, and very soon after the British made peace with the French and the new USA, the bankruptcy of the French monarchy led to the convening of the States-General and the start of the revolution. The monarchies' war against the revolutionaries became a Europe-wide conflagration, and after General Bonaparte took control of France, the conflict became global, even drawing in the USA. British troops occupied Washington in the same year as Napoleon's forces were abandoned to freeze, starve, or be picked off by 'partisans' in the Russian campaign. The major European economies were completely dominated by the war, government demands for equipment facilitated growth and innovation in industry. The British blockade of the continent forced many innovations (exemplified by the continentals' development of beet-sugar production) and novel methods for financing the state created new methods of banking on an unprecedented scale.

Those who benefitted from these developments in the war were not keen to abandon them when the war was over. Governments had to service their debts and to stabilise the financial system. The usefulness of colonies to the imperial powers had been re-emphasised, and the boldest capitalists planned to maintain and grow their businesses on a global basis after the war. For the next century, Smith's proposition was extolled in principle as the 'great doctrine of Free Trade', but applications of the principle were restricted and, in most of the cases when it was tried, the experiment was modified or reversed after a short time. Taxation and other intervention in the economy by any British government was deemed necessary for national defence, especially to develop the navy as the global force that was necessary to hold the whole imperial construct together, and Smith had conceded that government had to be paid for when he restated the traditional 'canons' of taxation. He wrote passionately against colonisation and was utterly ignored on that point. Imperialist expansionists often asserted that they were opening-up territories for 'free trade', which really meant compelling less-developed areas to enter the global economy on disadvantageous terms relative to the colonial power. Smith's critics noted, with glee, that when he was employed as a government advisor to recommend how to reduce public spending, the first result was that two extra clerks had to be employed to copy papers and letters for him.

Just as practical considerations twisted Smith's advocacy of free trade into a cover for colonisation, the concept of free trade, as such, was challenged from a new angle in the middle of the nineteenth century by Karl Marx, who approvingly quoted a comment that Smith had been 'a half-bred and half-witted Scotsman'. Marx studied avidly the textbooks and controversial publications that continued to use the term Political Economy in direct defiance of Smith's dogma. Ricardo, Malthus, Sismondi, Say, List, and Bastiat created a lively intellectual community that attempted to accommodate Smith's grand design in the real world. Thus, the mainstream of Political Economy developed the liberal view that a minimalist government could best let economic growth proceed organically, but they lived with the alternative reality of imperial power. Marx predicted that a catastrophically inhumane outcome would result if capitalism was free to expand unchecked.

The rapid popularisation of Marx's ideas by a minority of intellectuals and among the partially-educated 'lower orders' caused concern among the emergent middle classes, some of whom felt that Political Economy did not provide them with arguments that were sufficiently robust to refute Marx's prognosis. Hence, authors in several European countries were seeking a way of describing the economy that predicted less 'gloomy' outcomes than were predicted by orthodox Political Economy as it was consolidated in JS Mill's magisterial textbook, published in 1848 and retained as the core textbook at Oxford University until 1918 and at Manchester for a further decade.

In contrast to political economists, the new writers evaded the dilemmas which they would have had to resolve if they tried to accommodate their theory to the political and institutional structures that dominated the real world. They attempted to emulate the methodology of the natural sciences, by constructing a theoretical model of an imaginary market unconstrained by place, space, time, human physiology or psychology. They set Adam Smith's principle of self-interest as the motivating force of this fanciful universe, in which competition would be so free that Marx's warning of capitalism moving to a phase of monopoly control of the economy by the surviving capitalists could not occur. They developed Pareto's idea that the economy could find its own 'general equilibrium', in which free competition would eventually bring the system to a point where all accessible resources were deployed optimally to give the maximum total amount of satisfaction to the human race.

A majority of the people who became teachers of Political Economy in the expanding university system after 1870 accepted the challenge by WS Jevons, the professor at Manchester, that if teachers of economy wanted their lectures and writings to be accepted as 'scientific', their pedagogy must make extensive use of mathematics, as natural scientists had done for centuries. Contemporary physics and chemistry taught that everything that could be observed in the entire universe was built up from a limited number of elements, which displayed characteristics that Keynes later termed 'atomism and limited variety'. The new school who called themselves economists identified *transactions* as being the equivalent of 'atoms' in their economic universe, and they postulated that an economy – to be seen as a complex of transactions – would function most efficiently if no sociopolitical institutions interfered with the operation of the market.

This model was codified and promulgated in Alfred Marshall's *Principles of Economics* (1890), and over the next fifty years the self-styled 'Economics profession' spread their dogmas through the developing academic system. Many layers of modelling have subsequently been added to the scheme of theory that makes up Economics, and as successive policy prescriptions from Economists have contributed to the relative decline of the West, so the more extreme and dogmatic their assertions have become.

In this text, 'Economics' and 'Economist(s)' with capital letters refer to writing and to writers/teachers who follow the dogmas established by Marshall, his peers, and their successors.

By 1990, the orthodox dogma was centred on the absurd assertion that pure ratiocination can lead people to form 'rational expectations' (both as individual consumers and as business decision-takers), and this naïve notion was carried forward into the twenty-first century. It has already been noted that, even after the 2008 economic crash, the vast majority of professors ignored students' challenges about the validity of the subject. Just a few academics who wanted to appease their students introduced snippets from Marx, Engels, Keynes and other long-suppressed authorities to demonstrate that there was an accessible spectrum of historical material available. These optional marginalia to the syllabus in a few institutions did not directly challenge the complex modelling of vacuity that formed the core curriculum. Mainstream Economics has held steady; those students who could accept and assimilate the dogma became the favoured postgraduates who would carry the faith into the next generation, more doggedly oblivious to reality.

The vast majority of Economics graduates escape into the world of work, where they slough off the dogma without saying anything that would diminish the perceived merit of their qualifications as essential data in their curricula vitarum.

Marshall's system became known as 'Microeconomics' around 1940, after his former pupil, JM Keynes, had developed the concept that the state should deploy the public sector to influence the dynamics of the total economy, which came to be known as 'Macroeconomics'. Microeconomics remained largely an academic pursuit, confined to textbooks and classrooms in the postwar years down to the mid-nineteen-fifties, chiefly because most of the distribution of goods and services in Europe was volumetrically rationed and subject to price control. Alongside the bureaucratic allocation of available supplies between investment and consumption was a labyrinthine complex of 'black markets', which most people (and most firms) accessed at least occasionally when they needed to buy something that was not available to them officially. Neither the rationing system, with strict price controls, nor the black market was anything like 'the market' that Economists declared was the ideal mechanism for delivering satisfaction to human beings.

Thus, from the early nineteen-fifties, under Conservative governments and most notably during the premiership of Harold Macmillan (whose firm published both Marshall's and Keynes's books), wartime controls on the British micro-economy were relaxed, starting with the progressive withdrawal of quantitative rationing of consumer goods. Then, retail price controls were relaxed, followed by some controls on the creation of credit. But as they tried to foster a complex of open micro-markets analogous to the Marshallian theory, politicians also tried to create a macroeconomic environment where they deployed fiscal and monetary 'levers' to stimulate or damp-down the total amount of spending and investment in the economy, aiming to produce an equilibrium of full employment with stable, non-inflationary economic growth. Two sets of 'tools' were available for governments to use to this end. Fiscal methods are to increase or reduce taxes, and to increase or reduce government spending. Monetary methods deploy the Bank of England to adjust interest rates up or down (by changing the 'base rate' at which the

Bank of England will lend money to viable, approved financial businesses) and by increasing or decreasing the available money supply.

Virtually every supposed liberalisation of the UK micro-economy since the Second World War has been accompanied by the removal of state support from the 'supply side' of the economy, which led to increased unemployment of formerly-productive technicians and artisans, as well as to factory closures. The rate of factory closures and the abortion of investment projects also increased whenever a 'squeeze' was applied to the macro-economy, and British firms' plans for major investments, made in periods of economic expansion, frequently died or were dramatically curtailed in the subsequent credit squeeze. In cases where firms had been carrying significant spare capacity through a recession, and thus had the means to produce more goods or provide additional services when a macroeconomic stimulus occurred, consumers' increased demand could be met by indigenous suppliers. But even in that benign case, there was often an increase in the import of materials that were used as inputs to the increased output, and wages rose whenever firms had to compete for a small pool of skilled labour.

Thus, each relaxation of macro-economic controls (usually characterised by an increase in the creation of consumer credit) led to a surge in imports before there was any significant increase in the home economy's capacity to produce the most-preferred goods, due to the lead-time and the cost that were necessary for plant to be ordered, built, installed and brought into use. The combined effect of increasing expenditure on imports and the rising price of labour would raise the alarm that the economy was 'overheating', so the next squeeze would be imposed. This alternation of restrictive and then relaxed economic management, which became known as 'stop-go' policy, prevailed from 1950 to 1975.

By contrast, elsewhere in Europe, institutional structures ensured that there was much more secure investment in appropriate developments. The ubiquitous influence of the network of graduates from the French *hautes ecoles* ensured that French industry's plans were agreed with the appropriate ministries, before finance was secured through banks and insurance organisations that were controlled by holders of the *mandat*. In Germany, loans from the state-underpinned regional banks carefully directed selective investments that either reduced the country's dependence on imports or built-up export capable industries. Such investments, once initiated, were carried to fruition. The contrast between creeping British deindustrialisation and selective ongoing investment that was maintained elsewhere in northern Europe was well-established before the Thatcher government abandoned the stop-go chaos of bowdlerised neo-Keynesiansm by adopting policies that led to wholesale destruction of industry.

Company failures increase in periods when the economy is experiencing a recession, which may follow from a government-induced credit squeeze or from a systemic market failure. Alternatively, in periods when the number of transactions is growing strongly, successful firms buy less dynamic firms so that they can deploy greater productive capacity and more extensive intellectual property to optimise sales as quickly as possible. Both aggressive and defensive mergers and acquisitions of companies can ultimately create an oligopoly in each significant sector of trade and of industry. This is the situation where a few large suppliers can collude in a 'cartel', to control the market. Such an arrangement operates to the disadvantage of the firms' suppliers and customers.

Both Marx and Marshall observed this tendency, which was particularly powerful in the USA after the Civil War. Marx regarded this as a stage in the dehumanising progress of untrammelled capitalism, a stage on the route to monopoly; Marshall admitted that his idealist concept of a market could only be sustained if the natural behaviour of business organisations was inhibited by the rigorous application of competition (or 'anti-trust') law. Supposedly autonomous markets can only exist under the careful and constant supervision of a powerful state; self-generating 'free competition' is a myth, and the textbook model of progressively equalizing supply and demand is fantasy. Since the existence of regulatory bodies to ensure that 'competition' is directed and constricted in almost every sector of the economy, the public tolerance of an Economics that is based on utterly fantastic assertions of the efficacy of 'natural' competition is itself extraordinary.

The free movement of people around the world is increasingly inhibited by the fear of terrorism and by the rise of ethnic and cultural tensions as pressure of demand on schools, health facilities, and benefit systems becomes unsustainable. There is also growing pressure for international travellers to be vaccinated and checked for dangerous transmissible diseases.

International movements of weaponry, including chemical and biological components that can be used lethally, are controlled. The idea that allowing free trade in 'recreational' drugs will reduce international crime, especially along the southern borders of the USA, around the Caribbean and in Afghanistan, is confronted by the observation that countries importing heroin and cocaine openly would have to impose heavy taxation on the trade to pay for the significant long-term health consequences that could follow from more widespread consumption, so the mass smuggling of untaxed drugs of dubious purity would continue. Free trade, the highest ideal of Economists for many generations, is a fantasy; thousands of examples demonstrate that universal free competition is a toxic delusion.

The most successful firms in both domestic and international trade are those that have exclusive control of the relevant intellectual property, brands, patents, copyright, and trademarks. Such brands are all monopolies that the state protects in return for receiving fees for licences and taxes on sales. Individuals who own significant patents and brands, or who themselves become popular 'brands' as actors, sportsmen, authors, and suchlike, become super-rich. Massively disproportional wealth is also accessible to some operatives in the monetary trades, who must be licensed and underwritten by regulated institutions, a control that failed in the run-up to the 2008 crash and which remains highly fallible. Grossly exaggerated incomes are also allocated to chief executives and their close associates in many businesses, whose directors sit on each other's boards, forming an open conspiracy of past and present executives who serve as members of each other's remuneration committees. These individuals share a common interest in bumping up the share-and-salary packages that such individuals are awarded, often without adequate control being exercised over loosely-stated performance requirements. Paradoxically, the French author Thomas

Piketty has made a modest fortune for himself from owning the intellectual property in his representation of the socially disruptive phenomenon of increasingly extreme differentiation of the super-rich from the masses.

The Chinese authorities, who will continue to delay the full introduction of protection of aliens' brands, patents, and copyrights within their territory, have puckishly suggested that protected intellectual property is the denial of free trade, which is, of course, the well-understood but rarely spoken truth. A patent gives an inventor exclusive control of the registered idea for a period of years, during which the patentee may charge users for access to their property. The revenue thus earned may be used to enhance the inventor's wealth and lifestyle, or invested in the search for new ideas, after the taxman has taken his slice. Copyright is the right of someone who successfully claims first to have expressed an idea to take the credit for it, and to be paid a fee every time it is copied or cited, for a period that is usually longer than for a patent, especially where it applies to literary, musical, and artistic creations. Brands and trademarks can endure permanently, and their owners can relocate their domicile to a jurisdiction where taxation, macroeconomic policy, and the legal framework are seen as the most favourable to the proprietor.

The role of the state in the detailed development of the economy is by no means wholly exploitative and restrictive. A prime example of the productiveness of state activity lies in the fact that, for hundreds of years, government research establishments have been among the most successful generators of patentable ideas. This is especially true in relation to publicly-owned facilities and laboratories located in firms and universities that are working on defence or strategically innovative projects. State spending in response to current or potential military threats (including the space race and cyber security), as well as inter-state competition to harness new technologies, led to the emergence of thousands of commercially applicable inventions during the twentieth century. In 1970, Britain had a huge range of advanced product design and manufacturing facilities both under state ownership and in firms supplying the government and their sub-contractors.

Half a century of government spending cuts and privatisations has led to the disappearance of most of that capacity, and the redundancy of the skills that it fostered. The few relatively successful ex-nationalised firms that are still domiciled in the UK, such as Rolls-Royce, are owned by investors from all over the world and sell their products globally; short-term economic considerations have combined with an intensification of British government spending cuts to put even RR in jeopardy from asset-strippers and activist investors. Ongoing UK government retrenchment has meant that other major firms – notably BAE – are now dependent for their increasingly precarious survival on the strength of their sales to foreign defence establishments, and they are also dependent for new capital on investment by foreign agencies and firms. Such defence-related businesses are also vulnerable to pressure to refuse to deal with oppressive regimes and to inhibitions on making deals due to economically self-destructive anti-bribery laws. The one certainty that follows from reviewing recent economic history is that any policy that directly attempts to implement the Economists' fixation on 'competition' in a context of 'rational expectations' will be a calamitous failure.

Ministers in the Cameron governments tried to present a complacent picture of a 'growing economy' while everybody knew that inequalities of incomes were increasing, homes were much more expensive to buy or to rent year after year, exports were at best sluggish while imports were increasing, and that the system was dependent on financial trades that ministers and regulators partially struggled to understand. The absence of any advance warning, during 2006-7, from Economists of the impending credit crunch, to which Queen Elizabeth II referred during visits to the London School of Economics and to the Bank of England, proclaimed the intellectual bankruptcy of Economics. That abject failure of the whole 'profession' was followed by the predictions of doom that supported the campaign to scare the British population into voting to remain EU subjects, in the unnecessary and economically risky referendum that was called in June, 2016. The puerile responses that a few professors submitted to the sovereign many weeks after she had posed the question in the LSE reinforced public contempt for the academic chimera. The more Economists who supported George Osborne's arguments for the Remain side in the EU referendum, the more sceptical the public became.

There were always honourable exceptions to the hegemony of normative Economics. Some freethinkers, including a very few dissident Economists, issued premonitory warnings of a coming crisis before 2008, but the contumacious majority of Economists have stayed in post and carried on teaching, writing, and 'peer reviewing' ever more complex essays in irrelevance.

I wasted half a century of my own life trying to believe that there must be some validity in the fashionable form of Economics, which could surely be tweaked into a rational format by readmitting Keynes to the pantheon and incorporating his capacity for sensible observation of the world. Now I have decided to waste no more time on a failed pseudo-science and to offer my simple understanding of where Britain stands in the world economy in these very dangerous times, and how far Economics has contributed to the calamity. This book's second purpose is to recognise the ongoing validity of significant aspects of political economy, the science that was shelved (but never refuted) when Economics was adopted in the non-communist universities between 1890 and 1930.

During the deep recession that began in 2008, the electorate in the UK became so deeply conscious of the impotence of non-celebrity individuals and so acutely aware of the lack of strength and flexibility in the economy that the majority concluded that the political class is an ignorant and intermittently vicious enemy of humanity. In the first weeks of 2014 – eighteen months away from a general election – ministers and Economists began to proclaim a recovery in the economy. The published data showed rising turnover in the economy. At the same time, unpopular reductions in the rate of increase in spending on the health service and in social support systems were presented as inevitable for national survival. Through both the coalition government of 2010-15 and the improbable Tory majority governments that followed it, Britain's private and public debt continued to increase and Chancellor Osborne's cuts became deeper. Six weeks after he left office, the 'need' for even deeper cuts in the health service was disclosed. The referendum result is, in itself, proof of the widespread public belief that change is needed, not simply in the details of economic policy but in its entire orientation. This book is a modest attempt to present some indications of how that turnaround might be approached.

Chapter Two
First Principles of a New Microeconomics

Textbook microeconomics does not even state the basic principles on which economic systems actually rest. So here I will build the basis for an objective understanding of the massively regulated economic system on which all human beings depend. I can only present the results of my own observations; which involves giving names to everyday phenomena that are known to almost everyone, but which have not previously been defined and designated in this way. So here goes!

Economic Entities, Responsibilities, and Rights

Each person who is legally an adult in a genuinely free society is – in principle -empowered to own things, to buy and to sell, to work and to receive payment for work, to accumulate data, to learn and to form concepts, and to give and receive contractual promises. Very recently, global networking has enabled individuals to formulate their own attitudes and articulate their preferences more fully than at any previous time in history. In principle, economic freedom, under the rule of law, enables individuals to get the things that ensure their survival.

Most people in what used to be the most advanced economies, in the short period of affluence between 1960 and 2008, acquired purchasing-power with which to get things and experiences that provided them with a comfortable and enjoyable lifestyle. Since the crash of financial markets in 2008, there are strong indications that the majority of under-thirties in the UK and several other post-industrial countries will not attain the combination of assets and lifestyle experiences that is currently enjoyed by the over-sixties.

While global wealth has increased, income-generating opportunities for individuals have narrowed and the socio-economic stratification of people according to incomes has become more marked. Individuals who wish to become innovators find that investors are harder to find and to convince of the merits of ideas, and the terms on which finance is available become increasingly onerous. If they are able to establish successful businesses, they face demands for taxes and levies, while the use of many materials and processes is subject to a huge amount of restriction and regulation. The cornucopia of possibilities that has been opened by mass access to the internet has necessarily led to controls that extend far beyond anti-terrorist measures into a whole range of methods to protect children, holders of intellectual property, and many areas of the political establishment.

Every economic event follows from a decision that is taken by a living human person on his or her own responsibility, or on behalf of an entity that is empowered to act as a 'legal person', such as a company, a government agency, or a voluntary organisation. Every natural or legal person is an entity that can create, acquire, retain, sell, give, use, damage, destroy, or ingest material things; he or she can also receive services and undergo a massive range of experiences. Individuals can also take action to avoid exposure to experiences that they do not wish to undergo. Legal persons – organisations – can be granted rights, powers, and obligations that are similar to those that exist for a citizen. Every recognised person can own both material things and immaterial assets (such as shares in companies, bank deposits, and intellectual property) over long periods of time. Individuals and organisations make contracts that create liabilities to other organisations and individuals, which the counterparties can regard as their assets, and they can receive promises from other individuals and organisations which they can treat as their assets. The components of the micro-economy are:

1. human beings, and organisations that possess legal personality,
2. their assets and liabilities, including the processes by which assets are processed and transmogrified, and the means by which both material things and concepts are transported or transmitted.

These entities exist in (or adjacent to) the physical environment of the Earth and are heavily susceptible to direction, influence, and interference from the state (or community of states) which rules the territory where their material assets are located, and, in the case of immaterial assets, in the state where the assertion of proprietary, or the licence or the contract by which each asset was created or recognised, is legally logged and validated.

Human decisions set in train events that create, transport, transform, trade, retain, use, and ultimately destroy assets. Assets are material things, as well as experiences and situations that are sufficiently desired by people and organisations that they are willing to exchange other assets, including natural persons' talents, thoughts, and labour (their capacity to work), to gain control of them. It is easy to forget that the overwhelming majority of economic decisions that are taken in any period are default decisions to retain assets in their current use with their existing legal status, and to retain the pattern of assets, debts, and obligations that has been accumulated. Those default decisions imply the commitment of a significant proportion of the agent's income to a predetermined spending pattern, which limits the residue of income that is available for entering into new transactions.

Transactions in which the ownership or lease of assets is transferred from one person or entity to another are a vastly smaller proportion of the economy than the myriad unstated and often unconscious decisions to keep assets as they are. For hundreds of years, assets have collectively been known as 'wealth', meaning all the resources that are available to an individual, to an organisation, to a state, or to a community. Unless the responsibility of an individual or a legal person in relation to an asset is clear – and is enforceable at law – there is a probability that it will be less efficiently deployed in serving humanity than it could and should be. The wave of vandalism that defaced many European and North American cities with graffiti, forced the closure of public lavatories and made parks into no-go zones, most notably in the nineteen-seventies, emerged as a concomitant of the concept that the economy had by then become so affluent that confrontations to protect public goods or some classes of private assets were not worth the mental and physical stress that would fall on the building manager, the park keeper, the police officer, the school teaching assistant, or the would-be good citizen who might have intervened to prevent vandalism in less prosperous times. Individuals were coached by socially-challenging novels and plays and films, glossy magazines, lavish advertising, and peer pressure to concentrate on their own consumption. This entailed the acquisition of assets, heedless of the fact that the potential resale prices of more and more of the assets that they owned became less than the increment in debt that the owner had incurred to acquire them.

Most people spend periods of their adult lives sharing aspects of their functionality, especially as consumers, in family and other affinity groups. This interactivity was historically based predominantly on physical proximity to the other people in the group, but the internet and mobile communications have enabled manifold different types of relationship to form, and many non-domestic affinity groups transcend the boundaries of states. Households are still the most common groups that share assets (particularly material assets), among whom breeding pairs of heterosexuals predominate. But there are several types of group in which the participants pool some of their consumption and some of their assets and liabilities with the others, ranging from the genetically close intergenerational family to the frequently-changing diverse occupants of a student house. As the law and social morality have changed, members of affinity and domestic groups necessarily distinguish between:

A) The individual's personal economic activities and assets
B) Each participating individual's interest in the assets and activities that are conjoint in their family, household, or other group.

Many non-domestic aggregations of assets and liabilities under shared ownership are formed with specific purposes, such as business partnerships, or when people with similar interests or concerns form clubs and charitable organisations. Once such collectives are established, they can become licensed to exist independently by adopting an appropriate form of corporate identity, which can acquire legal personality that is separate from the individuals who constituted it. The people who are engaged in the functioning of the entity are legally required to differentiate clearly between things that are done for and on behalf of the organisation, and actions that they take in their personal capacity outside the organisation.

A sophisticated economy is created by individuals operating in and with licensed organisations, each of which is legally capable of constructing around itself an estate. Each of the components of the estate can be estimated to have a notional disposal or replacement price, as occurs with the probate of a deceased person's assets or to determine the compensation to be paid by the insurer after a fire or flood. The constituents of an estate are both material and immaterial, and they may be located in several countries, thus they are defined and regulated under various legal systems and accounting standards, but all assets fall within four discrete categories which have distinct economic properties (or characteristics) that give rise to four fundamentally different pricing systems, each of which has multifarious sub-sets. The broad outline of this differentiation was recognised by political economists in the eighteenth and nineteenth centuries, but not crystallised in the manner that is set out below. Economics has ignored the existence of the differentiation. This failure largely accounts for the irrelevance of the contemporary academic subject to 'real life'.

Four Types of Asset

The four categories of assets in the economy are, firstly:

1. ***Keyn***

Pronounced '*cane*' as in *sugar cane*.

This designation recognises JM Keynes's unique and original understanding of immaterial assets, as set out especially in his *Treatise on Money* (1929). The category (which Keynes described as 'chartalist assets') covers all the assets that are created by the human mind and recognised in law to exist. This includes natural and constitutional rights, cash, and the ownership of deposits with banks and with other savings institutions, plus the legal situation that makes persons the owners of land, of other 'real property', and of bonds, bills, stocks, shares, mortgages, pension entitlements, deferred savings, rights under insurance policies, and any other sub-category of financial asset, including any rights that are acquired in gambling contracts. All intellectual property is in this category also, because it is the result of human creativity expressed in a form that can be granted legal protection as being a possession of the creator, or of the organisation for and on behalf of which she or he was working when the concept emerged.

Over the past few decades, the Bank of England and its fellow central banks, as well as the other financial regulators, have accepted derivatives, swaps, and other gambling contracts as also being financial assets. When Keynes issued his greatest book, 'commodity futures' were a class of assets that linked directly to future deliveries of crops that were growing or minerals that were about to be extracted from mines within the timeframe specified in the contract. Uncertainty arose because a crop might fail, or be much bigger than normal due to optimal weather conditions, with a dramatic effect on prices, and a mine accident or the discovery of a new seam of some mineral might dramatically cut or increase the year's output as compared to what had been expected when the contracts were struck. Additional uncertainty arose from the fact that demand for the commodity, once it was available for delivery, might be more or less than what had been anticipated at any earlier date. Both on his personal account and as a bursar of his college, Keynes traded largely and successfully in those markets, drawing on his personal and academic interest in probability to manage the risks that arise in economic activity through the passing of time.

Since Keynes's lifetime, a vastly expanded range of types of futures have been created among a maelstrom of gambling contracts, including swaps, derivatives, and other deals that sometimes facilitate real-world trade when they are used by manufacturing and commodity-moving firms as hedges to mitigate the impact of unexpected variations in input costs, but which are mostly used simply for speculation by trader/gamblers, many of whom are funded and loosely supervised by incorporated financial firms. This business made a great deal of money for thousands of the participants as regulation was progressively relaxed over the years between 1980 and 2008. These activities generated a great deal of taxation and consumer spending in the centres where they were encouraged, and they will be a major source of friction in the upcoming negotiations on the UK's future relationship with the European Union.

This entire range of betting business should be kept wholly separate from the balance sheets of both retail and investment banks. Banks and investment funds should be permitted to invest in specialist betting firms, as shareholders and possibly as bondholders, under strictly defined conditions and with all such holdings properly registered, but they should not themselves be bookmakers, nor should they have bookmaking subsidiaries.

An expanding range of 'wholesale' betting in expanding financial markets can be encouraged on the basis of a realistic set of rules, governed by strong, subtle regulators who are possessed of draconian powers.

Properly managed gambling can be a huge source of international earnings for the London market, which has been the global leader in these innovations, but it should wholly be separated from the terrestrially-necessary trades of banking, insurance, stockbroking, and fund management that serve the real economy. The trading balance of the British economy was supported by the global earnings of the financial services sector between

1990 and 2008, and the whole spectrum of finance, from insurance to gambling with derivatives, remains vitally important as a contributor to the balance of trade. Thus it is depressing that successive British governments, bound by the rules and the conservative attitudes of the EU, have shirked from making the appropriate regulatory changes that hive off financial gambling into its distinct silos. Now the country's imminent partial emancipation from the European Union should enable a new era to begin in this sphere, while the nanny-state approach by the EU bureaucracy will prevent any potential rival to the London market from succeeding on a comparable scale. Such a separation of economically important finance from gambling should enable relatively straightforward arrangements to be made for 'passporting' mainstream British banking and insurance brands into the EU, on a reciprocal basis.

The defining characteristic of keyns is that they have no material substance; there may be certificates of their existence – such as charters, paper share certificates and bank statement printouts – but the actual keyns are either promises or declarations. These are set out in entries in the land register and in deeds to property, as well as in assertions of ownership of intellectual property, and in other forms by which a legally enforceable right to own a keyn can be expressed. In an increasingly wide range of cases where records are electronically created and maintained, no paper instrument is required for the contract or the asserted ownership of financial assets and of intellectual property to be enforceable. Sometimes, dangerous volatility can be brought to the price of shares if some shareholders 'lend' their shares to activists who want to use the votes that the shares carry; this should be illegal, the powers of shareholders should only be exercised by the responsible registered owners. The prices of new issues of shares and of bonds are based on the performance record and the perceived security of the issuer, weighted by the expectation of the buyers as to what predictable economic events might affect the financial results to be reported by the issuer over the proposed duration of the contract, and influenced by the present and anticipated levels of interest rates. Similar considerations should apply to trade in existing shares.

Within the parameters set by the law, by regulators, and heavily influenced by the incidence of taxation and the impact of monetary policy, people and corporate entities can create many forms of keyn (including many gambling contracts) by sheer act of will. If I can find a firm or an individual willing to extend credit to me, I can create a debt. Every such contract establishes a legally enforceable liability from me to the lender, which lasts throughout the life of the contract. A regulator may require my bank to give me a regular statement of the status of the loan that I have taken from the bank, with a reminder of all the attendant liabilities that fall upon me, and to notify me of any change in terms – such as interest rates – that apply in accordance with the contract. But the primary responsibility for ensuring that the terms of the contract are met lies with me as the creator of the obligation. Businesses create keyns in the forms of contracts, shares, bills of exchange, letters of credit, bonds, and other securities, which they sell to other economic entities, or exchange, or lease to each other.

So-called investment banking facilitates these streams of business, and lawyers make fortunes in formulating and challenging contracts. The market price of any existing keyn, on any day, depends on the potential buyer's current estimate of the capacity of the creator of the keyn to meet the terms of the contract under which the keyn was created; current accounting conventions call this the *fair value* of the keyn. Gambling contracts cannot be assigned an enduring 'fair value', they depend on contingent events and, if sold, they can only be priced according to the perceived probability of the materialisation, or avoidance, of the event that is the subject of the bet. A huge proportion of derivatives and other bets lapse, as allowed for in the contract that created them, long before they come to a point for settlement.

Virtually every personal or corporate estate carries debts, a mortgage, a credit card 'balance', an overdraft, a repayment due to a bondholder, obligations to employees, shareholders, or other stakeholders, or an emergent debt to the taxman. Some of these obligations are 'secured' by material assets; a house stands as security for the mortgage that is explicitly linked to the price for which it was bought, or a work of art may be designated as the security for a business loan. The debt is not owed by the cited asset, however, but by the person or organisation that created the debt, and the contract fails if the creator cannot ultimately settle it. Failures of this kind were the proximate cause of the crisis triggered by 'sub-prime' mortgage defaults by thousands of households in the USA in 2004-8.

Most transfers of credit from persons to financial institutions are instalments in a long-term process of repaying the principal and paying interest arising from the debtor's creation of liabilities in the past; the payments occur as direct debits and standing orders that, in aggregate, absorb a significant proportion of the individual's available bank credit month by month.

All keyns depend for their continuance in existence on the legal protection that is given to contractual rights, under the rule of law. Any economically active entity can distinguish three sub-categories of keyn in its estate:

A) **ik** *(an item of intellectual property,* or *intellectual capital)*, which is any legally enforceable status or right, including personal or corporate identity, and any concept, idea, image, process, design, or literary work that can be defended at law as being the property of a person or an organisation of some kind. Patents, copyrights, trademarks, and brands fall into this category.

B) **ka** *(keynic assets)*, these include bank deposits, shares, bonds, pension rights, the fact of being the owner (or licensed user) of any asset, entitlement to indemnification under insurance contracts, and entitlements under gambling contracts. These can all be recorded in the asset register of the estate.

C) **ko** *(keynic obligations)*, this category covers all the borrowings and debts that have been incurred by the estate, including the obligation to pay all consequential interest and service charges that are due when the time for each payment arrives. Commitments to meet gambling obligations, including historic obligations incurred in the course of 'casino banking', and all emergent obligations to pay taxes, are **ko**s.

(Note that *ik* is pronounced '*ick*' as in *quick*, *ka* as in *car*, and *ko* as in *cocoa*.)

A debt is not normally extinguished in the event of the destruction or diminution of a specific asset that was put up as security when the **ko** was created. For example, the mortgage obligation that was incurred when an individual, a collective, or a legal person bought a house remains outstanding even if recurrent flooding makes the house uninhabitable or if a fire destroys it. All **ko**s that an estate owner has created become due for settlement when the estate is wound up, which occurs following the death of an individual human being, or the closure of a business or charity.

A regular verification of solvency is required to enable corporate businesses to retain the right to exist; each such entity must prove that it is a 'going concern'. Both corporations and individuals are normally required to submit evidence of solvency – being able to pay any bills that may fall due to be paid within a defined period – before any other firm or person is willing to purchase a keyn that the would-be borrower wishes to create, and any buyer who fails to verify the security of the issuer accepts an inestimable risk of default.

The net keyn position (**K**) of an economically active person or corporate body is derived from:

$$(\mathbf{\mathit{ik}} + \mathbf{\mathit{ka}}) - \mathbf{\mathit{ko}} = \mathbf{K}.$$

2. *Jev*

Pronounced like '*dev*' in '*Devon*'.

In the middle of the nineteenth century, WS Jevons asserted that the only sensible way of showing the *value* of anything was to accept the buyer's subjective assessment; 'how many pounds, or pennies am *I* prepared to spend on acquiring it, here and now?' In the taxonomy used in this book, jevic pricing applies to those classes of material assets for which the buyer's willingness-to-pay alone determines the price, and the concept of *value* is left for the philosophers. Assets in the *jev* category can variously be categorised as:

- fine art (paintings, sculpture, etc.)
- antiques (including musical instruments, tools, etc.)
- archaeological finds
- geological, mineralogical, and biological specimens
- memorabilia
- rare and special books
- incunabula
- manuscripts
- ephemera
- curios
- and other classes of 'collectibles'.

When any of these things is sold, it is priced exclusively by the amount that the keenest financially capable intending buyer is willing to pay for it. In any case, the seller can state a 'reserve', the minimum price that she will accept, and the item is withdrawn from the market if offers do not meet the reserve.

Buyers are often guided on how much to offer by experts who verify the provenance and/or offer an opinion as to the 'quality' of the jev in relation to others in the same class, but the decision to make an offer for the jev is always taken by the buyer. For probate, and for an insurance or tax assessment of the cost of replacing it, each jev that is an inventoried item in an estate can be inferred to be sellable at approximately the same price that was agreed in the most recent sale of a closely similar object in the same category. The historical cost of producing and originally marketing the physical object has no bearing on the contemporary price of a jev that may be offered for sale.

The state and the courts protect the ownership of jev-related *ik* (such as the right to claim copyright on reproductions of an artwork that the estate owns), this is derived from the significant public and private wealth that is locked up in jev ownership. Acquiring jevs is part of the strategy by which wealthy individuals and some corporate entities accumulate broad portfolios of long-term assets. Legal costs may arise from verifying the provenance of works of art, or are incurred in defining or defending the status of the artists and the authority of verifiers of their works.

A majority of the paintings, statues, and other artworks by the greatest dead artists belong to museums and trusts that intend to own them permanently, so relatively few such items come to market and when they do the price is usually determined by auction. Prices do not necessarily fall if a series of pieces by the same deceased artist happen to come on sale in the same year, because the price of each jev is determined exclusively by the competition between the potential buyers who bid for the particular item at the time of the sale. Successful living artists sometimes limit the amount of output that they produce, to keep the price per unit high; others, like Picasso, leave behind a huge stock of unsold pictures as an endowment for their children or for their favoured good causes, to be trickled onto the market at a rate that keeps prices high over many years.

Costs are incurred in maintaining many jevs. Delicate artifacts and works of art must be kept in controlled environments to minimise material degeneration, and many jevs have to be protected from thieves and vandals by active security measures. These costs are justified by owners because jevs retain their perceived price estimate through time; a jev can be owned for many years, then be sold to acquire cash with which the vendor can meet **ko** liabilities, or seize an emerging business or consumer opportunity. When a jev serves as security for a loan, the contract by which the keyn was created usually specifies that the jev must be insured, so that if the jev should be stolen or destroyed, the insurer makes available the cash that may then be required to settle the outstanding keynic obligation.

Some people have the majority of their estate in the form of jevs, and very many estates include some jevs, but the proportion of wealth that is represented by jevs in the asset register of a typical organisation or individual – compared to the presumed resale prices attributable to keyns and quons in such estates – is usually relatively small.

The system of sale by auction can be applied in special circumstances to assets and experiences in any category other than jevs. In periods of significant inflation, houses may be sold in this way because the conventional methods of 'valuation' have ceased temporarily to apply, and there is a considerable literature featuring the sale (usually by a woman, or by a man who controls a woman) of a sexual encounter.

3. *Quon*

Pronounced '*kwon*', with a short 'o' as in *none, gone*.

Quons are goods and services whose prices are set to cover both:

1. the material costs of making and delivering the constituents to the point of consumption
2. the return that is demanded by the controllers of all the intellectual property that is incorporated in the utility or satisfaction that the consumer derives from the quon.

Quons are branded, or otherwise identified, so that each can be differentiated from all other products and services. This differential is the essence which qualifies the product, experience, or service to be a quon. While a jev is priced exclusively by the highest bidder's willingness-to-pay for the object, a quon's price is the outcome of a sophisticated marketing exercise that brings together the customer's willingness (and ability) to pay with the requirement of the owner of *the ik* that not only the material costs of production or provision must be met, but also the costs of establishing and maintaining intellectual property in all the protected constituents of the package *of ik* that are carried with the brand, plus the greatest possible premium that customers can be induced or conditioned to pay to gain or to continue to have access to a possession and/or to an experience that they consider to be special or essential.

If a free person has access to a reasonably up-to-date phone and access to an electricity supply that is good enough to charge the batteries, plus an internet connection, that individual has access to all the knowledge that is in the net – almost everything that has ever been known by the whole of humanity – and to a phenomenal range of entertainment, games, educational resources, culture, pornography, opinion, and nonsense. The user may be in the most primitive shelter on a remote island, or in a billionaire's pad in

Manhattan; both have access to abundant free data and to protected *ik* such as was never before accessible to even the most privileged members of our species. In the face of such access to intangible wealth, the once persuasive idea that economic science should be concerned with the allocation of scarce material resources is clearly inadequate. Immaterial assets can be accessed and consumed in abundance, by anybody, anywhere. Wherever the *ik* that is embedded in an immaterial quon (such as a computer game or a novel on Kindle) is protected, it can yield revenue for its owners and for any franchisees or licensees, and the combination of intellectual assets with material components creates this class of commodity – quons – to which sophisticated consumers aspire. The fundamental economic process that is underway at present in China is to enable a rapidly expanding proportion of the population to become consumers of quons.

A quon provides the consumer with:

1. ownership, or a lease, of a physical asset and/or of a license that provides access to the use of an immaterial quon that gives access to proprietary *ik*

or

2. the benefit (sometimes referred to as the *utility*) that is derived from being the recipient of a service function that deploys physical and/or mental activity in combination with relevant *ik*.

Consumers pay a significantly higher price for a prestigious quon than for a relatively lowly branded product that serves the same material function. Suppliers of quons will only continue to provide their brand while the full cost of making units available is recovered from customers, including marketing and after-sales costs, as well as all the costs for defence and ongoing development of the *ik*. Considerable time was taken up in the Burberry shareholders' meeting in 2016 by an explanation of why the company had destroyed a significant amount of stock, to maintain the quonic exclusivity of the items that had been sold successfully. To consume quons is the aspiration of almost everybody who knows of the existence of branded lifestyle products and experiences. Even genuine ascetics, who have made a deliberate choice to eschew all forms of material consumerism, use branded IT to access the social media to communicate with like-minded fellows and to recruit disciples. Firms need to buy patented and trademark-protected machinery and supplies, and the copyright software that is needed to keep them competitive.

The utility of ephemeral quons such as restaurant meals, pints of branded draught beer, and attendance at concerts, films, or sports events, is time-critical, time-limited, and often specific to location. The most durable quons – notably buildings and large items of capital equipment – can be maintained to hold that status for centuries, while many brands provide the specified consumer experience continuously over months or years, after which the material components and mechanical constituents may reasonably be expected to wear out, though many models become unfashionable before they are materially obsolete. Old tangible quons that have lost any second-hand marketability for their residual utility can become reclassified as jevs if they are kept in ownership until they become sufficiently scarce survivals that they gain the attribute of rarity; hence many people and some organisations selectively keep or collect what other people regard as 'junk' in the hope that items will be transmogrified to jev status and become subject to that different pricing system.

The brand by which a quon is identified may be the name of a designer, a restaurateur, a stage performer, or a company, and often quons are recognised by a product name or marque (such as Ford's Focus) that was dreamed up for a specific model within the brand.

In service trades, the material component of a quon may be attendance and performance by an authorised provider of legal or medical services, who needs – at the very least – an office or clinical space, plus access to data sources, administrative facilities, and supplies, or by an entertainer such as a lap-dancer who performs in a protected environment.

Buying a quon that incorporates access to *ik* does not transfer the ownership of the *ik.* As such, generally, the *ik* remains the property of the brandowner, and of the patent holders and any others who have created or purchased any of the intellectual capital that is utilised in providing the product or the service. The quon buyer acquires ownership of an assembly of physical components or services from human beings, through which it gains *access* to the *utility* that is provided by the brand-protected **ik**.

Most of the cash equivalents that are stated as 'fixed assets' that appear on the balance sheets of businesses are comprised of quons: buildings, other structures, and capital equipment including IT. Many of the **ko**s that are created in the economy enable firms to acquire spending power that is used to pay for the acquisition of quons that serve as the firms' productive capital assets.

4. **Marcom**

Marcoms are all the material resources that are extracted from nature, together with all processed material commodities that are not quons or jevs. Once a person or a firm has established the process for preparing a marcom for market, the supply can be continued for as long as the prices that are offered by customers for the units of output are equal to, or above, the cost of producing them, including the cost of capital and remuneration for the managerial input. Assuming that the output meets the customers' requirements for durability, hygiene, and safety (often overseen by regulatory bodies) the producer can continue to offer the output – up to the full capacity of the plant – until conditions change. Such changes include the exhaustion of mineral supplies, the obsolescence of plant through wear-and-tear, the adoption of alternative materials or productive techniques by the firm's competitors, regulatory changes, and the cessation (or significant reduction) of demand. The relationship between demand and supply is changing constantly, responding to the myriad complex of events that alter the circumstances of both producers and purchasers of the commodities.

Marcomic material commodities, manufactured products, and services are not identified or protected by any significant **ik**, and they have none of the quonic utility to human consumers that is conveyed by brands. This category of asset broadly covers what Marx called commodities, and also widgets as presented in textbook Economics. In theory, if capital were available to fund continually increasing productive capacity, the price of any marcom could be forced down by competition between producers until it was equal to the exact cost to the supplier of providing the last unit that would be demanded at that price, assuming that the market was a sufficiently effective transfer mechanism for the final buyer and the final seller to locate each other and strike an 'equilibrium price'. In practice, the pragmatic decision to cease allocating more capital to increase material production would be taken well before a reductionist search for the marginal customer was undertaken, The nineteenth-century Economists' concept of 'equilibrium' – which could only be a momentary phenomenon – will never set the context for action by human beings in the material world.

The revealed preference of human beings for fashionable quons means that billions of marcoms are required, to be incorporated into a widening range of ever-more-complex quonic end-products every year. Also, billions of acts of service that are sold for marcom prices are essential to the delivery of myriad quonic consumer experiences.

A whole chain of processes is performed to convert raw materials into the material components that contribute to a sophisticated quon, and a parallel input requirement is needed by providers of quonically-priced services. Some firms are 'vertically integrated' so that the one organisation controls all the stages in a long sequence of production of increasingly complex marcoms in their own plant. Other firms outsource the supply of components, many of which they can buy 'just-in-time' from other firms. Some products acquire the status of quons even though they can be seen simply as components in more complex end-products; one of the best examples of this occurs with aero engines, where *Rolls Royce* and *Pratt & Whitney* are trusted international brands that give added confidence to travellers on *Boeing* or *Airbus* aeroplanes. Where the branding of patented or otherwise protected components is perceived to be a significant advantage – as *with Intel Inside* – the quonic status of such components is unequivocal. In other cases, a makers' mark is put on marcomic components for stock-control and quality-control purposes in the user's plant, but that implies no quonic attribute for the marcom concerned.

Especially where they supply similar components to several firms, marcomic component-making firms periodically take the risk of over-producing output during phases of reduced demand which their controllers believe to be temporary, so that they can meet the anticipated surge in demand as soon as an upturn occurs. Meanwhile, they keep their plant running and retain at least the core of their workforce in place. To pay for such a strategy, the firm has to sell some of an accumulation of keyns that are held as reserves, or draw down cash reserves, or risk borrowing money to fund their operation. As the recession that followed the 2008 financial crisis became more prolonged, banks faced a growing dilemma of 'zombie companies', firms to which loans had been made, who needed to extend the duration of the loan, or to increase the quantum of the loan, without which they would collapse and the bank would then have to write off the loan. Sometimes, demand for marcoms declines unexpectedly, in other cases, an anticipated rise in demand fails to materialise, or is less than was planned, so that the suppliers' need for cash forces them to sell the accumulated stock as surplus or scrap.

In agriculture, planting has to take place well before demand for crops is materialised, so when it actually crystallises, the demand for the crops may be severely deficient relative to the available supply in a year with an abundant harvest, precipitating a fall in prices. Alternatively, demand may exceed supply, either due to growth in demand or contraction of supply caused by a drought or a crop disease, or the exhaustion of a mine, in which case the price of that product will rise and some demand will probably be unsatisfied. In the case of major industrial minerals, including oil, in 2015-16 the offered output exceeded demand, resulting in a price collapse. This risk arises when the capacity to produce the marcom has been increased too much, because competing suppliers' past estimates of future demand prove to have been excessive. In different circumstances, imbalances range from trivial volumetric inequality of demand with supply to severe glut or dearth, and such variations are endemic in the trades in crops and minerals. The consequential volatility of prices and returns to business owners can be mitigated by surplus-holding schemes which can ensure that not too many suppliers quit a sector when there is a short-term glut, or switch their productive resources to sectors where their investment might result in a glut there.

The amount of capital that has to be invested to sink a deep mine or to exploit an oilfield is so great that firms with such embedded capital draw down reserves to maintain their assets through all but the most extreme gluts, with a view to optimising returns over the long period during which they expect that the capital investment should remain viable. Such provision depends on the companies concerned having powerful management resources and confident, long-term investors. Supply chain management draws increasingly on game theory, and there are opportunities for astute managers of firms to exploit suppliers and customers who lack vigilance and rigour. A whole array of speculators hover around the supply chain, taking advantage of every twist in the supply-demand balance to make their own turn; therefore, the constant vigilance of regulators, supported by governments, is necessary to ensure that essential supplies continue to be available over the long-term, and that heavy capital investments are not unduly rendered redundant.

Two important inferences emerge from this recital of the facts of marcom market structure. While the processing of marcoms may happen in large and small factories, as plant design evolves, the provision of the basic input materials – which are archetypically marcoms – often requires massive capital investment, as in oil wells, mines, and large-scale farms. The output of marcoms is offered in markets that are dominated by the demand of those who convert the output into manufactured marcoms that are later to be sold on to makers of quons and neoquons. The majority of workers in the material sectors of the economy are employed in the marcom trades, and their employment is subject to the vagaries of those markets. Just as large corporations are needed to accumulate the capital that is necessary to sink mines, to equip farms, and to maintain plant in which to make steel, so the prices they charge are subject to the demand of the firms higher up the supply chain nearer to the quonic transmogrification of the output, the point at which the label is affixed that precedes the offer of the product to the potential final consumers. Despite the fact that more of global consumers' spending is on quons every year, the bulk of materially productive employment remains in the marcomic sectors of the economy.

This largely explains the persistency with which the wages of the many who are productively employed remain low, relative to the wages of the privileged few; those employed in the completion and marketing of the final product, alongside higher management and the professionals who create and guard the corporation's *ik*, who command high salaries, generous commission, and share options. On the other hand, large corporations that have made massive investments in fixed plant and equipment have an interest in maintaining the staff who are necessary to operate the plant, so they are more likely to offer continuity of employment, even in periods of reduced consumer demand, than risk not being able to function effectively as demand recovers. This means that large corporations have to pay heavily to keep plant and staff in a state of readiness to function, with the consequence that their declared losses during depressed periods are even greater than they would be if more ruthless cut-backs were made.

Therefore, during recessions, large firms are less likely to shed employees than small firms, who have to respond quickly to diminution of their cash flow. This was very heavily instanced in the recession that followed the 2008 financial crash, and in the chaos following the commodity price collapse of 2015. Small firms are highly vulnerable in adverse market conditions, while large marcom suppliers have traditionally been more robust because their owners are prepared to accept reduced (or even negative) revenue at some stages in the business cycle in order to be in the offing for substantial revenue distributions when the demand is high. Many small marcomic firms are operated on a short-term basis, in times of high demand, sometimes by entrepreneurs who serially establish firms on the upturn and terminate them on the downturn, though this is only feasible where relatively small amounts of plant are needed for the process. Large marcomic firms needing large-scale plant to achieve operational efficiency need to operate according to the very different strategy through time that maintains their capacity to produce output in the event of future recovery of demand. These complex interactions must be recognised by any democratic government that asserts a wish to enable the mass of productive employees to have a stable and sufficient standard of living. More of the implications of this issue will be discussed later in this text.

Makers' marks are attached to many of the marcoms that are directly consumed and used by humans. This enables health, safety, and other regulators to trace the marcoms back to their originators if any aspect of the product is alleged to be unsatisfactory. Increasingly precise regulation of retail sales and 'class actions' against manufacturers and distributors (often led by chancing lawyers) have caused many firms to cease to offer marcoms for direct human consumption due to the risk of being sued for detriment to a user. Retail chains address this risk, while offering competitively priced goods, by putting their own brand on products that they buy as marcoms after checking the supplier for health and safety compliance, and the produce for acceptability with customers. Such 'own-brand' goods are *neoquons*, where the retailer provides the assurance that is conveyed by their own house brand.

In cases where a category of marcom has been withdrawn completely from retail sale, consumers must thereafter exist without that consumer experience. The withdrawal of consumer marcoms from the marketplace can have a significantly adverse effect on many humans' standards of living, especially that of the poor. A declining proportion of the increasing total output of marcoms is directly consumed by human beings, and this will continue as long as living standards are rising. Each individual consumer's distribution of spending between quons, neoquons, and marcoms is a strong indicator of that individual's material standard of living.

Quon providers need to secure their supply chains, and thus it is in their interests to offer contracts on terms that enable their suppliers of marcomic inputs to maintain and renew their capital equipment, and to treat their staff fairly. The medium-term demand for marcoms is constantly in flux due to the development of new materials and innovative production techniques. The introduction of new categories of quons and neoquons, and of new generations of established brands for which new or modified input components are required, also changes and widens the demand for marcoms. The demand for any marcom provider's output can also be affected by the entry of new competitors to the market, by changes in the pattern of demand for quons of which the marcoms are components, by the introduction of new methods of marcom production, by the development of new input materials, by regulatory changes, or by competitors' bankruptcies. Volumetric demand and offer prices for marcoms are constantly in flux, and it is clear that supply and demand do not trend towards the equilibrium that is envisaged for widgets in Economics.

The Economic Consequences of English Jurisprudence

Britain is unusual in many ways, but one area in which England, Wales, and Northern Ireland are most peculiar among developed countries is that they do not have either an elected or an autonomous judiciary. The current crop of judges like to assert that they are independent of the government, and over the four decades of Britain's membership of the EU the judges were increasingly willing to use European legislation and case law to interpret Acts of Parliament very differently from what Members of Parliament state they intended in passing the legislation. That supposition of independence merely emphasised the judicature's lack of the more important form of independence. The judges are products of the profession of confrontational advocacy, which has grown massively in numbers over recent decades, and has established itself as an unproductive drain on the economy and a potent force for the destruction of social cohesion.

Civil cases are determined on the same basis as ice-dancing contests. The judge rewards advocacy skills, according to his insider perception of the relevance and intricacy of the arguments that are deployed, just as skating judges award points for 'content' and 'execution'. Establishing the truth is no longer the perceived objective, and justice has come to mean 'whatever the courts let counsel get away with'. Some judges, called 'recorders', one day hear cases, and the next week are down in the well of the court working as barristers, disputing with their fellow barristers whom they heard from the bench last week. Assertions that individuals are able to switch roles between judge and advocate, and from defender to prosecutor, without any susceptibility to cronyism, are merely ludicrous, and when British advocates are moved up to full-time judicial office they remain members of the tightly knit communities in their Inns of Court. Criminal cases are notionally decided by ordinary citizens sitting as a jury, but, in the event, the judge, the prosecutor, and the defending lawyer collude on what evidence they will permit the jury to hear, and the judge frequently steers – or openly directs – the jury to reach a dictated verdict.

It is economically advantageous for the legal professions when defendants in criminal trials are either acquitted or given minimal sentences followed quickly by parole, so that a high percentage of the criminals can soon be brought back to court (with their solicitors in support) to face further trials for new offences which represent new jobs for barristers, who may swap the roles of prosecutor and defender next time around. The invention of new defence arguments and new forms of psychiatric 'assessment', however specious they may initially appear to be, enriches the whole profession when they are brought into general use, as does acceptance by judges of obfuscatory and dilatory tricks by lawyers that extend the number of chargeable hours taken up by cases, and which increase the number and complexity of appeal hearings. The tradition of adherence to the Ten Commandments and dedication to the concept of truth has not survived the decline of religion, and there is now no consistent moral restraint on the inventiveness and greed of advocates. Equally dangerous is the emergence of contrarian lawyers who take on cases in which they press for extreme interpretation of human rights principles, including arraigning civil and military state employees, with the intention of weakening the state.

In many other countries, advocates and judges take different career paths, and thus the judiciary is separated from the profession that presents defence arguments to them. Charles Dickens wrote that, 'The one great principle of English law is to make business for itself', and that situation has not changed for the better in the century and a half since. Whilst admitting the advocates' phenomenal capacity for speed-learning, as well as their intellectual versatility and verbal fluency, the public despises them and the 'no-win, no-fee' solicitors who instruct them, because they have largely invalidated the concept that trials seek to establish the truth. The residuum of honourable lawyers may not have recognised the cumulative effect of their profession's dereliction of morality and their contempt for the public interest over recent decades, and some of them may even try to repudiate these observations, but the preponderance of evidence is against them.

Notwithstanding the appalling default of the courts, lawyers' inventiveness in creating work for their professions has been indispensable in developing the forms of contract that create and define keyns of all kinds. The existence of personal identity can only be articulated and asserted because the law recognises persons. The concept that persons (including legal persons) can create and own intellectual property – *ik* – is the highest economic achievement that has been made possible by the judicial system to date. The concepts that have become contemporary *ik* are derived from charters, licenses, patents, and copyrights that were developed in the English legal system (which grew from the very similar pre-revolutionary French legal system), and many of them have been developed to the ultimate extent in the USA, which, in the main, has derived its legal system from Great Britain. These legal concoctions have made possible the emergence of the modern economy of quons and keyns, and the hope of permanent prosperity for all rests upon them. The validity of any *ka* or *ko* is entirely dependent on defensible contract terms, quons can only exist as symbiotic repositories of material possessions with integral access to *ik,* and neither jevs nor marcoms can be traded or insured properly if the legal ownership and status of such objects is uncertain.

These are crucial facts of productive economic activity that depend absolutely on the creativity of legal practitioners, in a world where the component of quon prices that is taken by the owner of the intellectual property that is essential to the consumer experience often exceeds the total cost of the material components of the quon. Registering, regulating, and defending intellectual property is crucial for businesses, and makes some people very rich. The best specialist lawyers thoroughly understand the classes of intellectual property, Economists who notice intellectual property as a phenomenon of the economy descend into tortuous irrelevance, usually exploring the undergrowth that has accumulated in the shadow of Schumpeter's agonised attempts to accommodate the concept within the normative Economics of his era. The difference in wealth between the median earner among intellectual property lawyers and the median earner among Economists is the best evidence that the lawyers are way ahead of the Economists in their appreciation of economic realities and in the materiality of their contribution to the economy.

Intellectual property is a vital component of personal, corporate, and national capital, and the nation's wealth conspicuously includes the *ik* that is embedded in productive plant, and in the stimulation of productive new inventions. Further potential capital investment arises from the inflow of export earnings (and licence fees and remittances) that can be derived from the use of a country's intellectual property abroad. Britain's current account deficit on material trade is now so great that the residue of net earnings from the export of *ik* is insufficient to make a satisfactory contribution to capital investment within the country.

Much intellectual capital is deployed to provide for lifestyle consumption, bringing no return that directly augments the nation's material capital. But if the effect of the consumption is to improve the mental state, the fitness, the inventiveness, and the willingness to work of the population, then it can indirectly be very productive. A consumer's lifestyle choices can be categorised as 'unproductive' consumption if the recipient makes no countervailing contribution to the generation of increments to the nation's capital in the form of materially or intellectually productive resources. Tragically, many millions of people in Europe and North America are inadvertently unproductive even though they are of normal working age and in a reasonable state of mental and physical fitness. Most people have restricted incomes, especially those who are dependent on state benefits, and only a miniscule proportion of their spending is returned indirectly to the economy as investment, while in many cases their pattern of consumption makes them obese, prone to smokers' diseases, and to the effects of alcohol or 'substance' abuse. Millions become intellectually vegetative, to an extent that they could not seize an opportunity for productive employment should it arise.

The Autonomy of Economic Agents

The term 'economic agents' simply means, 'all the individuals and legal persons who are empowered to make decisions and enter into contracts within the economy'. Demand for a vast range of both durable and ephemeral quons depends on the ability of potential customers to create debt to get the purchase price. The pattern and the pace of the growth of quon trade depend very significantly on the supply of credit. Individuals and households can increase their consumption of quons by creating keyns. Such a process can be sustained whenever the increasing total of **ko**s that are created by individuals is serviced by the growth in their real earnings.

Individual and corporate economic agents exist in space and time and are surrounded by risks, threats, and opportunities. Differential access to education, information, and means of communication influence the relative productiveness of human beings. The vast majority of producers of both intellectual and material outputs do their jobs as participants in firms. Every personal and corporate estate expands or shrinks, as well as changing in composition, over time. In an increasingly crowded and competitive world, individual adults must constantly be reminded of the basic fact that they can only expect to retain control over their lifestyle choices if they contribute effectively to the economy as producers and as responsible consumers. Mature citizens allocate their income between acquiring goods and services for direct personal consumption and accumulating a portfolio of **ka**, by buying insurance, by contributing to a pension fund, and by saving and investing.

The liberal assertion that free trade was the ideal principle for managing an economy was confronted by political and legal reality as soon as it was formulated. In nineteenth-century Britain, regulations and restrictions were deemed to be necessary to protect factory children from overwork and abuse, then night work for women was banned, then all workers were protected by laws which banned dangerous activities and the exposure of workers to toxic and abrasive substances. With the spread of democracy, popular legislation that acted against free trade was consolidated by compulsory state education, by measures to promote public health, by building regulations, by the recognition of trade unions, and by the enactment of thousands of other Acts of Parliament that specifically repudiated the idea of untrammelled market freedom. Most specifically, the liberal political class failed to recognise the phenomenon that was the most fundamentally inimical to the concept of free trade, the rise of *ik*. The importance of intellectual capital – and of the means of defending it as the exclusive possession of its creators (and of those to whom the inventors sold or leased it) – became the most significant determiner of the wealth of individuals and of the success or failure of the majority of firms. Economists simply buried the accumulating heap of irrefutable evidence to this effect in the 'too difficult' tray.

Immediately after the United Kingdom surrendered most of its then-existing North American colonies to become the USA (while keeping the territories that became the world's second-biggest country, Canada) a second overseas empire was focused on India. The other existing colonies were supplemented by claiming new possessions. Throughout the nineteenth century, trade between the colonies and other states was controlled strictly from London, while British and Irish settlers occupied Australia and New Zealand and continued to develop Canada.

JA Hobson formed a radical analysis of these processes as a correspondent in the 'Boer War', and published *Imperialism, A Study* in 1902. Lenin thought that Hobson's idea (which he adopted as his own) was so important that it justified the redesignation of the enemy as 'imperialism' rather than 'capitalism' in his own version of the concept in *Imperialism, the Highest Stage of Capitalism* (written in 1916 and published in 1917).

While a form of Leninism was established in the USSR between the two world wars, elsewhere colonialism continued to flourish, until major components of the French, Dutch, American, and British empires in south Asia were seized by the Japanese in 1942-3. The West Europeans' overseas empires were subsequently sloughed off, largely at the behest of the United States (with the enthusiastic assistance of local Leninist 'fellow-travellers'), over the three decades after 1945. Meanwhile, the Soviet and Maoist regimes – the 'second world' – applied resources that they could little spare to support the establishment of indigenous 'socialist' regimes in the 'third world'. While imperialism lasted, massive wealth was accumulated in the imperial capitals, and so was was available to be dissipated during the twentieth century, partly in waging war and partly in funding the welfare state. Twenty-first century politicians have not begun to recognise the full implications of the fact that the accumulated treasure that was derived from centuries of imperial success has been dissipated, without hope of replenishment.

Adam Smith is generally accredited with having been the originator of the doctrine of free trade, yet even he explicitly recognised that some sectors of society and some human conditions require the state's protection, and that some massive engineering works – such as action to control river and tidal flooding in a constantly changing environment – can only be undertaken under government direction. He declared that the wealth that pays for welfare and for public works – alongside defence forces, police, and other essential services – is generated by people, acting on their own accounts or as agents of estates or of corporate entities. He asserted that if economically active agents were constrained by oppressive regulation, or by taboo, the generation of wealth must be sub-optimal.

This argument does not allow for the limitation on everybody else's freedom to copy ideas for which patents or copyrights have been given to individuals. Yet it was during Smith's lifetime that protracted litigation resulted in the reduction of the scope of the patents that had been granted to Sir Richard Arkwright at exactly the same time as Smith was writing his supposed masterpiece. Economic growth accelerated hugely as entrepreneurs began to use inventions that were derived from ideas that Arkwright could no longer claim as his exclusive property. However, the case left him as a very rich patent-holder in respect of the inventions that the courts accepted to be his original concepts; anyone wishing to deploy devices incorporating those patents still had to pay Arkwright for that use.

The Arkwright case showed the vital importance both of defining *ik* precisely and of limiting the scope of any particular patent to its unique essentials. Patent and copyright law has greatly been refined over the subsequent centuries in response to litigated outcomes, and lawyers are still making fortunes in crucial cases, such as those between Apple and Samsung in 2012-16. A storm of lawsuits would have arisen if Tim Berners-Lee had not handed over his undoubted right to the underlying *ik* of the internet to humanity at large. Attempts by some US biotechnology companies to capture data that can be discovered in nature and publish their discoveries as being their invention of globally important generic *ik* is a major source of friction between Europe and the USA. Attempts by firms to pre-empt scientific discoveries by claiming anticipatory ownership of *ik* look likely to develop into the next major test of patent law. The world needs an international convention to set clear definitions of how *ik* can be asserted and defended. The worst outcome would be a breakdown of the shaky internationalisation of patents, copyright, and brand protection that at present exists, without a superior system being set to replace it.

A simple spreadsheet can display an estimation of the resale prices that could be fetched by selling all the assets of any estate; expressed as a series of numbers of currency units, this can be set alongside a similar estimate of the estate's liabilities. Between the mid nineteen-eighties and 2007, money-lenders encouraged tens of millions of individuals in the supposedly more mature economies to establish a net deficit on their estates' balance sheets, defying the commonsense principle that households and firms should have a positive overall balance on the 'book value' of keyns plus quons plus marcoms plus jevs in their estate. If a person dies with more unsecured debt than the net valuation of his or her assets, their creditors have failed in the risk management of the credit that they extended to that individual. Before granting credit to any corporate or personal estate, simple common sense requires the lender to verify the sufficiency of the assets that are held in the estate to serve as security for the new loan in addition to all the borrower's existing debts, together with verifying the sufficiency and reliability of the borrower's anticipated income flow during the term of the loan, and that cash-flow projection frequently depends on the potential productiveness of the borrower's *ik*.

Quons, jevs, and stocks of resalable marcoms can serve as security for *ko*s that a person or a firm creates, as can *ka*s that they own which have been issued by third parties. The total valuation of quons (**Q**), marcoms (**M**), and jevs (**J**) in an estate, plus-or-minus the net keyn position (**K**) of its owner, produces the **net balance** (**N**) for a person or for a corporate (or collective) entity,

$$\{Q + M + J\} +/- K = N$$

Companies must have a positive net balance at all times; trading when insolvent is illegal. State corporations and quangos usually have a governmental guarantee of solvency, backed up by supposedly rigorous control criteria. Any other form of organisation is viable if the net position on its balance sheet is positive, according to conventional accounting standards. In terms of this text, if:

$$\{ik + ka + Q + M + J\} - ko > 0$$

In the above,
K stands for **net** valuation of inventoried keyns, **K** = {***ik*+*ka***} − ***ko***
Q stands for valuation of inventoried quons
M stands for valuation of inventoried marcoms
J stands for valuation of inventoried jevs
ik is all forms of intellectual capital
ko is keynic liabilities
ka is keynic assets.

It is up to the potential investor or lender, in any case, to verify that the valuation of a would-be borrower's assets is sound and truthful.

Chapter Three

More About Keyns

The term *keyn* identifies a vast range of immaterial assets without which the global economy could not function, plus a huge range of other financial 'products' and bets, all of which are contracts for the payment and receipt of money, and some of which can be deployed as hedges against the potential cost arising from material risk events. Some of these contracts enable a range of individuals and businesses to aim for significant profit from charging fees to churn such assets, enabling star traders and their managers to enrich themselves. The range, scope, and detail of keynic contracts is constantly changing, but the basic relationship of debtor and creditor, the deployment of money as the denominator of the contract, and the essential distinction between long-term and short-term contracts, does not change. The risk of loss is present in all keynic contracts, and it is notorious that the probability of making a significant loss is lessened by the extent to which the market participants who enter into the contract have relevant experience, understanding, and knowledge. Both advanced understanding of the forces that are in play and arcane data that are withheld from the common herd make keyn markets far from a level playing field, and no extent of legislation and regulation could ever remove the range of advantages that some players will always acquire.

The frenetic expansion of the interaction of neo-traditional bank financing with gambling, which peaked in 2006 (and crashed in 2008), did not change this reality, and still now governments and central banks maintain regulatory systems that evade unequivocal assertion of the fundamental difference between banking that enables normal economic activity to continue and to develop, alongside gambling. A sensible recognition of the essential difference between the two spheres of activity will enable legislators to recognise gambling contracts as a range of special classes of keyns that require regulation as such.

A keynic asset (***ka***) remains in existence for as long as a contractual agreement between the two relevant participants in the economy remains in existence;

- the creator of the ***ka*** accepts responsibility for the obligation or debt (***ko***) that they have accepted as the necessary concomitant to the advantage or asset that they have acquired by creating the ***ka***
- the counterparty (or a party to whom the contractual rights are assigned at any point during the life of the contract) holds the ownership of the ***ka***.

All through the period of existence of each ***ka***, interest, and/or service charges, and/or dividend payments, and/or instalments of repayment, and/or some other form of recompense – as specified under the terms of the contract – are due to the owner of the ***ka***, from its creator, or from another economic agent that legally inherits or adopts the creator's obligation during the currency of the keyn. Many ***ka***s expire on a specified date, or on the occurrence of a specified event, when the creator (or their successor) may be obliged to make a final settlement to the then owner of the asset.

A keynic obligation (*ko*) is:

- an obligation that is accepted by a human being or by a legal person in consequence of a contract by which that agent accepted the commitment to make future payments

or

- an obligation that arises from a lawful imposition that is placed on an economic agent, such as a tax or license fee, or any legal liability that arises from the tenure of land or property, or in the course of parenthood or employment, or from a variety of other situations.

An obligation to pay a legally levied tax, fine, or license fee is a **ko** that inescapably falls due to be settled by a person or an institution. In a democratic state, it is assumed that the taxpayer's consent to the imposition of levies, taxes, and license fees has been expressed through the electoral process, and that each organisation is managed by people who accept their obligations to pay fees, fines, and taxes as a necessary concomitant of the entity being recognised by the state as a legal person.

Intellectual property (*ik*) consists of the right of a human being or of a corporate entity to possess any of the following:

- legal personality: the right to exist and to make contracts,
- real property, in the sense that the relationship of a natural or legal person to the material asset is a fact in law, is defined by law, and the circumstance of being the owner depends on legal protection of that status,
- the ownership of any product of intellectual activity (by an individual, a small group of people, or by employees acting on behalf of a firm) that is identifiable and definable, such as a copyright piece of writing, a design, or an advertising slogan, that the relevant courts can recognise and enforce as being exclusively the property of a human creator, or the property of an organisation to which the creators have contractually ceded control of their inventions and discoveries made within the context of their contract. It is extremely unwise for any plurality of people, even a married couple, to establish joint ownership of intellectual property without formally agreeing the terms on which the property is to be owned if they split up, or on the death or incapacity of one or more of them. It is credible that artificial intelligence will actually produce inventions within a

few years. This will raise significant issues about the ownership of intellectual property that is generated in this way: no doubt the legal professions are already preparing the ground for such issues to be addressed.

- ownership or control of any situation or status that is granted to the person or organisation under the law. The prime example is the ownership of land; other examples include licenses to use patented processes, the license to practice as a doctor, extraction rights for oil, minerals, or water, a franchise to run a branded coffee bar, or an employment contract,
- any other immaterial asset (not being a *ka*) whose existence is recognised and defended by a properly empowered court.
- **negative *ik*** is an economic agent's liability in respect of any emergent debt, including any unfulfilled component of a contract to provide cash, quons, jevs, or marcoms, or a contract to perform some service. If non-performance leads to a failure to fulfil the terms of a contract, the obligation can potentially be transformed by a legal process into a debt, a ***ko***. The price at which a ***ka*** that came into existence in this way may be sold thereafter depends on the offer that a buyer is willing to make at the time when the asset is put up for sale. Until about 1990, price setting for any material or financial product was located at a point on the Earth's surface, and was thus fairly easily subjected to regulation by the regime on whose territory the contract was made, but in cyberspace there is now a globally accessible marketplace, with many hundreds of millions of potential traders who have widely differing levels of economic sophistication.

The inevitable absence of any materially objective system for pricing *ka*s becomes a serious problem after the collapse of a political regime, a monetary system, or a market bubble, when some classes of *ka*s cannot rationally be priced at all. Some, like imperial Russian bonds, will never again have any value, except as a special-interest range of jevs. Until this millennium, the owners of **ka**s were allowed to make cautiously positive assumptions about a long-term median price that (in stable conditions) would apply to temporarily non-marketable keyns that they held in their portfolios. Under sensible accounting standards, they could state those price assumptions in their formal balance-sheet and justify the basis for the estimate to their auditors and to the taxman.

That proven system was superseded by Economics-inspired international accounting standards in force during the 2006-16 crisis of confidence in the leading financial markets. Under those rules, every **ka** was 'marked to market', which meant it had to be recorded in the owner's accounts as being sellable for the same price as identical 'products' that were traded on that date. Most holders of long-term keyns had no intention to sell, and owners recognised that if more units of any class of keyn were offered for sale on a trading day than the market was conditioned to absorb, the price would fall significantly. If holders of a class of keyn learned that a large number of other owners were trying to sell, in such volume that the price was declining rapidly, 'confidence' in that whole asset class would come into question. In the deepest crisis of 2008, many assets became unsellable because no one was willing to buy into a class of **ka** that had become 'distressed' or 'impaired'.

Credit rating agencies are firms that purport independently to assess the strength of financial assets. Early this century, most of them abjectly failed to recognise emergent disasters, in Independent Insurance in the UK, and globally in Enron. Right down to August 2008, they blithely continued to offer good ratings to totally insubstantial 'securities' and to their issuers. A massive global insurance corporation, US-based AIG, was highly rated until the week of its collapse, disregarding the fact that a small peripheral division of the firm had underwritten enough bankers' debt to swamp their whole corporate balance sheet, through selling a new class of betting slips. There is no valid independent method for assessing the relative security of **ka**s in future time. It was reckless and deeply shameful that regulators insisted upon – and continue to require – agency ratings to be used as surrogates for judgment by the directors of investment firms and their clients and counterparties.

Economic Crises

No observation of human decision-making can be taken as definitive, however professionally and objectively the evidence is collected, but there are some recurring behaviours that can be taken as typical over most cultures and the past few centuries. In the inter-war years, JM Keynes referred to 'irrational optimism' as a major factor in creating booms in asset prices, notably of bonds, shares, and futures. Developing that point, Hyman Minsky spent a long academic career, from the nineteen-fifties, examining these crucial relationships, though he was largely ignored by the mainstream of the 'Economics profession'. Ten years after his death, in the wake of the 2006-8 crisis, his work began adequately to be recognised, with an increasing number of commentators admitting that there had been a 'Minsky Moment' as the inevitable consequence of the facts that neither regulators nor participants in markets had understood the relationship between **ka**s, **ko**s, time, and money. As Minsky had foretold decades previously, during the bubble period, financial institutions massively increased both the volume and the variety of the **ko**s that they created and the range of **ka**s that they bought. Assuming that participants in a booming market borrow to enable them to participate in the accumulation of assets, Minsky classified borrowers in three broad groups:

1. "Hedge borrowers", firms and individuals who can pay the interest, and if necessary repay the principal of their loan, with cash derived from a sufficiently extensive portfolio of assets over which they have full control
2. "Speculative borrowers", whose incomes enable them to service the debt, but who need to re-borrow or roll-forward their loans because the balance-sheet of their firm or estate is not sufficient to enable them to close off the loan at their discretion by liquidating assets to which they have current access. People and firms get themselves into this situation when they assume that in the medium-term the asset that was bought with the borrowed sum will appreciate in price sufficiently to enable them to settle the debt when they sell the asset (and, if they have planned well and been lucky, make a profit for themselves as well)

3. "Ponzi borrowers", who rely on the resale price of the asset rising sufficiently to enable them to service the debt (both interest and capital repayment) if they need to sell it. If the market is not rising at that time, they cannot pay either the interest due on the borrowing or the capital sum owed.

Minsky showed how, when an asset bubble collapses and prices begin to fall, the most extreme Ponzi borrowers are immediately found to be unable to service the *ko*s that they have created; their failure raises questions in the market generally about which other borrowers are in this category and the prices for resale of the *ko*s that they have issued collapse, often to zero. As the Ponzi borrowers fail, the viability of speculative borrowers next comes under challenge, and some of them become unable to service their *ko*s as more creditors demand settlement while asset prices continue to fall. Finally, if market prices fall sufficiently and remain depressed for long enough, the weakest of the hedge borrowers could also be unable to meet their obligations as they fall due for settlement. There is no systemic terminal point for a collapse of the market, so the powers-that-be, the state, and/or the central bank, or a supranational agency, must intervene to prevent the collapse of the material economy when the system of payments becomes unsustainable.

Minsky pointed out that houses, in particular, can be treated as speculative assets whose prices rise in proportion to the increase in the amount that financial institutions lend to property purchasers. There is no solid basis for the level of house prices, such as equivalence with the material cost of constructing the house. Especially in the period 2001-6, lenders increased the assumed resale prices of property assets, including hotels, shops, and industrial units, as they loaned more on looser terms to wider categories of borrowers (e.g., by increasing the multiple of the occupants' annual income that could be borrowed against a mortgage). The house-selling boom in the USA and in parts of Europe that peaked in 2005-6 was greater than any previous bubble, largely because securitisation enabled primary lenders to transfer the ownership of the 'retail' *ka*s to 'wholesale' market participants. Mortgagees' debt became progressively more widely spread around the market, so more and more firms held assets that were at risk to the impact of falling property prices when the expansionary mood gave way to pessimism.

When the shift of sentiment occurred (triggered by defaults on sub-prime mortgages in the USA) the fact that all property assets were perceived to be potentially overpriced meant that the price collapse spread virally. Neither regulators nor risk managers in the lending institutions had taken account of the increasing probability of the bubble ending in a Minsky Moment; most of them had never heard of Minsky, and consequently they reaped the whirlwind. Governments allowed a few significant firms to collapse, but very quickly they recognised that economic stability as such was at risk and thereafter they took concerted action with their central banks to shore surviving firms up, with loans and in some cases by partial nationalisation. In the same period, the International Monetary Fund and the European Union (acting together with the European Central Bank in eurozone countries) forced the member countries where the system was most out-of-control to 'restructure' their sovereign debt to the disadvantage of domestic bond-owners. Alien speculators, most conspicuously hedge funds, bought 'distressed' state bonds on the world market at knock-down prices, then negotiated with the issuer governments to secure a privileged debtor status that enabled them to make a profit in return for not voting against the rescue packages. Thus, the beleaguered governments were enabled to shore up the stronger components of their financial markets with the support of the international institutions and subject to their draconian oversight, sometimes subject to also being screwed by the speculative holders of state securities.

It took a thousand years to develop the financial markets that eventually became superficially so sophisticated, and actually highly precarious, by the year 2006. There was a long process by which participants in markets became aware of the possibilities for creating ***ko***s that were notionally secured by assets, and of the legal institutions that gave credibility to ***ko***s and ***ka***s. Keynes used the word 'chartalist' to define such assets because, in the end, such assets can only have validity if they are recognised and protected by the state. The establishment of a legal relationship between a human being (or a corporate body) and a material asset was originally expressed in royal charters which granted the ownership of land, licensed the existence of abbeys, and authorised the autonomous existence of cities and city guilds. The word 'real' in the terms 'real estate' and 'real property' derives from 'royal'.

The price payable for the ownership of a plot of land, expressed as a sum of currency, is constantly changing, depending on the current macroeconomic context, the availability of credit, and the state of expectations, and it is powerfully influenced by demographics, planning regulations, and location, where it becomes more or less fashionable for activities to become concentrated. The price of any item of real estate is also significantly influenced by the perceived desirability of the material assets that exist on and under the site. Where the land has previously been built on (as with cleared 'brownfield' sites) and is deemed to be eligible for redevelopment as residential land, the resale price of the site depends on the potential developer's estimate of the relative desirability of the houses or flats that can be built at that location, within pricing patterns that prevail in the overall housing market.

Land that is designated for industrial or commercial use commands prices that derive from the potential productiveness of the activities that will be undertaken in the buildings that are (or can be) put there. In the case of agricultural land, the valuation of the ownership depends on the fertility of the soil, the climatic zone, the level of demand for crops and livestock, any licence for the tenant to abstract water, and on geographical location, which influences the cost of delivery of crops to markets. Where access to minerals in the Earth's crust is permitted, the costs and potential gains from extracting these minerals largely determine the price of the land, and of the mineral rights if they are separately available to be owned or hired. In all cases, a positive probability of the land being granted a change-of-use under the environmental planning laws, perhaps when an extractive process has been exhausted, will increase the potential resale price. Even under the feudal system, it became possible for potential buyers of land ownership to borrow some, or all, of the purchase price against a mortgage, and from this stage, the prices of parcels of land became determined both by the income-generating potential of the land and by the terms on which mortgage finance was available.

Competing potential buyers of a piece of real estate may take a more or less positive view on the development potential of any site, or of the maintenance costs of the structures and other installed assets. They can assess present and prospective macroeconomic conditions and prospects differently, and will have differing amounts of circulating capital at their disposal, differential access to borrowed credit, and different possibilities for raising new capital from the market by selling bonds or shares. Consequently, they may formulate significantly different offers for the same property. The rental income that the owner can demand from an occupant of the site depends primarily on the *location* of the plot in relation to its usefulness for human activities, making allowance for taxes, planning regulations, licensing constraints, and transport costs. The cash rent of land is further weighted by the form and duration of the tenure that is offered.

Assets, Money, and Credit; The Evolution of the System

At various times and in various places, conquering monarchs and revolutionary regimes have declared all the land within a state or a province to be the property of the government or of the 'community'. Sometime after every such event, control over land – starting with exclusive access to some of the most desirable plots – has been allocated on lease or license to politically useful tenants. Ultimately, owners again emerge who control the land, 'land' sometimes including the birds and insects that fly over it, and the vegetation, the water, the rock, the structures, and any minerals that are on or underneath it. Socialists assert that the surface and the resources of the Earth should be the common possession of humanity, but most governments allow land ownership (or long-term secure leasing of land from the state) to continue and to develop, on the grounds that it is the most efficient means to secure effective management of this most basic of all material resources outside the human body.

To meet his tax bill, to secure a return from the ownership of the land, and to recoup the costs that periodically arise in asserting the control of his patch of land, any landowner must invest in farming the land, or lease the land to a farmer, or sell access to the land for amenity purposes, or lease the land for access to mining or for occupancy by buildings, or to some other purpose that produces income. The landowner or the licensed tenant of the landowner must at all times have sufficient control over the use of the land to protect the investment that is put there in the forms of crops, amenities, and structures. The establishment of European states' power over the Americas, Australia, New Zealand, and much of Africa led to the European concept of real estate being implanted, which conveniently ignored most of the customary rights of the aboriginal (i.e., pre-colonial) inhabitants.

Leaving aside *ik* in the form of peerages and knighthoods, which are economically insignificant (except as a source of slush funds to Lloyd George and, reputedly, to Tony Blair's new Labour project), next to land in historic significance among forms of *ik* is the right to create money, to mint coins, and to print currency notes. Until the First World War, under English law the word 'money' meant 'coins made by the Royal Mint'. From 1819 to 1931, the Bank Charter Act fixed the price of gold of a carefully-specified fineness at the equivalent of £3.85 per ounce. The Royal Mint issued gold sovereigns that were worth exactly £1, while officially minted silver and copper coins represented fractions of a gold pound. Banknotes could be issued by the Bank of England, and by other banks that were licensed to do so, all of whom were obliged to maintain the parity of each pound represented on all of their notes with one sovereign for one pound.

The Bank of England's note issue was supported by a reserve of gold bullion that was protected every night by a detachment of guardsmen, and the amount of the gold reserve could be increased as the world gold supply increased. With an increasing stock of the underlying asset held at the bank, the circulating money supply could be increased, the mint could issue more gold coins, the Bank of England could increase its note issue on the strength of its gold reserves, and other banks that were so licensed could also increase the number of notes that they put into circulation. British note-issuing banks other than the Bank of England were obliged to back the notes that they issued with a proportionate reserve in the form of gold sovereigns, and/or Bank of England notes, and/or deposits placed by the issuing bank in the Bank of England that could be encashed on demand in the form of sovereigns or Bank of England notes. Over the century when that firm gold standard was maintained, the availability of gold within the system set a limit to the money supply that could be created, so there were periods of deflation when the expansion of the economy was curtailed by the limitation on the expansion of the currency. But for most of the time, the evolving banking system enabled the existing money supply to be circulated very much more quickly, supplemented by an increasing 'fiduciary issue' of notes created by the Bank of England which developed confidence in recognising how far their paper pounds would be accepted, always given the promise that notes would be exchanged for gold should the holder of any Bank of England notes demand that.

The Bank of England managed the system robustly until 1914, then key clauses of the Bank Charter Act were suspended to enable the First World War to be financed, partially, with the issue of supplementary paper money from the Treasury. A 'gold exchange standard' for the pound was 'restored' at the 1819 parity, for international transactions only, in 1925 when Winston Churchill was Chancellor of the Exchequer. That attempt notionally to re-establish the pre-war gold parity of the pound sterling was heavily criticised by Keynes (*The Economic Consequences of Mr Churchill*) and it became untenable after the Wall Street Crash of 1929. Since 1931, by law, tangible UK money has comprised chartalist notes issued by the Bank of England, supplemented by Scots and Northern Irish banks' notes and by coins from the Royal Mint.

I can change five £1 coins for a £5 note, or vice versa, but no material 'value' attaches to any of the currency units. The scrap metal price for a £1 coin is miniscule and the salvage price of cancelled paper money is even less in proportion to the purchasing power of the monetary units. The notes and the coins are government-guaranteed **kas** that everyone uses because a medium of exchange (which also serves as the unit of account for cashless transactions) is essential for modern living. Keynes had explained chartalist money before the First World War in his little book on *Indian Currency and Finance*; after the war he developed the exposition in his magisterial *Treatise on Money*, which was published in the year of the Wall Street crash, exactly when an unambiguously keynic form of money had to be established in the United Kingdom.

The Present State of the Monetary System

Every sovereign state, and any monetary union of states, has its own fiduciary ('take it on trust') 'money'; this is objectivised in a supply of coins and notes which are declared to be 'legal tender'. All participants in economic activity within that territory are legally obliged to accept payment in the designated currency as settlement of any debt, unless the settlement is lawfully contracted to be paid in some other currency or medium (such as 1kg gold bars). Trade within a country is conducted and transactions are recorded in terms of the national currency, while most international contracts cite the US dollar or another major currency (e.g., yen, euro, or British Pound) to quote prices and to make settlements.

Keynes suggested the creation of global chartalist money – bancor – during the wartime negotiations that led to the creation of the World Bank and the International Monetary Fund. The US saw greater advantage for themselves in using gold and the US dollar as the templates for a new world order, so the US dollar became the unit of account and the main medium for settlements between member states. The USA was able to maintain a statutory linkage of the rate of exchange of its currency to the price of gold ($32 = 1 ounce of gold) until President Nixon cut the link in August 1971. Since then, the world gold price (usually expressed in US dollars) has fluctuated, rising strongly when there was reduced confidence in fiduciary money and falling back when the major economies seemed to be growing sustainably with low inflation. Gold is sometimes still described as a 'store of value', but nobody considers contemporary banknotes to have that attribute. Only really naïve people could believe – or even hope – that a stash of £50 notes will buy as much consumer satisfaction in ten years' time as they will buy today.

A recurrent fear expressed in Keynes's writings was that of the currency being debauched, in the absence of a supranational monetary authority that would maintain a stable global standard on the lines of bancor. It would thus have horrified Keynes to have lived to see 'Economists' Keynesianism' develop during the nineteen-sixties into a machine for the excessive creation and circulation of money, which is exactly what is meant by the term 'debauching the currency'. The economic chaos of the seventies was the predictable outcome of the process, and the subsequent failure of monetarist politicians to recognise that they had established no sufficient means of controlling the velocity of circulation simply compounded the problems that came to a head in 2008.

Yet even in the prolonged aftermath of the 2008 crisis in the global financial system, there has been no hint of a will on the part of politicians to surrender control of their national currencies to an International Reserve Bank. The euro is the exact reverse of a step towards a global currency; it was created as a vital component in the structure of the *Festung Europa* that was being built to limit the exposure of the EU to the competitive tempest that will batter the post-industrial countries over the coming decades. The creation of the eurozone was a political project and the adoption of the euro was accompanied by so much false presentation of data by applicant governments and by complicit central banks that the fallout from the crash in 2007-8 inevitably exposed the flakiness of the common currency. It disclosed some of the lies on which the eurozone was constructed, and the legacy from that history of unsustainable falsehood may yet bring about the collapse of the system.

Since 1971, it has unequivocally been clear that national currencies, joined subsequently by the euro and by Special Drawing Rights created by the International Monetary Fund, are the only money that is available in the world. There is nothing 'backing' the British pound or the euro. The virtually uncontrolled development of banking and related activities after the 'big bang' in the nineteen-eighties enabled clever people to make very good livings by enabling the available money supply to be deployed momentarily to settle transactions, then moved on to another use. By devising ever-more-sophisticated forms of contract, and slicker means of making momentary use of credit, a widening range of financial traders has been permitted periodically to accelerate the circulation of money, to their profit.

Throughout modern history, each phase of very rapid development in the financial system is followed by a 'crash' (or 'crunch') when over-extended traders have not been able to deliver the cash or credit that is contractually required to be available. The risk that the failure of payments by one or two firms might become contagious forces the central bank and/or the government to take action to stabilise the immediate situation. The action often has to be extensive, and sustained over a period of months, or even years, as has been the case since 2008. Every time there is a bail-out of the banks, it is apparent that the system of money and finance depends entirely on the state, and on the central bank, which is an arm of the state. Yet between crises, it suits governments to pretend that their central banks are 'operationally independent' of the government; this myth is carefully set out in the constitution of the US Federal Reserve and in the foundation documents of the European Central Bank. It suits politicians, in most cases, for most of the time, to be able to assert that the monetary system works autonomously, according to national laws and international conventions. The mask slips occasionally; in the extreme crisis of 2007-8 the British prime minister claimed that he was 'saving the world' (or, at least the monetary system), but that is an extremely precarious place for a politician to be positioned. The electorate is unsettled by such talk, insofar as they understand it, which is not very far. After every crisis, the politicians and the voters want as quickly as possible to return to the fairytale world where honest and able monetary technicians in the central bank fully understand what they are supposed to be doing.

In daily life, even in the most developed societies, despite the easy availability of non-cash means of payment for use by firms and individuals, notes and coins continue to circulate in massive volume. Cash is used by less sophisticated individuals who do not understand how to use electronic transactions, people who do not have access to electronic means of payment, or those who refuse to use them for fear of hacking. Much more significantly, cash is king for drug dealers, secret gamblers, unauthorised minicab drivers, ponces and their victims, recipients of disability benefit when they do odd jobs, illegal immigrant workers, sellers of stolen goods and, say, fake watches, and many other participants in the multi-billion-pound black economy.

The cash that circulates from 'respectable' citizens into the black economy slides back into taxed areas of business through shops, street markets, pubs, bookies, box offices, and other legitimate outlets that are still largely cash traders. Retail banks make a charge for receiving cash from other retailers, or for issuing change to them, because handling cash is time-consuming; cash also brings a risk of robbery, occupies physical space and is dirty. Yet, notwithstanding their efforts to reduce the extent to which their customers require them to trade in notes and coins, the retail banks provide access to cash for small businesses' tills and for personal customers who insist on having ready money to buy drinks in the pub and vegetables on the market, and also to pay for illicit drugs, commercial sex, and for untaxed cleaning or plumbing services in a way that avoids their spending pattern being tracked through the record of their debit and credit card transactions. But it is essential to note that the vast sum of officially-issued cash that is in circulation, supplemented by the decades-worth of forgery, is trivial within the total flow of cash and credit through the global economy.

Despite the survival of physical cash, the majority of significant legitimate purchases within a mature market economy are settled by making transfers of credit, payment by mobile phone, debit card, touch-cards that the British idiotically describe as 'contactless', BACS transfer, credit card, cheque, banker's draft, direct debit, standing order, and other means that are authenticated signals to banks to make transfers of credit from one named and numbered account to another. Since securitisation became common, retail banks have discouraged depositors from holding significant sums to their credit in their current accounts by depressing interest rates and levying service charges on some deposits. In the first years of the new millennium, there was a pervasive delusion that clever people using computers had become masters of the universe. In place of retail banks collecting a flow of savings from the mass of the population, lending to persons and small businesses (retail lending) was funded by credit transfers that could be passed ever faster from one 'wholesale' borrower to another in cyberspace. As long as the frenetic circulation could continue to accelerate, the sustainability of the wholesale funding that was available to retail lenders was not challenged. Customers were offered such easy access to credit that millions of them saw no point in saving. The (mostly elderly) account holders who retained significant personal deposits saw their income vanish as interest rates approached zero after the 'crunch', and their bitter condemnation of this experience will deter their younger relatives from engagement with traditional forms and concepts of saving.

Interest rates are specified in many kinds of keynic contract, and are thus aspects of *ik*. 'Base rate' is set by the central bank, which is in some countries called the 'monetary authority'. Base rate is charged to the firms that are allowed to borrow directly from the central bank; typically, these are government departments and agencies, licensed banks, and some other specialist money-trading businesses. As the crisis unfolded during 2007-8, central banks assured institutions within their currency areas that enough transferrable credit would be made available to ensure that 'too big to fail' institutions could continue trading, provided all the affected firms obeyed constantly-evolving rules, which in some countries involved draconian terms for deferment of payments on commercial contracts and restructuring of large tranches of the national debt.

The rates of interest that were specified in many keynic contracts were flexible, so that during the life of the contract, the rate could go up and down in line with changes in the base rate. Until the crash, LIBOR – the London Inter-Bank Offered Rate – was supposedly a representative average of the rates at which participating banks were borrowing from and/or lending to other banks, as reported to the London banks' trade association. After the crash, it was disclosed that some banks guesstimated a 'normal' daily rate, and that many wantonly untruthful reports had been submitted, to reflect the commercial interests of firms and of individual traders rather than objective reality. Even after the exposure of this scam, LIBOR continued to be published. Billions of poundsworth of new contracts cited this template interest rate on every trading day, and trillions of poundsworth of contracts citing LIBOR continued in force, because regulators (all over the world) accepted the traders' argument that it would have been impossibly complex to replace it quickly with anything else. Some bankers were penalised and some banks were fined, but the economy demanded the continuing creation of contracts to serve both material markets and the many virtual casinos, and so the discredited system was revamped and continued.

Contract law requires that there are two parties to any transaction: a buyer who is to receive some service, asset, or other benefit, and a seller who is to deliver the service or asset to the buyer. The seller is required to *perform* whatever it is that they promise under the contract, for which the buyer is obliged to pay the *consideration* that is the agreed price for the performance.

There might be a significant period of time between making a contract and the date when the final delivery of performance is due, which is usually the date and time when the final component of the consideration is due to be paid. A contract to supply new aircraft or to build a major bridge takes several years to complete, and modern contract terms are structured to enable the two parties to complete the deal even though both the job specification and the purchasing power of money may change dramatically during the contract period. Both parties to long-running supply contracts are aware that economic and political conditions may change significantly during the contract period. The buyer wants to be as sure as possible that he can make payments in the specified currency on the due dates while managing the risks that regulatory change, inflation, deflation, or currency exchange-rate fluctuations will make future settlements more expensive than had been anticipated at the time the contract was negotiated. The supplier wants to reduce the risk of having to pay higher than estimated future prices for input materials and for labour, and to be able to make up for delays due to unusually adverse weather or political problems – possibly including terrorism – by managing purchases to take account of deviations from the critical path that is planned for the project. Hence, the treasurers and finance directors of large non-financial organisations use sophisticated keyns, including some gambling deals, to mitigate the perceived risk of potential variances in future prices and input costs that could derail their tightly budgeted business plans.

The Crisis of 2008

The London merchant banks were established between 1700 and 1900. Their speciality was to devise and trade in *ka*s that met the growing demand from governments, local authorities, and businesses to borrow money. At first, they operated within the UK, but they quickly developed international business. They also assisted companies to make share issues, to sell bonds, and otherwise to add to their available capital resources. When the British financial markets were largely deregulated in the nineteen-eighties, most of the surviving merchant banks merged with stock-broking and stock-jobbing firms to form greatly enlarged 'wholesale' financial conglomerates that did business on their own account and offered advisory services to a huge range of firms, trading with each other and with retail banks. These firms became highly opportunistic, empowering their star traders, dealers, and advisers to open a vast range of new lines of business and to expand the most attractive opportunities to the full. Thus, when the markets froze after the crisis in autumn 2008, it was clear that on a mark-to-market basis many of their assets were incapable of being priced.

The British authorities that had let the crisis occur – the Bank of England, the Treasury, and the piffling Financial Services Authority – could be in no doubt that if they had been alert to developments in the markets they could have (and should have) prevented the crisis. Thus they colluded in a complex bail-out that potentially cost taxpayers hundreds of billions of pounds and risked unleashing massive inflation. The material economy went deeply into recession and living standards declined, but, thanks to the bail-out, the financial sector began to release finance sufficiently to restore inflating prices to the property market.

Systematic, radical restructuring of the conglomerates, though widely recommended, has not taken place. Some prudential measures have been applied, chiefly requiring the surviving players to accumulate greater reserves in their banking divisions, but essentially, minus Bear Stearns and Lehman (which had both had their home base in New York), the conglomerates slithered towards business as usual.

The complexity of the markets and the products in which the conglomerates had been power-brokers grew over several decades. In the nineteen-seventies, they devised the first generation of derivatives to facilitate speculative bets that were each derived from the risk profile of a real-world contract type, such as insurance against hailstorms destroying growing crops in the US mid-west. Subsequent phases of development in this market added more speculative risks, further removed from any reference to the material economy. Derivatives were followed by spread bets that enabled punters (many of whom were traders employed and funded by firms in the securities industry) to speculate on movements in financial markets and in commodity prices. Clever programmers created algorithms that enabled machines to trade with each other at vastly higher speeds than human brains could encompass, which required the creation of even more sophisticated programs supposedly to prevent such high-speed trading from running wild and undermining the system. The vast majority of such contracts had no role in funding industrial investment or the construction industry, or even as financial reinsurance.

The trend moved further into Wonderland in the late 1990s, when the traders began to issue what grew to become many billions of dollarsworth of 'products' created by structured investment vehicles (**SIVs**). The SIVs were each given a separate legal identity when they were created for specific purposes, such as wholesale funding for 'bundles' of securitised mortgages and credit card debts. Primary securitisations recognised the purchase of a bundle of loans owed to retail banks and mortgage lenders, the credit they received from the sale enabled the lenders to buy a new bunch of *ka*s created by individuals, by partnerships, and by small to medium-sized firms. Some of the securities that were created in this way were resold in the wholesale market – maybe several times over – to become part of the asset portfolios that were consolidated into **CDOs** (collateralised debt obligations) and **CLOs** (collateralised loan obligations) issued by SIVs and by funds of funds, most of which were affiliates or spin-offs of securities firms and of hedge funds, though one firm, a subsidiary of the US-based insurer AIG, ruined that massive global organisation.

The dealers in these products traded with each other electronically within and between currency zones and increasingly in cyberspace, creating, swapping, exchanging, repackaging, and otherwise churning bets that were classified as futures, options, derivatives, and other innovative 'securities' which enabled the expanding complex of fictional assets and liabilities to be kept moving through the markets. Programs were adopted by all the wholesale banks and securities traders, supposedly rationalising their attempts to achieve a rolling match of maturities of assets against liabilities across all their terrestrial and cyberworld contracts. The balance of ***ka*** with ***ko*** was supposedly verified by a real-time assessment of ***VaR,*** the perceived total 'value-at-risk'.

VaR provided a summary estimate of the supposed 'fair valuation' of an organisation's portfolio of assets and of contingent liabilities, derived from the current market prices that all the assets would fetch and the maximum possible loss that the organisation would face if it had to pay out on all the bets that it had underwritten. This assessment was supported by forecasts of whether the ***ka***s and the ***ko***s in the firm's book of business would continue to balance at a series of time points in the future if no further contracts were entered into. This indicated which sorts of transaction should be added to the existing portfolio to eradicate adverse potential future imbalances. By 2005, the methodology had been extended in some banks and securities firms to postulate a ***TCE***, a tail condition expectation, or ***Tail VaR***, which alongside other more complex methods of risk evaluation helped them to recognise – when the 'crunch' struck – how seriously they had mismanaged their portfolios by mixing the residue of traditional banking with a book of bets. They had ignored the simple fact that as soon as any firm tried to liquidate a significant tranche of any of the asset classes in their portfolio, this would instantly change the balance of supply and demand, and thus the price of the 'products', which would undermine the valuations on every firm's asset register under the accountants' 'mark to market' regulations.

In the first years of the new millennium, the global securities firms put intense pressure on their highly intelligent but historically ignorant traders, and offered them extraordinarily inflated cash incentives to devise, buy, and sell innovative contracts, which all the others followed, creating concentrations of risk successively around each novelty. All such risks were logged and overseen by the compliance experts in the conglomerates, and over the years after the crash it was to become apparent that most of these products were so robust, and the contracts that created them so clear, that they remained valid, and the profits receivable on them strengthened the firms' balance sheets. However, as marcomic industry in several of the advanced countries continued to shrink under competition from the emergent economies, an increasing proportion of securitisations supplied credit that financed rising property prices and household borrowing. This seemed to be a slick and painless process, as each new batch of consumer borrowing could be securitised and passed on through the 'wholesale' market. The banks and financial firms' asset-and-risk portfolios appeared constantly to meet the dynamic equilibrium requirement according to whatever mathematical model was currently in fashion. This was a world totally different from that which Keynes had inhabited, where the predominant industrial sector retained massive unused or underutilised shipyards and factories, and was surrounded by former employees who remained skilled and willing to work. To apply stimulatory monetary and fiscal measures in the context of the inter-war depression could restore a healthy mixed market of financial and material activities, which could thereafter grow autonomously.

In the entirely different circumstances of the post-2008 recession, Britain had no significant mass of mothballed factories, so almost the entire focus of policy-makers had to be on stabilising the finance sector. But wholesale finance took stabilisation for granted and went for growth, beginning with the low-hanging fruit, housing. Hence, people were enabled to borrow to become house-buyers, enabled to offer ridiculously rising prices, especially in the greater London area and the few other hot spots where there was the greatest shortage of desired properties. Keynes's proposals to stimulate the thirties economy would have the effect of reducing inequalities between the regions of Britain and the sectors of its economy; moves to stabilise the financial system after 2008 emphasised regional and sectoral inequality. The distribution of votes between the Remain and Leave sides in the EU

Referendum gives a clear picture of the geographical impact of these factors in England and Wales.

After the financial big bang, financial conglomerates and some retail banks became increasingly adventurous in lending for commercial property, as industrial investment (and consequently the availability of industrial employment) declined as the global market in manufactured marcoms was increasingly captured by emergent economies. Thus, year on year, an increasing proportion of consumer spending was alienated to purchase imports of marcomic components and of marcoms that would become neoquons on the supermarket shelves, as well as imports of quons and components for quonic services. A torrent of propaganda assured owner-occupiers who did not move home that their equity in their homes was increasing in step with the rise in prices of the similar properties that were sold, and all home owners were encouraged to borrow against the supposed security of their equity to buy and to hire more quons. Thus, ongoing acceleration of credit creation and circulation was transmitted via the housing market into borrowing more money to buy quons, while brandowners increased their profits as cheaper marcomic components enabled branded products to be assembled even more cheaply.

The central banks and regulators in the US and the UK allowed the credit bubble to develop until 2006, when defaults on sub-prime mortgages in the USA made it impossible for managers of lending firms not to notice that an incalculably large proportion of the contracts that they put on the 'asset' side of their accounts might not be recoverable. At the interface between the retail and the wholesale sectors, several securities firms, including some of the largest, became unable to compute their value-at-risk and to set it alongside any 'valuation' of their countervailing assets. At an early stage in the development of the crisis, Lehman Brothers was compelled to declare that it could not instantly demonstrate its liquidity, so it was taken over by the regulatory authorities and the liquidators sold its more obviously viable trading operations to other firms. Subsequently, over several years, the disposal of Lehman's assets was to prove that the company's resources were amply sufficient to meet all its liabilities, and to pay the hefty fees levied by the liquidators. Yet the strength of Lehman's assets could not be demonstrated when a state of crisis was perceived to exist.

In the UK, the solvent Lloyd's banking group was 'persuaded' to take over HBoS (the uneasy product of a merger between the Halifax Building Society and the Bank of Scotland) which was found to have greatly overextended its commitment to speculative markets and lent recklessly on commercial property. When the scale of the disaster became clear, the merged Lloyd's Group could only be 'saved' by the nationalisation of most of its equity. The Royal Bank of Scotland, all on its own, had replicated the HBoS fiasco and it was also nationalised.

In October 2008, the 'banking system' was perceived to have failed, governments enabled their central banks to prop up the hastily restructured conglomerates, and ministers were directly involved in the rationalisation process. Emulating an innovation by the US Federal Reserve, in March 2009 the Bank of England initiated its greatest-ever open market operation – effectively 'printing' new money with which to buy government bonds from the banks – under the new name of 'quantitative easing' (QE). The Bank of England's new scheme provided the banks with liquidity with which to repay depositors and bondholders who demanded the cash to which they were entitled. The most overstretched UK building society, Northern Rock, was split into a viable firm that could soon be sold to Virgin Money and a 'bad bank' whose assets could eventually be sold on at significant discounts by a state holding company. This model was to be copied in other countries where similar cases were identified. If that range of interventions had not been undertaken, ordinary trade and industry would have become inoperable, cash machines would have emptied, and the payment of wages and of taxes would have ceased.

As a consequence of QE, central banks' balance sheets grew massively, while the keyns that they bought for the money that they created from nothing enabled the banks to balance their books. Over the next decade, securities that banks had not been able to sell in 2007-8 were bought by the central banks and piled up on their asset registers. While QE seemed to be generally positive for the massive US economy, the UK's material economy stagnated and the balance of payments plunged deeper into deficit. QE by the European Central Bank started later than in the UK, was explained with even less clarity than in Britain by officers of the ECB, and players in the diverse European markets showed little comprehension of the scheme. Nevertheless, QE grew into the engine that facilitated the greatest-ever debauchment of the world's leading currencies; central banks' governors and boards held – and accepted – responsibility for conducting this exercise, without any concept of how to stop doing it or what its ultimate effect would be. That remains the situation at the time of writing.

Money and Macroeconomic Management

Interest rates that are quoted in contracts are determined by the lenders, who take note of forecasts of potential changes in base rate and in currency exchange rates where they may be relevant to the decision. The lender in each case also takes a view of the viability of the borrower over the period of the contract, and in the twenty-first century it appears that the risks of lending to a participant in the material economy are greater than are the majority of finance-to-finance transactions with which the lenders are more familiar. Before the 'big bang' in the nineteen-eighties, the traditional rule was that the weaker and more uncertain the perceived income-generating potential of the borrower, and the less extensive and secure its asset portfolio, the higher a rate of interest would be demanded on any loan advanced to them. The liberation of financial markets coincided with the destruction of much of British industry, and ever greater numbers of contracts were bets with other participants in the financial markets in deals that became increasingly detached from terrestrial reality as the inventiveness of the traders matched the expanding power of computers and the growing range of algorithms. The traders in derivatives, futures, swaps, and a huge range of newly invented securities and bets bought the highest agency ratings for their 'products', which increased their acceptability to counterparties who had no significant comprehension of the products or the risks to which they could give rise.

The causes of the credit crisis of 2007-9 can be seen in systemic and psychological terms, as illustrated above by Minsky's thesis, which makes more remarkable the extent to which governments and central banks ignored what was happening in the financial markets around the turn of the century. Although Minsky's principles remained in relative obscurity, central banks could not be acquitted from the charge that, throughout the build-up of the bubble, they ignored the more traditional – and equally valid – guidance that was available from Fisher's Law (aka the *Quantity Theory of Money*). The law is summarised in the simple equation:

$$MV=PT$$

Where M is money supply, V is velocity of circulation (of all media that can be deployed as spending power), P is the level of prices, and T is the number of transactions at those prices. In the predominantly materialist economy that existed until the nineteen-sixties, the purpose of the monetary system was to facilitate and support material trade. By 2000, while purporting to control the media of exchange that fell within central bankers' definitions of money, **M**, governments, central banks, and market participants effectively ignored **V**; this spectacular negligence freed the banks and the speculators massively to increase their turnover. Banks and other financial firms churned the credit that they made available to each other and moved the recognised money-supply ever more speedily from one transaction to the next, while keeping the notional total of officially recorded 'money' within the stated target range. Some of the incremental turnover was used by the wholesale financial market to securitise loans and mortgages that were issued to the public by retail banks (and by building societies, savings and loan companies, and similar businesses), and by credit card companies and by a huge raft of other licensed lenders, all of which became increasingly adventurous in the types of contract that they created with firms and individuals.

In the period from 1990 to 2010, the emergence of new firms producing marcomic components in low-wage countries enabled retailers in the formerly industrial countries to contribute to rising living standards by selling an increasing range of quons and neoquons, at constant or falling prices year after year, and thus the post-industrial economies were even more de-industrialised. While inflation was apparently 'restrained' because retail prices of neoquons and lower-esteemed quons were falling, the 'valuations' of houses and of well-located commercial property increased massively. Government ministers and central bankers, led by the magisterial figure of Alan Greenspan at the US Fed, seem really to have believed that the 'money supply' was under control. Economists, politicians, and commentators supposed that modified monetarism was achieving an ideal combination of economic growth with very mild price inflation that was reflected in the consumer prices indices. Only in 2008 did it become obvious that the supposed control mechanism had been irrelevant to the rampant growth of speculative intra-finance-sector transactions.

During the era when the monetarist delusion prevailed in British politics (broadly, 1980 to 2007), various lobbies and interests developed the pre-existing dozens of definitions of 'the money supply', which ranged from

- banknotes and coins only
- widening to banknotes plus coins plus bank deposits
- extending to still wider definitions that included all types of 'instruments' that may be traded by banks and securities brokers, including more betting contracts.

In the much simpler world that had given rise to Fisher's Law (in 1911) it was recognised that if an increase in the supply of money (**M**) and/or in the velocity of circulation of a growing variety of means of making payments (**V**) is significantly lesser or greater than the rate of growth in the supply of goods and services in the economy, the resulting imbalance **must** impact on prices (**P**) and/or on the amount of trade (**T**) that takes place. Keynes described Fisher's Law as 'a truism', a simple statement of the obvious, but that in no way implied that it was invalid or irrelevant. It was axiomatic that price stability for marcoms could only be maintained if the effective money supply that was accessible to economic agents in any period – **M** multiplied by **V** – increased (or diminished) in line with the growth (or the decline) of material economic activity (**T**) in which human beings participated. Whichever definition of **M** was selected for any expository or regulatory purpose, if the product of **M** times **V** increased more than **T**, the prices at which transactions could be concluded (**P**) must go up. If **M** expanded faster than **T**, price inflation could only be avoided if **V** decelerated at the rate that compensated for the potential impact of the excess of **M**. Fisher assumed that 'credit money', **M'**, has its own – faster – **V'**; which means that an increase or decline in the accessibility of credit can quickly become disruptive to the economy. So if the perceived money supply is controlled, but the increase of credit is uncontrolled, the circulation of money-and-credit (the purchasing power available at any moment) is unlimited.

In the world that had fallen prey to the monetarist myth after 1980, the millenarian debt bubble became so destructive because monetarist regulators apparently felt so cocksure about their mastery of their naively-defined 'money supply' that they effectively ignored the constantly-varying (usually increasing) rate at which power-to-borrow was developing. Totally removed from any sector of the material economy, the autonomous financial market's expansion of the range of types of keyns, and the speed of transaction, accelerated **V** to the extent that the volume of assets in existence passed beyond the control of even the biggest market participants and thus made the noughties crisis inevitable.

In the slump of the nineteen-thirties, it had been apparent that as unemployment increased, the aggregate purchasing power of the population declined. The velocity of circulation and the number of transactions declined, and as firms competed for sales there was downward pressure on prices, which impinged most heavily on marcom-making and trading sectors. Quon prices held up better, because the more privileged sectors of society – the customers for the then much smaller luxury market – better retained their purchasing power; indeed, some quonic brands grew through the depression because their marcomic input costs (including the cost of labour) could be reduced. Jev prices were highly volatile because many sales were driven by necessity as owners faced ruin, while the super-rich could still compete to buy the most-desired jevs.

Although vastly smaller than in 2008, the global stock of keyns in 1929 included the bulk of the government debt that had been incurred during the First World War and the credit that had been generated in the irrational Wall Street optimism of the mid-late twenties, plus the credit that had been extended in emulation of Wall Street in the smaller markets all around the world. Hence, the 'crash' that first hit New York keyn prices on Black Tuesday, October 29, 1929, reverberated throughout the financial world. It was a novel event of cataclysmic proportions. Central bankers were keen to prevent the situation being made worse by hyperinflation, which (in the nineteen-twenties) had destroyed Germany's capability to service the debts that had been imposed on their new Republic under the Treaty of Versailles. In order to keep control of their own states' financial markets, central banks reduced the money supply broadly in line with the shrinkage of the economy, which further intensified the depression.

In those conditions, as **P** and **T** were declining, a significant deceleration in **V**, and even more so in **V'**, was inevitable, as millions of people were compelled to reduce the number and magnitude of transactions that they could undertake in the material economy as their incomes and expectations declined. This pressure was also reflected on firms, especially in the marcom sector, which had to cut back on expenditure as sales declined; many such businesses went out of business, and millions of their employees became unemployed. As this saga unfolded, JM Keynes saw that the obvious way to break the slump was to stimulate **V**, the rate of circulation of money in the economy.

'Economists' Keynesianism'

Keynes determined that the key to a recovery was psychological. Both in their personal spending and in releasing funds from the firms that they control, real-world market participants are likely to spend more of their money, sooner, and to borrow more for investment, if they expect their own incomes and the trade that they do to increase thereafter. When they are presented with credible signals that the economy is getting stronger, they will want to take advantage of the upturn. Thus, if the government makes good news by reducing taxes and increasing its spending, more goods and services will be bought and sold, with the result that more people will be more fully employed. Keynes' *General Theory of Employment, Interest and Money (1936)* postulated that a judicious combination of increased government spending and active management of interest rates during a depression could support the necessary acceleration of **V** by unlocking unused circulating capital to pay for wages and commodities. That would cause further demand to appear in the economy through the 'multiplier' effect. The government should also be willing to increase **M** as much as may prove necessary, once the economy was expanding again, to maintain stable prices. The ambition and innovative capabilities of the banking sector would speed **V'**, financing the growth of the economy until it came close to 'full-employment equilibrium', at which point the brakes (reduced state spending, higher interest rates, and tighter control of the money supply) should be applied in order to prevent 'overheating'.

The *General Theory* was later presumed to have provided a partial rationale for the government's spending and borrowing policies that facilitated rearmament between 1936 and 1939. But Keynes's prescription was not used directly by the government in that period. Nevertheless, in the later nineteen-thirties, a major programme of house building was encouraged by Neville Chamberlain, as Chancellor of the Exchequer and later as Prime Minister. This was funded largely through lending by building societies, with government guarantees, while the state and local authorities invested in the necessary roads and ancillary infrastructure.

Lloyd George had promised 'homes for heroes' in a 'land fit for heroes' during the Great War. That promise had been put on hold by the austerity measures of 1921, and then it was deep-frozen by the state spending cuts of the mid-nineteen-twenties, even before the financial system went through the trauma that followed the 1929 crash. Successive governments supported the supply of electricity to extended areas of the country by both private companies and municipally owned power stations. But much the most significant stimulus to **V'** in the late nineteen-thirties arose from the government's spending on ships, aircraft, tanks, and ordinance to be ready for a Second Great War that was becoming inevitable. Firms that had supplied the better-off sections of the population with fashionable cars and radio sets during the recession could adapt their plant to manufacture tanks, aero engines, radar, and communications equipment that the forces would require, while domestic radio receivers were to be the most effective medium for morale-building, the dissemination of information, and propaganda through the war years to come.

The demands on resources that were thrown up by the Second World War required a total command economy, and the experience of the former conflict was drawn upon heavily in contingency planning before the war. Every price that could be controlled was to be controlled, and quantities of every marketed commodity were to be rationed for allocation to 'priority' consumers. Keynes was drawn into the centre of government, managing the monetary system with innovative skill that earned him a peerage and with an assiduity that may have undermined his heath.

The war was won, but it has frequently been suggested that the subsequent peace was a period of loss and decline for the United Kingdom. For two decades after 1950, successive UK governments adopted policies based on a bowdlerised interpretation of the 'General Theory', here characterised as Economists' Keynesianism, aimed to bring about 'full employment equilibrium'. This concept was developed as a macro-economic equivalent of the notional equilibrium that Economists asserted would be achieved in each segment of each market if competition were allowed freely to determinate outcomes. The fiscal and monetary devices that Keynes had proposed should be used to relieve a severe depression were now to be employed even during mild recessionary phases. This repackaging of policy prescriptions fostered the delusion that the Chancellor of the Exchequer could so closely 'fine tune' the total economy that unemployment would be minimised, while growth would be stable and continuous. However, within less than a decade, it became apparent that the aggregate effect of such measures was to provoke Keynes's nightmare of inflation. Wage and price inflation were of concern in the sixties, and the 'spiral' of increasing wages pushing up prices that stimulated a new round of wage demands became rampant in the seventies.

The post-war 'neo-Keynesian' Economists did not sufficiently recognise that the increasingly voracious demands of the national health, welfare, and benefits systems, the increasing cost of education (including modest expansion of higher education), and the continuing demand for defence spending in the 'Cold War', on top of the cost of servicing the national debt, were constantly increasing the national budget. Hence any tightening of fiscal policy (reduced state spending or raised taxes), or of monetary policy, tended to impinge on the private sector, on local government, and on the nationalised industries.

During and after the war, all the pundits were agreed that there should be a focus on investment in industry to produce real economic growth. British producers had to be enabled to compete with US exporters (who had been able to invest heavily to meet the demands of the US war economy) and with the newly-designed output that came from new plant that was being built by desperately determined Germans and Japanese whose countries had been devastated in the war. However, British governments depressed incentives by imposing 'super-tax' on high earners, and limited the capacity of industry to accumulate capital by imposing purchase taxes on domestic sales of produce and by imposing corporation tax on company profits. National insurance levies were taken from all employees and from their employers, alongside Pay-As-You-Earn income tax, which tended to disincentivise employees who had expected to receive immediate benefits from winning the war. A combination of low productivity, rising wages, and high taxation led to the premature closure of older plant, which resulted in redundancy of skilled personnel and reductions in industrial capacity.

In addition to the deterrent impact of taxes, domestic demand for consumer goods was limited by restrictions on the creation of credit for consumers (e.g., making people pay significant cash deposits to buy houses or consumer durables, and/or reducing the number of months over which credit could extend). Tightening of these rules became characteristic of successive 'credit squeezes', which indeed reduced demand, to which suppliers responded by reducing their investment plans, and/or by closing low-productivity plant.

Inevitable Failure

In economies that were subjected to the inflationary effects of Economists' Keynesianism, very few house owners were prepared to sell at lower prices than they had themselves paid, and so the property market stagnated during credit squeezes. Similarly, wages proved very resistant to downward pressure. By contrast, the periodic relaxation of credit creation in phases of monetary expansion led quickly to increased wage demands, more imports, and higher house prices, which had their impact before any investment in basic industries or high technology could come to fruition. Consequently, there were repeated deferments and reductions of industrial investment, a massive increase in the prices of the housing stock, wage inflation, and an expansion of personal debt. An inescapable policy priority of successive governments was to maintain the key elements of the welfare state, which had been promised during the war. The impossibility of giving an increasing number of beneficiaries more generous benefits from a stagnant or declining economy was self-evident, so successive governments tried to support expansion of the economy by facilitating an increase of personal indebtedness that enabled aggregate demand to increase.

Economists presumed that the government's receipts from income and purchase taxes would increase with economic growth, and thus maintain the welfare state. But as demand increased, the state and more of its individual citizens were borrowing money with which to buy imports. The massive loan that Keynes arranged from the Americans just before his death, which was intended to give war-weary Britain extra help to reconstruct the economy, was found to have bought in nylon stockings and cosmetics, more than industrial equipment, when it had all been spent. The nation's propensity to import consumer quons in preference to advanced industrial equipment has continued, and was the main driving force for the massive trade deficit in the second quarter of 2016.

Between 1956 and 2008, public policy moved from the command economy that had been masterminded by Keynes during the war, towards a mishmash of measures that were naively intended to enable the economy to function according to Economists' perception of a free-trade system. Under the ideologically-purist Labour governments of 1945-51, such ideas got short shrift, especially because the Berlin Airlift and the conquest of China by the communists made it obvious that elements of the war economy must continue in the Cold War. Then the Conservatives were in power from 1951, and they were forced to recognise the limits to Britain's global impact when the Franco-British force was compelled to withdraw ignominiously from the Suez fiasco in 1956.

It was suddenly and urgently necessary for the reformed Conservative government under Harold Macmillan to restore the morale of the nation, and their preferred method was to give people a sense of affluence, so that they could make their slogan in the next general election "You've never had it so good!". The spectre of Adam Smith was brought back from the limbo to which Keynes had hoped it would remain confined, so that Economists could refresh their models that simulated free trade determining prices throughout the economy, including wages – the price of labour. Such models were, self-evidently, very far from the contemporary reality.

In the postwar period, most jobs were covered by 'wages councils' or similar bodies, each of which served an industrial or commercial sector (or a major component of a sector), whose job was to reach agreement between employees, employers, and government officials on what would be a fair wage for each category of employee, given all the circumstances. The driving idea behind this was that the war could only have been won if each sector of the economy fulfilled the tasks assigned to it. Labour disputes, causing either a go-slow or work-to-rule, or a full-scale strike, could ensure that the affected sector failed to produce what was necessary, so settlements were required. In cases where strikes interrupted production, perhaps most notoriously in coal mines in east Kent while the Battle of Britain was raging above, such disputes were deplored as deeply damaging both to the economy and to the nation's morale.

Once the war was over, a minority of Economists soon began to advocate the demolition of the system whose objective was to produce synthetic sectoral consensus, in favour of genuine negotiation that would set wages according to market forces. In the real world, powerful trade unions and the Labour party ensured that negotiations would continue to be directed to securing nationwide settlements. But when Macmillan's government was in place, a majority of Economists, and a growing number of politicians who followed their views, argued that wages should be set locally by workplace units according to local conditions. This fissiparous approach operated with increasing disadvantage to the economy, however, especially where union representation was captured by 'activists' of whom the most conspicuous were in the printing and motor-manufacturing sectors. In those areas, nationally agreed minimum wages were subject to supplementation wherever 'wildcat' tactics could be deployed to compel employers to pay especially high rates for the most powerful groups of workers.

Newspapers can only succeed if they are topical, so the printers and their support workers could demand conditions and rates of pay that almost everyone else recognised to be excessive, and if they did not get them, they could simply strike. If the news of the day was lost, the publisher's revenue was lost, if the strike went on for weeks, the newspaper would be bankrupted by having to maintain its premises and maintain its journalists with no output, no sales, and no advertising revenue. Hence for decades the press was held to ransom by the corrupt hegemony of the unions. Similar practices arose in significant sections of the motor industry, with the effect that there were frequent stoppages of production which meant that customers with the means to pay could not always get the model of car that they wanted, so they accepted an imported alternative, and inward cash-flow to the British manufacturers became uncertain.

Beside the sectors where bandit trade union leaders had seized dominant positions were other sectors where counterproductive special conditions applied. Before 1960, Britain had invested almost exclusively in coal-fired electric power stations and in coal-gas retorts to produce 'town gas' for domestic and business use. Therefore, coal miners could stop the economy.

The Thatcher government's frustration at this situation eventually led, in the early nineteen-eighties, to a resolution that was long-planned. Newspaper printing, motor building, and coalmining for power generation were much cited as industrial relations failures that represented a sort of national 'disease'. This distemper was exacerbated by some of the union leaders and activists who were motivated by hard-left anti-capitalist views (frequently bolstered by direct affiliation with the Soviet bloc) who actively wanted to ruin the capitalist system, regardless of the impact that this would have on the apolitical majority of the workforce. The union leaders assumed that, during the seventies, the workforce had become generally prepared to strike for higher wages as a result of two macroeconomic drivers that had had the effect of raising prices for consumer goods rapidly. 'Organised labour' had become habituated to demand compensatory wage increases and to enforce the demands by calling strikes.

Disruptive Forces, Trade Unions, and Oil Producers

The first driver towards accelerated consumer price increases was the devaluation of the pound in 1968. From 1948 to 1968, the pound had been held at a fixed rate to the US dollar, under the rules of the International Monetary Fund (£1 = $2.80). During the sixties, Britain's already endemic balance of payments deficit with the rest of the world increased, so that by mid-1968 the Labour government of Harold Wilson recognised it to be unsustainable. A quick fix was sought in reducing the exchange rate of the pound to $2.40, which was intended to make British exports cheaper and thus potentially more attractive to foreign customers. The beneficial impact of the devaluation was countered by the fact that imports to Britain became dearer. The addiction of British consumers to US entertainment and other imported quons continued, and business purchasers of imported marcoms still needed them as inputs to the manufacture of goods for both home and export markets. Increasingly savvy commentators in the media enabled consumers better to measure the rate at which the prices of the things they bought were rising, and in their capacity as employees they demanded compensation for this 'inflation'.

The hoped-for effect of devaluation on exports and on the balance of payments was quickly vitiated by rising incomes, so during 1969 the government introduced a policy intended to slow down the rate of increase of wages. A much respected left-leaning Minister, Barbara Castle, was selected to find a means of ending what had become known as the wage-price 'spiral'. Her civil servants and advisers devised a system of prices-and-incomes control, which was explained in a substantial document entitled *In Place of Strife*. The unions refused to participate, and some senior members of the government refused to endanger their standing with the unions (who financed the Labour party) by supporting the policy. The initiative collapsed and, in 1970, Labour lost a general election to the Conservatives, whose leader, Edward Heath, scrapped the notion of managed voluntarism that had been proposed by Mrs Castle and introduced an 'industrial relations court' whose job would be to enforce the decisions of a 'prices and incomes board'. Fines and other penalties could be levied on people who disobeyed the court's judgements, and the entire trade union movement refused to collaborate with or obey the court. An impasse was reached, strikes became endemic over many sectors of the economy, and the balance of payments became worse than that which had triggered the devaluation.

Before any resolution of the confrontation over the wage-price spiral had been found, the second great macroeconomic disruption occurred, in 1973. After prolonged cogitation and careful planning, the Organisation of Petroleum Exporting Countries (OPEC) determined to change from being a discussion group to being a cartel. They agreed that they would all sell oil and natural gas at roughly triple the prevailing average global prices (according to the quality of the output from the various oil wells and gasfields) by imposing new taxes and higher royalties on all sales. Thus the oil-importing countries were to be compelled to transfer wealth to the oil exporters. Some of the member countries of OPEC had large populations existing on low incomes, and could use the money instantly for development; other member countries had small populations and could plan to use the money for investments that would support them when the oil ran out. Inevitably, much of the money was used to prop up dictatorships with advanced weaponry, much of it swanned away in corruption, and much enabled ruling groups to indulge in the wildest of conspicuous consumption. For the importing countries, and especially for Britain, the consequences were devastating. The railways had been 'dieselised', most goods and passenger miles were travelled in cars and vans and busses, and air travel had become important both in business and for holidays; every aspect of life depended on oil-fuelled transport.

No prices-and-incomes policy, and no industrial relations court, could reverse the tide of rising prices that flowed into the UK economy, provoking wage demands that sought not only to meet the actual level to which prices had risen but to anticipate the next year's price inflation as well. By the end of 1973, the Conservative government had sat out a miners' strike, which caused rota-cuts to electric power supplies in all regions of the country, and the 'three-day week' in which firms were only allowed to draw on gas or electricity supplies for three days a week (except for minor amounts to maintain refrigerated units and preserve security). Output and productivity rose during the period of the three-day week, but in general the balance of payments was worsening and 'industrial relations' had effectively been destroyed by the number and intensity of disputes.

Early in 1974, the Heath government called a general election, seeking powers, in effect, to rule by decree (as had been done in ordering the three-day week), and they lost the election, by a tiny margin. The Labour party formed a minority government supported by disparate groups of MPs such as Scots and Welsh Nationalists who extracted promises for the enactment of policies that rewarded their constituents. While some support on an issue-by-issue basis was offered by the tiny Liberal party in parliament, it proved impossible for the Labour leader, Harold Wilson, to build a coalition with them. A second election in 1974 elicited almost the same result, leaving the country to flounder with another precarious Labour government.

The Labour Party held office, but could hardly be said to have power, between 1974 and 1979. A cobbled-together compromise deal with the trade unions was reached on the basis that a Labour government was preferable to the Tories in the eyes of most of the union members, so the union leaders tried to moderate the extent to which wage demands rose above the level of prices. The economy was in chaos, a situation not perceptibly mitigated by the replacement of Harold Wilson by Jim Callaghan as Prime Minister. The balance of payments worsened, state borrowing increased, and interest rates rose.

Nine years on from the 1968 devaluation, the balance of payments was so bad, and the pound had declined so far in exchange for other currencies (under a 'free float'), that the government had no option but to seek a loan from the International Monetary Fund. The purpose of the loan was to enable the government to stabilise the exchange-rate for the pound and restore the credibility of British state debt. The ministers knew that any IMF loan would be set on terms that implicitly blamed the 'neoKeynesian' economic policies that had been followed in the fifties and the sixties for the crisis. The clique of US Economists who were now at the height of fashion with the IMF were self-styled 'Monetarists'. They advocated the proposition that if a government controlled the money supply effectively, that would set a limit on the amount of spending that their economy could experience. If a sufficiently stringent monetary policy was pursued, focussed on stringent control of government spending within 'cash limits', monetarists argued that inflation could be squeezed out of any economy, which could then operate according to models derived from Adam Smith's dogma of free trade. Thereafter, the economy could grow autonomously and everybody could become better off.

The Chancellor of the Exchequer duly signed a 'Letter of Intent' to the effect that the government would pursue monetarist policies, which were sent to the IMF, and the Labour movement – the trades unions and the Labour Party – went into meltdown. The Labour Party was split dramatically between those members who argued that the country must conform to IMF demands in order to bring some 'sanity' back to economic management, and those who declared that the monetarist proposals were contrary to the socialist principles of the Labour Party and of the wider labour movement.

Most trade union leaders tried to persuade their members to adhere to their support for the Labour government as the least-worst option and thus to modify their demands. This argument failed to have effect, as disparate groups of union members organised strikes to try to make employers concede wage rises in accordance with rising costs of living. Hence came about the 'Winter of Discontent' (1978-9) when rubbish plied high in the streets and in some local authority areas burials were not available for the dead when cleansing and cemetery workers went on strike; these were just two conspicuous examples of a massive national breakdown of industrial relations. An election early in 1979 brought the Conservatives to power under a new and largely unknown leader, the first female Prime Minister, Margaret Thatcher.

Thatcherism: Worthy Intentions, Disastrous Outcomes

Mrs Thatcher and her key allies embraced Monetarism, and were determined to make it work. With the Bank of England, they set maximum targets for the expansion of the money supply, and they set limits on the amount that every department of state and each public sector organisation could spend from the central budget. Interest rates rose dramatically as competition increased to get access to the curtailed supply of credit, and cutbacks and redundancies began to affect all publicly-funded entities. The economy entered a recession, house buyers faced higher mortgage rates, finance for industry and commerce was squeezed, and job opportunities were reduced. A deep recession beset the country, which could in small measure be attributed to a 'second oil price shock' late in 1979. Monetarists argued that the imposition of their policies would force participants in the economy to develop 'rational expectations' in place of the crazy free-for-all that had run riot in the seventies, and, indeed, the squeeze on cash and credit and the high interest rates did cause a severe shock to millions of individuals.

The government was widely seen as a right-wing clique that was trying to punish the mass of the people for the economic chaos of the seventies, inflicting pain for ideological reasons. Meanwhile, in opposition, the Labour Party rejected the moderate leadership that had accepted the IMF agreement, and elected the most left-wing leader in its history. By the time of the next election, they had prepared a manifesto so radical and unrealistic that Denis Healy (who, as Chancellor, had signed the Letter of Intent) called it "the longest suicide note in history". Although the Conservatives were widely regarded as viciously antisocial, an increasing proportion of the public was prepared to admit that their policies were having the effect of curbing excess in the wage-price drama. With Labour having made itself 'unelectable', Mrs Thatcher easily won an election in June, 1983, and thereafter the Conservatives had a clear field for a decade.

The deciding factors in the election were not the inanity of the Labour manifesto and the bumbling appearance of the party leader, Michael Foot, but the effects of Britain's astonishing victory in a war to drive out the Argentinians, who had captured the Falkland Islands (a British colony in the South Atlantic). It was widely agreed at the time, and has since been affirmed, that almost any other politician of her day would have agreed to American offers to mediate, which would have put a thin cosmetic on a British acceptance of the loss of the islands. Mrs Thatcher, however, exploited the 'can do' willingness of the chiefs of staff of the armed forces to attempt an invasion and reoccupation of the Falklands. This stretched to the absolute limit the resources of the 'conventional' forces, as it was clear from the start that neither the US nor the USSR would tolerate any British nuclear strike on Argentina. After a campaign that tested the stamina of the British marines and infantrymen beyond any reasonable limit, demonstrated the inadequacy of their equipment (even including their boots), and suffered severe casualties, the Argentinian occupying forces were forced to surrender. The British nation (having been acutely concerned at the human cost of the war, and the probability of another national humiliation) experienced both relief and pride in the outcome. Thatcher was momentarily a national hero, as were the troops and sailors who returned to almost ecstatic welcomes at the ports and in a march through London. The good feeling ensured that the bitterness that had been engendered in much of the country by the government's economic policies was insufficient to prevent the Conservatives winning the next general election comfortably.

With a secure majority in the House of Commons, the government set about the permanent reconstruction of the economy. This included removing from the trade unions the potential to overcome any policy set by a government, Labour or Conservative. Even at the cost of destroying the industries in which they were employed, and accepting the destruction or abandonment of billions of poundsworth of viable plant and of potential output, Thatcher's team were set on defeating the left-led mass trade unions. Thus, in March 1984, plans were announced for the eventual closure of more than sixty coal mines, the programme to start immediately.

Arthur Scargill, the head of the National Union of Mineworkers, led a majority in the national executive who accepted the view that unless their union took dramatic action while coal was still in high demand, the government would remove coal from its historic role in the economy and thus destroy the union and its members' livelihoods. Declining to hold a national ballot of members, the union launched upon a strike that the Thatcher government was prepared for. Mountains of coal surrounded key power stations, and the police were briefed to prevent pickets from the miners' union denying access to their workplaces for power station and other relevant employees. The strike was launched in the summer, well away from the period of peak winter demand for power, and miners in some districts declined to join the strike. The ideological Marxists in the NUM saw this as their last chance to deploy the massed might of organised labour to strike against the capitalist system through this assault on the power industry. Mrs Thatcher was quite happy to accept this challenge, as a vignette within the campaign that she and Ronald Reagan were conducting against the 'evil empire' based in Moscow. In apparent confirmation of Thatcherite suspicion of the links of Scargill's clique to the USSR, a levy was imposed on the wages of miners in the Soviet block to support the supposedly 'starving' miners' families in the UK. Scargill's subsequent refusal (or inability) to account for that money was to cause much bitterness amid the disillusion that beset many ex-miners and supporters in later years.

Coal, steelmaking, cutlery, wool, ceramics, automobiles, and a long tally of other industrial sectors were denied subsidies or short-term tariff protection by the government when they came under pressure from foreign competitors. Thus, alongside the deliberate plans to close coal mines and shipyards, the dramatic decline of much of the rest of British industry was allowed to occur by default of the government, which looked forward to a much cleaner future for the UK as a post-industrial centre for finance and cultural activities. Much of the country became both post-industrial and bereft of sufficient employment opportunity for the people who had been skilled and well-paid artisans, and for their children. The balance of payments for material goods became permanently adverse at this time; an overall balance was struck some years later by the profits received from British-owned businesses around the world and by financial services activity in London.

The government sold nationalised industrial sectors (steel, for example) and utilities (electricity, gas, water, railways, and telecommunications) through privatisations. The mass of new investors who were offered small packages of shares on favourable terms cashed-in their holdings as soon as a 'profit' was available and the shares largely passed into foreign hands. Due to this alienation of ownership of privatised businesses, divided payments went outside the UK. Japanese and German-owned motor factories were planted in the UK with enthusiastic support from the government, which ensured that their preferred sites for factories easily obtained planning consents, and that their operations received grants and tax concessions that had not been available to the former British industries. The profits from these investments could be taken overseas, at the discretion of the owners, further reducing the security of the balance of payments.

Government ministers, however purblind they may have been to the fate of huge areas of the country, could not wholly be ignorant of the destruction of material production that took place. They accepted the disappearance of the old industries because it removed the possibility of any reassertion of militant mass trade union activity. A strike by the workers in a chain of shops or a bank simply handed business to their competitors, and a general strike by bank staff was inconceivable save in the case of a total breakdown of the socio-economic order, when it would have nil effect anyhow.

Until the nineteen-eighties, the financial services sector had been controlled by a relaxed mixture of legislation and custom. Bankers and stockbrokers had been subject to peer-group censure since the emergence of those occupations. Wilful deceit or a default due to incompetence in a bank not only brought a risk of loss to depositors with that firm, but could destabilise the whole payments system, and similar consequences could arise from stock brokers making a fraudulent claim about the prospects for shares or bonds that they were offering for sale. Thus a simple system of discreet whistle-blowing had been developed, by which dangerous or ungentlemanly activities were shunned and 'cads' were frozen out of the business.

At the start of the eighteenth century, the reckless speculation known as the 'South Sea Bubble' ruined hundreds (maybe thousands) of investors and led to the passage of legislation which limited the formation of companies with limited liability shares to any firms that might be authorised by specific Acts of Parliament. Later in the eighteenth century, the canal companies obtained parliamentary authorisation, as did the railways in the first half of the nineteenth century. Nevertheless, some companies failed; one of the most spectacular such incidents was the collapse of the conglomerate that was built up by the 'railway king' George Hudson, who saw that consolidating local railway lines into a national network was feasible. However, the limitations of the available methods of financing, and Hudson's sharp practice, caused the collapse of his endeavour in 1849. Meanwhile, the overloading of parliament with petitions for company authorisations led to the passage of a Companies Act in 1844, the precursor of the present legislation, which enabled properly-funded and transparently-managed joint-stock companies with clearly stated aims and objectives to be registered without a specific Act of Parliament. Banks could be either partnerships or incorporated companies, but traders in shares and bonds operated as individuals within partnerships right through to the Thatcher years.

Then, amid the dramatic social and economic changes of the nineteen-eighties, interested parties in the financial trades easily persuaded the government that their sector needed to be modernised. Mergers of banking companies had occurred throughout the nineteenth and twentieth centuries, enabling the resulting firms to meet the changing needs of their customers, including very large industrial and commercial organisations. Opportunists now argued that the historical distinction between stock-brokers and stock-jobbers was out of date, and that the separation of those functions from banking was also obsolescent.

Hence, the Thatcher government brought in the 'big bang' of 1986, when centuries of regulation and generations of 'gentlemanly conduct' requirements were ditched, in favour of a corporate free-for-all in 'wholesale' finance. Stock-brokers, bill-brokers, and stock-jobbers merged with banks, merchant banks merged with banks, and gigantism vied with claims to offer a 'boutique' service as to what sort of firm best suited which sort of customer in what circumstances. More important than the institutional changes were the related innovations in the mode of operation of the markets, and in the range of 'products' available, which have been outlined already. Assets were churned, transmogrified, repackaged, and churned again, at increasing speed as computers improved and the algorithms used in the markets developed even faster than the technology through which they could be expressed.

In the lead up to the 2008 crisis, some of the most innovative speculators in bonds, shares, oil, and other commodities, and in all the related derivative gambling contracts, were self-styled 'hedge funds'. A hedge is a row of bushes and trimmed trees that marks the edge of a field or a garden, and can provide privacy and concealment. The pioneers in this sector of finance began trading as sophisticated, secretive, trend-bucking and sometimes counterintuitive clubs for specialist long-term investors, mainly high-net-worth individuals, and thus the name 'hedge fund' was a legitimate description for such entities when it was adopted in the nineteen-seventies.

Latterly, the majority of firms that operate under this designation have traded in derivatives that supposedly shadow markets in commodities, shares, currencies, and securities, and they played a significant part in precipitating the 'credit crunch' when they selected which institution should be 'sold short' next. 'Short selling' consists of buying an option to buy shares, or 'borrowing' shares at a fee that is a tiny fraction of the current market price of the shares, then offering the shares for sale, in sufficient volume that their price is forced down. The short seller then buys shares at the low price to which they have been driven, holds them for the shortest possible time, and takes a profit when they sell them to their contracted customers. The simple cure for this abuse is to categorise selling shares that one does not own at the material time as fraud, which it is. So called active investors do buy (as well as borrow) shares in businesses, frequently to force the firms to strip out assets and reduce their commitment to long-term investment; thus they put short-term 'profit' over the potential for long-term benefit to the economy.

Making Sense of the Post-Crash World

The **solvency** of any estate can be demonstrated when the total of intellectual property (*ik*) that is owned by an individual or a corporate entity, plus its financial assets (*ka*) and the current estimate of the potential resale price of its holdings of quons and jevs and marcoms, exceeds the aggregate *ko*.

$$(ko - (ka+ik+Q+J+M)) > 0$$

A person can only legally acquire the liquidity with which to make an increment to their pattern of consumption, or to meet an unexpected and unavoidable obligation to pay a debt, fine, or tax, by adopting one or more of the following means:

- sell material assets, usually quons or jevs, with the opportunity-cost of having ready cash but no longer having those assets,
- sell *ka*s, such as bank deposits, bonds, or shares; the opportunity-cost of this option is surrendering any maturity premium that might accrue to owners at the point when the *ka* is liquidated,
- take out a mortgage, loan, or hire purchase agreement; the opportunity-cost is that future income will be committed to servicing this *ko* throughout the contract period,

- hire the quon, which commits a slice of future income throughout the contract period and might provide less complete control over the consumer experience than does outright ownership,
- increase earned income, by expending greater effort, and/or spending more time at work, with the opportunity-cost of allocating less time and probably less energy to lifestyle activities.

Most of these options became inaccessible to many individuals and businesses in the Atlantic economies after 2007. While the temporary decline in city employment in the UK was exploited by independent school headmasters to recruit a few numerate schoolteachers, many more people saw little benefit in acquiring career-orientated qualifications that were already heavily oversupplied, and it became hard for the unemployed to gain valid work-related experience. Since then, there has been a more stratified approach to recruitment for city careers, which has slowly restocked the financial trades with ambitious and innovative people, but even before the vote for Brexit there was a high level of uncertainty about future employment prospects.

An economically active person flourishes when she or he can maintain a strong income flow, combined with careful management of debt and effective control over the asset mix in their personal estate. Humans are condemned to the ageing process, and must plan to meet the financial and social implications of longevity. In financially unstable periods, such as the present, it is impossible for many individuals to maintain savings plans, even if they are lucky enough to retain their jobs.

There is considerable historical evidence to support the proposition that, in stable economic circumstances, significant tax incentives have encouraged people to save, especially when consumers' access to credit is controlled. The prime methods are to refund income tax proportional to the amount saved or invested in a pension fund, or to place the tax rebate into an approved savings product. The decline in saving among the mass of citizens was one of the most significant developments of the twentieth century. In 1914, 40% of British households had at least one Prudential saving or insurance product, and at least another 30% of households were covered by other home-service assurance companies. By the millennium, Prudential's penetration had declined to 14% of households (many of these holding only old policies on which collection cost exceeded the premium received), and the overall coverage of households by life assurance was declining as policies lapsed, matured, terminated, or were paid out on the death of the assured individual. Savings and investments by households decreased from the later nineteen-fifties until 2007. The 'stakeholder' savings and pensions plans that were devised for lower earners under the aegis of the Blair government made no significant contribution to the replacement of the abandoned savings culture among the population. The most conspicuous (but quantitatively trivial) take-up of stakeholder plans has been as a tax-beneficial avenue for modest intergenerational cash transfer by an affluent minority.

The wildly irresponsible abandonment of the state earnings-related pensions scheme (SERPS) by the Tory government was an unmitigated disaster, which was compounded in the nineteen-nineties by taxation of absurdly miscalculated actuarial 'surpluses' on company pensions funds. This led to employers taking a 'pension contribution holiday' which shrank the funds in real terms until the unabashed leaders of the 'actuarial profession' admitted that they had been grossly underestimating the longevity of pensioners and thus the amount that should be accumulated in employees' pension funds.

This succession of failures under Conservative governments was compounded under Labour rule by 'brilliant' Chancellor Brown's savagely detrimental impact on the personal pensions that provident individuals had been encouraged to buy instead of SERPS, by his reckless tax-grab from the funds, and later by his 'advice' that occupational pension funds should sell shares to push falling markets further down after the 'dot-com' bubble burst in 2001. The 'default' pension scheme that was imposed on the lower orders by the 2010 coalition government will provide such exiguous additional retirement incomes for contributors (while taking many of them over the income threshold where they lose state benefits) that it will further discredit the very idea of personal savings and investment The era of pensioner poverty will approach its peak probably around 2030, and then continue through the mid-century.

Millions of people who saved voluntarily, through their pension funds and in other ways before 2008, saw that their funds' investments had greatly been diminished after the crunch, and many thousands among them are sufficiently sophisticated to recognise that a worse personal impact of the financial collapse will probably be experienced when significant inflation (potentially hyperinflation) circumvents the pensions providers' obligations to savers at some date in the future. Hence the very significant change in pensions policy that was announced in the 2014 British budget was at first welcomed by holders of personal pension funds. For ninety years, it had been a legal requirement that holders of such pensions, on retirement, must apply the bulk of their accumulated saving to buy a lifelong income called an annuity. Because actuaries had made desperately stupid miscalculations of average life expectancy and had insisted on pension funds holding bonds rather than equities (shares), the annuity providers were offering lower than expected pensioner incomes to new retirees every year.

Henceforward, individual fund-owners were to be able to spend or invest the money as they wish; they could blow it on cruises and luxury consumption over a few years, or support their children's house purchases, or buy an income via an annuity or through other investments, or, most likely, make some combination of all those choices. The macro-economic consequences will be significant; many more retired people will ultimately become wholly dependent on the state pension (and other benefits, such as housing and council-tax benefit) when their private 'pension pots' have been spent, which will increase the government's need to borrow or to increase taxes. Another macroeconomic consequence will be that the large investment funds that annuity providers have historically invested in the stock markets and in infrastructure projects will be reduced, as fewer people bother to invest in pension funds, with deleterious effects on capital investment and economic growth.

All this will make it more difficult for the economy to achieve sustainable long-term growth. The shrinkage of the available pool of investment capital will further weaken what is left of the shattered system of material production, distribution, and exchange. Textbook Economics offers no help, but fortunately many thousands of women and men who are known as 'economists' have developed practical skills and useful knowledge. They could apply their skill and experience to assist in the formulation of viable policies that can mitigate the potential crisis, if they finally free themselves of the Smith-Marshall dogma that has blighted the economy.

The turnaround in Britain's performance in the last two Olympic Games has inspired the entire nation; it is within the capabilities of the people to transcend the athletes' achievement by building anew the economy that led the world for well over a century. There is no lack of ability, inventiveness, ingenuity or imagination; all the evidence shows that Britain possesses these in abundance, notwithstanding admitted gaps in a range of practical skills that follow from the population being unconvinced that good long-term employment prospects will follow the training programme that is needed. The nation has been demoralised by generations of stupid policy and social exploitation. That cannot be the end of the story. The example of the Olympians and their huge support structure shows the truth of the adage, 'Where there's a will, there's a way!'

Chapter Four

Quons, Brand, and Price

For much of the twentieth century, in the non-communist world, the word 'materialist' implied disapproval about hedonistic consumption. Then, in the last years of the century, the invisible ear that guides the development of everyday speech responded to a shift in shared perceptions among human beings. By 1975, British consumers' attention had overwhelmingly become focused on branded things and experiences, and for any commentator in those circumstances to stigmatise what had become a normal aspiration would have seemed absurd. The increasing cohort of consumers who chose 'organic' milk and vegetables, and 'fair trade' coffee, required certification that their purchases met these preferences; certificates of verification of origin for such products are a class of *ik*, so buyers who make these options have voluntarily extended the scope of intellectual property.

Nothing that is consumed by humans in the modern urban economy is a simple 'gift of nature', gathered and used without the intermediation of other people or of corporations, without the use of capital equipment, and free from licensing systems and legal authority. 'Fresh air' is available to urban humanity only because governments enforce costly pollution control. If I grow lettuce in my garden – which is mine according to land law, and has planning consent for horticulture – I may use only genetically approved seed. My use of water from my own well or water butt is controlled under abstraction regulations and health and safety laws, and any fertilisers that I use must conform to licensed standards. Even if one could ignore taxation and interventionist state spending, regulative restrictions would still be pervasive, even in domestic life, in a free country. The Economists' ideal of self-interest guiding individualists in an environment of free trade is absurd.

As participants in the global economy, human beings learn that petrol prices in Australian and Icelandic service stations respond to events that affect output from oil wells on the Siberian steppes, the Arabian Desert, and the Nigerian coastal swamp, and that oil price movements can be exaggerated by exploitative hedging activity or undermined by new technology. Constant change in the supply-and-demand situation for commodities has knock-on effects on the pricing of alternative and complementary commodities. Lamb becomes more expensive when beef vanishes from the shops because cattle are slaughtered in a foot-and-mouth disease or BSE scare, and East African coffee prices rise in response to unseasonable Brazilian frost. No economically aware person can be in doubt about the direct personal relevance of speculation and of other influences that affect commodity prices.

Applying this awareness, corporate managers in many sectors of industry take steps in partnership with keyn traders to mitigate the adverse potential impact of input price movements and potential supply constraints on their cash flow projections by buying futures, options, and insurance, and through using a range of contingent funding techniques that suit their business model and their appetite for risk. These activities can mitigate the impact of risk events, but cannot completely transcend them. Financial devices to hedge against changes in the availability and price of commodities do not have any direct material impact on the production of the marcoms themselves. A group of commodity exporting countries can form a cartel – as happened more than forty years ago in the case of the Organisation of Petroleum Exporting Countries – that can increase the taxes and royalties that the import-dependent countries must pay to them. Any notion that material markets can move 'in the long run' towards a 'general equilibrium' of supply and demand in free markets, where decisions are based on 'rational expectations', is naïve fantasy.

Water and minerals are available on and under the land and beneath the oceans thanks to the 'bounty of nature', but their extraction depends upon a complex of keynic, quonic, and marcomic transactions. By the time a consignment of iron ore has been extracted from a mine in Australia and put on a train for shipment to Korea, the process has incurred (at least) the following costs:

Ik purchases and exposures:

- fees for exploration licenses,
- fees for verification of the legal status of the land,
- fees for confirmation of the landowner's right to extract the material,
- royalties to the landowner,
- regulatory fees and payments,
- tax,
- compulsory insurance premiums,
- licenses (company registration, planning consents, extraction licence):
- payments to any trade association or cartel,
- {and, in many countries, bribes}
- plus contract prices paid for:
- quon purchases
- specialist exploration services,
- branded equipment,
- engineering consultancy and services,
- skilled management and labour,
- unskilled labour,
- risk management services,
- optional insurance premiums (and any alternative risk financing),
- transport services,
- energy supply,

- water (and/or water abstraction rights, which are *ik*).
- keynic exposures where the activity can only occur when it is funded from either shareholders' resources or from borrowed capital,
- marcom purchases, payments for items used in mining, processing, and transportation that do not incorporate quonic *ik* and are therefore used at the extracting firm's risk.

Finance and Management

In companies' accounts, agricultural, mining, industrial, and logistical activities are often presented within 'cost centres', each of which can cover a complex of sites and premises and a sequence of processes. Cost centres vary in scale and in longevity. In manufacturing, a cost centre might be the whole of a factory or warehouse that repetitiously performs a very limited set of functions millions of times a week for decades on end, or it may be a team that is charged with designing a specific variant of an established product with a work programme and a budget to carry out that single one-off task, once, according to a tight time schedule.

'Fixed cost' comprises payment for all the resources that are necessarily allocated to a cost centre before it can do anything at all. This includes the cost of providing the site, the building, and the machinery, as required, in good order, together with connection to the energy and water supplies, and access to storage facilities and means of transport, plus the costs of achieving regulatory compliance, optimisation of the facility in accordance with the prevalent carbon trading regime, securing the presence of competent management and of a trained workforce, including cleaners and maintenance people. Taxes and license fees that fall on real estate also form part of the fixed cost of any economic activity that is conducted on that site. The great majority of materially productive cost centres have a designed capacity of output that can be achieved from normal working. The fixed cost remains a 'given' until reconfiguration of the facility is determined. The fixed cost per unit of output – average fixed cost – diminishes as it is shared between more items of produce.

The 'variable cost' that is attributed to the functioning of a cost centre comprises payment for resources that are used when the plant is operating, and the total variable cost falls or increases broadly in proportion to the level of output in successive periods. Most material inputs can only be sourced in indivisible packages – such as a pack of 1000 screws – that must be bought even if only one screw is needed to make the marginal unit of the product, the last one that is demanded. The variable cost that is attributed to a cost centre rises when each indivisible input is accessed and then falls as the batch of the input is more fully utilised. Average variable cost per unit of output decreases with increasing output, up to the point when the cost centre can gain the maximum benefit of the economies of scale in purchasing indivisible inputs, including the fixed cost element of taking on each additional employee.

Absolute optimisation of fixed-plus-variable cost over a vast array of variables would be attainable, if at all, only for a moment in a constantly-changing business environment. When the output from a cost centre declines sufficiently to require a reduction in workforce, significant redundancy costs are incurred, and a huge range of costs arises from the closure of plant, often including action to remove pollutants from the site, so a reduction in operational capability can have an extremely high marginal cost.

In accounting for material economic activities, financial controllers monitor the cost that is incurred at each point, and in many cases they estimate the embedded cost of work-in-progress as it passes 'downstream' through each of a sequence of cost centres that create the material components of an 'end-product', in the hope of defining the points at which the greatest 'addition of value' is presumed to occur. It is much more difficult to assess the 'value-added' by providing corporate services such as brand promotion and suppressing theft of a firm's *ik*, and to decide which costs of services are essential and which may be dispensable. Hence the easier range of tasks – tightly controlling the costs of materials, of energy, of warehousing, and of transporting material things – can more rigorously be carried out.

In deference to health and safety rules, including pollution control and energy efficiency, material processes are extensively regulated by the state, and in all cases these requirements generate compliance costs, which could equally appropriately be allocated to manufacturing and process cost-centres or charged as central corporate obligations.

A manufacturing or logistical facility has a designed capacity, but that can usually be exceeded by at least a small margin to meet exceptional demand. Using a facility at more than its planned working capability puts stress on the machinery and facilities, and so potentially increases maintenance costs and the potential incidence of breakdowns. In most cases, staff must be paid extra wages if they are to be persuaded to work more intensively and/or overtime, and sometimes temporary labour must be recruited and trained to meet an increased workload, with an increased potential for errors to occur. Additional supplies of water, energy, and other inputs have to be bought, at spot prices that may be significantly higher than the contract prices that had been negotiated for the planned normal usage.

The aggregate of these variable cost increments can cause the unit cost of providing incrementally more units of extra-marginal output or activity to exceed the notional price that is attributed to those units of output through the normal accounting process, even for a highly-popular quon. The chief executive may take the view that the brand will suffer reputational detriment or loose future orders if intending consumers cannot be supplied, thus the high marginal cost of operating over-capacity is accepted. Although such extra-marginal cost is usually reported as an increment to manufacturing or service-providing cost, it is more properly a cost of brand image building and customer retention.

Economics and the Real World

Academic Economists begin their 'analysis' of the functioning of business entities by assuming that the sole purpose of the producers of goods and providers of services is to take their output of 'widgets' to the point-of-sale at which autonomous buyers review competing supplies and engage atomistically in transactions on the basis of two unrealistic assumptions:

- that the participants in a transaction have access to all the information that could conceivably influence their decision,
- that in a 'unit of time' each decision-taker (a buyer or a seller) concentrates solely on the potential costs and benefits of entering into this transaction, and is under no external pressure (such as hunger, exhaustion, thirst, sexual stimulation, taxation, or coercion).

Models built on this base have been expanded into millions of words and set out in highly complex criteria for competitiveness, on which basis Economists assert that 'imperfect' reality should so be regulated that actual market behaviour would be compelled to approximate to the model. Militating against this assumption are the facts that human beings have animal needs and moods, and their behaviour is affected by competitive and collaborative instincts, imperfect knowledge, differential education, and intellectual competence, and constant consciousness of the myriad options, opportunities, and pressures that they experience simultaneously. Both on their own account and as managers of corporate entities, human individuals make pragmatic decisions within a context of a complex of regulations, and they have a varying level of awareness of (and appetite for) risk in different aspects of decision-making and at different phases in their life cycles and careers, none of which conform to the simple binary assumption of the microeconomic orthodoxy.

Right from the first stages of designing a consumer product or experience that is to be offered for purchase as a quon, precautions are built-in to minimise the risk that consumers will claim redress for detriment arising from their use of (or exposure to) the brand. Hence, with notable exceptions – such as tobacco products and high-risk sports – marketing campaigns usually stress the safety and reliability of quons. Educating consumers in the safe use of the product is often an important part of the marketing and after-sales process. Customer complaints are dealt with promptly, warranties are acted upon smartly, and, when it becomes necessary, product recall is effected quickly and with appropriate publicity.

In addition to meeting the basic legal requirement that all 'goods' must be fit for purpose and manufactured to comply with health and safety requirements, a quonic brandowner is expected to respond positively to any failure of the product to meet the consumer's expectations. The brandowner's after-sales obligation is normally limited to the initial purchaser and, in appropriate circumstances, to other economic agents that use the quon by licence of the original purchaser during the warranty period. Most cars remain functionally satisfactory for a decade or longer, though the full brandowner warranty usually expires after three years. The brand owner sometimes publicises an emergent failure in a model long after the expiry of the warranty period, as a cost of maintaining the image of the brand to support future sales. Some brands – notably of medicines and of foodstuffs – are explicitly *not* guaranteed after the clearly stated 'use by' or 'best before' date that is shown on the packaging, and suppliers such as retail pharmacists offer facilities for disposal of out-of-date quons that could become dangerous or be misused.

The demand for a brand – particularly for some classes of durable quons – can significantly be increased when there is an option to hire rather than buy the consumer experience. Many authorities have suggested that leasing consumption experiences, rather than buying durable quons, will be a defining feature of sophisticated consumerism in this century. A firm of lift manufacturers can lease 'vertical transportation' to the residents of a block of apartments, rather than sell a lift to the builder. The provider installs, maintains, and periodically updates the lift, charging the managers of the property a regularly recalibrated rental that can take account of inflation, of increasing costs arising from changing technology or regulatory change, and of the developing expectations of users of elevators. Under this type of contract, the users can always have a state of the art vertical transportation experience.

Hiring a quon shifts the focus of the initial transaction away from an expression of the potential buyer's capability to raise a cash price at a specific date, onto the predicted capacity of the lessee's income stream to bear the rental payments that will continue throughout the contract period. Over the period of such a lease, lessees must meet the cost of maintaining the lessor's capital, and the costs of brand defence and product development, within the hire charge. This principle applies to the billions of pounds' worth of quonic capital equipment that is leased throughout industry and commerce, as much as it does to consumer quons hired by households.

Differential hire charges for similar quonic experiences, facilities, or services reflect differentiation in product design, quality of service, brand reputation, snob appeal, material robustness of the components, and other characteristics which vary in importance through time and across categories of products and services. The relative importance of the various criteria is determined by consumer expectations. Some brandowners – for example, in healthcare equipment and sophisticated printing technology – refuse to sell the equipment that they build; they insist on leasing agreements which stipulate that they must control specified maintenance services, hoping to inhibit piracy of their *ik* by not equipping users of their output with manuals from which technical secrets could be captured. Brandowners with new products or significant variants of known products often need to stimulate expectations in their customers before the product can become the object of their desire.

Quonic Pricing

No branded quon can be offered on the market for a sustained period if the proportion of its ultimate retail price that is received by the brandowner does not cover the full costs of creating and protecting the brand, including:

- Reputation,
- Patents,
- Brand names,
- Marque and product type names,
- Logos,
- Trademarks,
- Copyright descriptive writing,
- Copyright images,
- Designs,

- Marketing research,
- Marketing, including advertising and 'Corporate Social Responsibility',
- Contract terms, including warranties, guarantees, and limits to liability,
- Methods of securing revenue that are most convenient to the purchaser,
- Pursuit of makers and sellers of fakes, including prosecution and publicity,
- Management of the media to prevent or refute 'knocking' stories,
- General publicity to maintain and enhance favourable brand awareness,
- After-sales service,
- Provision of complementary products (filters, cleaning materials, etc.) without which the equipment cannot work effectively,
- Replacement of 'unsatisfactory' units under warranty,
- Effective user-friendly complaint and customer query handling,
- Capability to meet clients' liability demands,
- Assurance of environmental acceptability.

Some of the costs of establishing these attributes predate the assembly of the material parts of individual units of the product, and others arise at or after the time when the ownership or lease of the quon has been added to the asset register of the consumer's estate. Some costs arise directly from the differential performance of individual units in the hands of diverse consumers, while others of the above heads of expenditure serve the general promotion of the brand over several years and sometimes across a range of *marques*.

No quon can have an objective 'value'; it is an amalgam of material components with the utility that consumers perceive to exist in their having access to the brandowner's ***ik***. Any quon within a consumer's estate can be allocated a notional resale price for purposes of insurance, tax, or probate in terms of a 'true and fair' estimate of what a buyer will offer for it at the time and place where she assesses its potential utility to her.

Price differentials are not the major criterion for choice between brands that lie within any segment of a highly stratified market in the minds of the majority of consumers who intend to buy a durable quon and have decided broadly how much they can afford to pay. Image, design, social *cachet*, reputation for reliability, and a host of other non-price factors exert huge influence on the consumer's selection between the competing brands. Each brandowner offers the quon to distributors at an indicative wholesale price (often as a basis for their negotiation with retailers) in each currency zone, within a total tariff 'basket' that is designed to provide sufficient aggregate income for the firm to make a profit from this particular quon, after meeting:

- the after-sales costs that may arise in this year relating to units of the brand that were sold in past years and are still in use,
- the costs of manufacturing, logistics, and warehousing in this year,
- the costs of marketing and selling the items that are to be sold in this year,
- the costs incurred in protecting the brand's **ik** from pirates and detractors, and any costs arising from doing deals with unsavoury or corrupt regimes,
- this year's spending on developments for the future, many of which will not be implemented.

A firm that operates manufacturing and distribution facilities in a dozen countries and supplies customers in more than a hundred and fifty sovereign states, each with their own taxation and regulatory regimes (which are often further complicated by state and local taxes, inspectorates, and bylaws), faces a mass of political, currency, and tax risks, as well as the risks that are posed by the natural environment, by any process plant that they control, by the variability of the materials and of the workforce, and by the costs that arise from the after-sales expectations of the consumers. All these factors create differentials in the local shop price that is set for any branded quon in different parts of the global distribution system.

Each intending buyer is free to check out the range of available alternative purchase possibilities within the accessible market before making a decision on which segment to enter, then determining which brand to buy. A middle-sized family saloon car is not competing with stretched limos or with Chelsea 4X4s, or with minimalist runabouts. The competitors within the family car segment of the market comprise other brands of middle-market hatchback saloon. Each buyer makes a selection from the models that are offered within the accessible segment, taking account of the complementary costs arising from the purchase, notably fuel and insurance in the case of motor vehicles.

Any firm or individual that controls a quonic brand, even in a highly competitive mass market segment, cherishes a *mini-monopoly* over its registered brand name and over the copyright to its advertising slogans and trademarks, as well as over any patents that it owns, and in all the other significant areas of *ik* that it commands. It seeks the maximum possible differentiation from other brands, both subjectively in the consumer's perception and objectively in the array of protection that the firm acquires and asserts for its *ik*. In the special cases of high fashion clothing and of some ephemeral accessories, items can retain their brand labels when they are released in end-of-season sales for a fraction of the price that was quoted when the design was launched. This dramatic price periodicity does not harm the brands because the ephemeral nature of fashion is fully understood, and highly competent consumers' attention is focused on the *ik* that inheres in the next new season's designs. This pricing strategy is not replicable in the majority of the other segments of the pattern of quonic demand and supply.

In many quonic market segments, it is more efficient to protect the *ik* that has been invested in a model by dismantling unsold units and re-using the fungible components, rather than to let recognisable output become available at a discounted price in some secondary marketplace where it can potentially undermine the *cachet* of the entire brand. Factory shops enable some businesses to sell 'surplus' stock and 'seconds' whose components cannot be disassembled for incorporation into new branded produce. The rapid transmission of information on the internet makes informal offloading of any surplus stock even more risky for brand reputation now than it was in past generations. A landmark case in France in the middle of 2008 concluded that brandowners are entitled to compensation from a trader or a trading platform that facilitates sales of fakes of their quons, thus extending the range of protection to the *ik* in a brand.

Producers of highly desired luxury brands must be careful about making any decision to increase output in anticipation of rising demand, lest they find that the market falls away after a short-term surge in demand. The image of a top-of-the-range brand would not be enhanced if a significantly increased supply of the quon was put on the market at a reduced price. Such a change would probably be perceived to have devalued the decisions of existing consumers who had paid the previous, higher price. From the firm's point of view, it is irrational to decrease the inward cashflow per unit sold that provided a greater margin to cover risks to *ik*. It would be self-destructive to diminish the unit profitability of the brand, in order to gain a cohort of less wealthy customers who may make greater demands for after-sales service, and whose use of the brand might tarnish the image of the product in the eyes of higher net worth people. These strictures do not necessarily apply when the price is lowered sensitively to dispose quickly of the residual stock of a marque or a model that is being discontinued.

Competitive downward price adjustment can be effective in specific short-term circumstances, for example, if the objective is to finish off a competitor in a market segment where demand is limited or is declining. Directors of brandowning firms consider the possibility of merging with other brandowners, or attempting a pre-emptive acquisition of a competitor, when brands are facing new sources of competition, when the consumer experience is passing out of fashion, because of the approaching expiry date of crucial patents or of other time-limited *ik*, because input materials are becoming inaccessible, or because some phase of the production process – or the product itself – is becoming unsustainable on environmental or public health grounds. Firms that own obsolescent brands commonly carry legacy expenses, including:

- pensions obligations, including commitments to ex-employees who have retired or moved on to other jobs while retaining deferred benefits,
- uninsured employer's liabilities to present and past employees,

- uninsured environmental liabilities for pollution around factories that may already have been sold or demolished,
- potential after-sales service demands from customers, some of which relate to brands and products that have been discontinued but nevertheless bear an ongoing contractual obligation for a successor brandowner to manufacture spare parts or complementary products such as filters,
- potential contingent liabilities to counterparties,
- potential liabilities to past and present customers,
- costs of maintaining the integrity of the firm's accumulated *ik*, which may include valuable residual assets that were formerly incorporated in quons that are no longer on sale.

Firms in Context

One scheme for trying to achieve long-term corporate viability, which was at its most fashionable in the early to mid-nineteen-nineties, was to create conglomerates. A 'holding company' bought a range of firms that controlled an array of dissimilar brands in different market sectors. Proponents argued that the resulting ragbag of disparate marcoms and quons that the firm produced from widely spread factories could be distributed more efficiently to buyers from rationalised warehousing systems, or sold direct to consumers from unified product catalogues. These hopes generally proved to be exaggerated, though some past failures may have succeeded in the present state of online trading. The multifarious manufacturing plant were often located where firms had been able to claim the biggest industrial development grants in some past era, and in changed times they incur unnecessarily complex logistical costs. Conglomerates typically increased their gearing to finance each successive takeover, so they could not quickly invest enough additional capital in their acquisitions to rationalise manufacturing or warehousing onto consolidated sites.

A conglomerate also had to meet all the defence and developmental costs attaching to the *ik* that was integral to the brands that it wanted to maintain or develop. To reduce this costly tangle of problems, some conglomerates sold viable brands that could be designated 'non-core' businesses. The firm that buys ownership of such a brand takes possession only of the complex of *ik* that is identifiable as the source of utility in the brand. Fat fees are paid to advisors to undertake all the 'due diligence' that is needed to ensure that the buyer of a brand takes control of the plant and machinery, the key people and the *ik* that they require, and nothing more. The conglomerate that divests itself of the brand is left carrying the *ko*s that have been incurred in preserving the brand up to the date of sale, and the costs of slimming down the firm's infrastructure into the shape that the new owner is willing to buy. Hence a typical demerger carries vendor costs for redundancies and writing-off of debt, as well as the notional cost that the divesting conglomerate has kept on the balance sheet to settle the heritage obligations. A similar transference of a set of business assets can be effected, without passing on the company's debt burden, when a 'pre-packaged liquidation' is arranged.

The record of mergers and corporate acquisitions (M&A) shows that, in general and especially in mature sectors of the economy, post-merger profits do not improve upon the profits that were record by the component firms as they had been before the merger. Banks, accountancy practices, and law firms draw huge fees from facilitating corporate mergers, and those payments constitute a drain of wealth out of the 'real economy' into the service sector. As a general rule, even the most successful mergers produce organisations that are significantly less than an optimal combination of the former component parts at their best. Similarly, many very highly leveraged buyouts of companies by speculative venture capital incur financing costs that can partly be serviced by raising prices, but this can soon meet with sales resistance from retailers or from their customers. The next most obvious means to increase short-term profits is to 'strip out cost' from the business, although such a programme almost inevitably has a detrimental impact on the firm's ability to defend and develop *ik*, but this is not a significant concern to an opportunistic corporate raider who intends to sell the business before the spending cuts cause perceptible diminution of the perceived utility of the brand or of the efficiency of plant and systems.

Non-destructive mergers and acquisitions occur most naturally where demand is growing rapidly for brands that incorporate a new technology or a new consumer concept. In those conditions, the more aggressive firms in the sector absorb their rivals to gain control of those companies' *ik* and market share and productive capacity. In recent years, this has been particularly marked in the fields of information technology and online games, but the history of Hewlett Packard since the millennium is a spectacular example of such a strategy that has repeatedly soured. Aside from the special cases of emergent markets and novel quons, M&A activity is often an indicator of sectoral decline. Thus, one can expect that facilitating defensive M&A, especially in Europe, will provide revenue for bankers and lawyers throughout the coming decade, as global competition slices away the historically cosy markets that European brandowners have enjoyed. We will also see a continuance of the purchase of US and European companies for control of their *ik* by firms based in India, China, and other emergent economies.

The Psychological Context of the Quon

Understanding the factors that cause some brands to be preferred by buyers is important in assessing the utility of *ik* to brandowners, and the contribution of *ik* to the pricing of shares in a firm. Psychological research on consumers' perceptions, backed by an improving scientific understanding of the biology, chemistry, and electrically measurable activity of the human brain, indicates that brand recognition occurs in the egocentric and image-conscious right-side frontal area. Choices that respond to activity in this region of the brain are highly significant to people, and it is apparent that individuals invest emotional energy in the pride of ownership and in the sensation of luxury that comes from using preferred quons. It is also increasingly clear that the 'hardwiring' of the brain is not completed until the very late teens, so younger people cannot be assumed to have perceptions or preferences that are similar to those of mature adults.

Because they are addressing these prominent forces in human nature, the cost centres within a brandowning firm that address the psychologically sensitive aspects of consumer relations such as design, marketing, image protection, and after-sales service – sometimes including green credentials and maybe even a claim of corporate social responsibility – can leverage demands on the chief executive of a corporation that greatly exceed the influence of cost centre managers whose role is to produce marcoms within the supply chain.

Some of the most highly desired brands cover physical products that are materially less robust, less durable, and less finely styled than some of their competitors, and some of the most highly-reputed services are far from the most perfect available, yet the most financially capable celebrity customers demand to have those most-preferred brands for reputational and emotional reasons. The millions of daily demonstrations of this blatant and persistent refusal by consumers to act 'rationally' are a further proof of the practical irrelevance of pristine academic Economics. So-called Behavioral Economics attempts to explain reality without repudiating the formulaic mainstream of the subject, and it could become useful if its practitioners were freed from their redundant intellectual impedimenta.

Psychological and social mechanisms determine the quonic desirability of a brand and indicate the utility that a potential consumer attributes to that experience. The need to preserve and, whenever possible, to enhance the benefit that the consumer believes that she or he gets from the quon compels the owner of the brand to accept the increasing *ik*-related costs of achieving synergy with the aspirations of consumers. This is the most relevant factor in attracting adherents to social media, which are significant in building and breaking brand reputations over all markets. Human consumers are egocentric. A brandowner's failure to deliver the product or the experience on time in the desired quantity might in some cases cause the customer to want the quon with more passion than before. Some individuals may accept gracefully the excuse for short-term non-performance that the supplier proffers. Alternatively – as in any matter where emotions are engaged – the consumer might turn away from the pursuit of that experience to look for an alternative source of satisfaction.

In each market segment in which he or she has a quonic consumer aspiration, the individual aims to secure access to the brand and the model that will provide them with the highest level of satisfaction that they can afford, in the context of their spending power (including available loan finance), and of their preferences, which can include regional or sectoral loyalties. Brand marketing aims to achieve the perceptual segregation of the consumer experience by users of that brand, and the brandowner must ensure that the means of delivering that consumer experience are constantly fit-for-purpose. The most preferred quons are enjoyed in a context of mutual self-interest. Consumers of the most expensive brands collude with brandowners to protect the exclusivity of the ***ik*** that consumers have accessed, and in so doing they promote the brand. Keeping a durable quon in a pristine state for its 'product lifetime' is more often assured by the actions of the consumer than of the supplier, however tightly drawn might be the after-sales service requirements on the supplier, or the maintenance conditions that are imposed in a lease of a consumer experience.

Regulation and Quonification

Almost all foodstuffs that are available in advanced countries are now subject to close regulation – exemplified in animal 'passports', certificates of origin of fruit, etc. – and consequently if products in such categories are not otherwise branded, the retailer must take responsibility for the chain of certification. Providing such assurance for the consumer is a very significant feature of contemporary retailing. This regime was threatened by the scandal that erupted early in 2013, when horse meat was found in 'beef' meals, and pork was identified in 'halal' meals in supermarkets. The recovery process required much more rigour in the verification of authenticity of ingredients and an inevitable escalation of product prices.

This scandal gave an unexpected impetus to a process that began in the supply of milk in the UK. For a long period, farmers received barely the cost of production of fresh milk at the farm gate, and were for several years at a loss to understand where the mark-up was generated that enabled the supermarkets to sell the same commodity profitably. From the consumer perspective, labelling and certification make packets of milk acceptably quonic. Wily farmers understood that mechanism before the favourable 'correction' in commodity prices moved in their favour after 2008. They now make a good return on part of their output by creating their own-label products and by using Farmers' Markets, where increasingly rigorous measures are enforced to ensure that participants stick to the 'own produce only' rule to preserve the added utility of the generic 'Farmers' Market' brand. The food adulteration scandal in 2013 made local certification of origin of food even more attractive to the public, and consequently farmers' markets and local butchers (providing evidence that they sourced their meat locally) received a new boost to their sales.

Nothing but a recognised quon meets the full set of conditioned expectations of the sophisticated consumer, yet only a minority of consumers can afford to command a wholly quonic pattern of consumption that meets all their needs and aspirations. Most parents cannot routinely buy highly priced quons for everyday use, so leading large-scale retailers offer their own-brand products that feature fashionable design, sturdy structure when that is appropriate, and a promise of replacement in the event of product failure. A store chain's self-certified foodstuffs and own-brand canned meats, school uniforms, and electrical goods are 'warranted marcoms', which are normally sold as **neoquons**. In the mature economies, specialist firms produce and package such products, which they sell as marcoms to retail companies. The shop price of a neoquon is almost invariably less than the price of a leading brand that offers similar functionality. Buyers of durable neoquons are often given the opportunity to purchase an extended warranty that will refund the price of the product, or replace the item, if it fails to deliver its specified performance during the cover period.

This trading model is generally more profitable for the participating firms than is the establishment of less prestigious brands which are designed to be sold at a lower price than the most fashionable brands. Nevertheless, many firms have achieved long-term profit from marketing second- or third-tier quons when enough customers accept the brands as the best affordable option to which they can aspire; this subset of quons is likely to increase as millions of consumers in the post-industrial societies get used to lower material living standards, especially if finance is available to fund start-up businesses that supply such brands. There is always a chance that a second-tier brand might make the leap into a more esteemed market segment over the medium-term.

In the sophisticated cities of the most advanced countries, market stalls, pound shops, and cut-price stores sell surplus stocks of 'deleted' branded goods and a range of marcoms that meet the legislative requirements to be 'fit for purpose'. There is also a significant 'under-the-counter' trade in marcoms for which no trader will accept liability. Some openly sold marcoms bear a maker's mark, but that does not denote a brand that the consumer would wish to announce that he owned, though it may well indicate the maker's desire to build his product into a brand. A broom or a hammer that is bought as a warrantied marcom from a market stall can be as effective for its purpose as a much higher-priced quon that performs the same function, but in the absence of a brandowner's guarantee, and of verification of the range of *ik* that is inherent in a quon, the commodity is priced as a marcom.

The idea of a 'consumer's surplus' applies most obviously when a consumer has the choice between buying a well-regarded branded refrigerator (for example) for £800 and a neoquon of similar appearance and capacity at £250, plus an optional £40 for an extended warranty. The consumer who opts for the neoquon foregoes the experience of being a premium quon consumer in that arena, but he has a consumer's surplus of £510 (or, if he dispenses with the extended warranty, £550) to spend on other things. Alternatively, £550 can be seen as the opportunity-cost to the consumer who pays the higher price for accessing the intangible benefits that attach to buying the preferred quon. Purchasing quons at reduced prices in a sale, or importing them from a country with a different taxation regime, without dilution of after-sales service from the brandowner, also generates a consumer's surplus, usually at the cost of significant time spent by the buyer on effecting the purchase and on the pursuit of any after-sales benefit in cases of personal imports from abroad.

Individuals who have utilitarian requirements for durable goods, but cannot afford (or choose not) to buy either quons or neoquons, can enter the second-hand market in search of cars and electrical equipment, pushchairs, furniture, and a range of other durables, including clothing. No contractual brandowner obligations attach to the material residue of former quons and neoquons that are resold as (specifically non-jevic) 'second-hand' items, especially after the terminal date of the makers' product liability. Nor do retailers accept any responsibility for the utility or safety of neoquons that they once sold, beyond the expiry date of their warranty. A wise second-hand trader sells items 'as seen' and leaves all the riskier elements of such trade – and all the dodgy items – to be offered for private sale in the small ads columns of local newspapers, on corner shop notice boards, and in their internet equivalents.

For several centuries, a vast array of products has been made specifically for use by the armed forces, purchased on a basis of quasi-quonic pricing. The design of a device may be owned by the Admiralty or the Ministry of Defence, in which case the manufacture can be franchised out to the supplier that submits the most efficient tender in cases where there is no government arsenal, factory, or shipyard that is available and competent to perform the task. Alternatively, the *ik* may be owned by a corporation that contracts to supply its quon to the government at a negotiated price. Also during and after the Second World War, a huge range of consumer goods ranging from 'National' orange juice and cod liver oil for infants, through quality-certified margarine and soap, to 'utility' clothing and furniture, was distributed to the general population under the control of government agencies, in rationed quantities, at controlled prices. In the event of a non-nuclear global war, or following the near-collapse of the economy in an extreme future depression, a similar system could be reintroduced to distribute a minimum per capita supply of subsistence goods through a rationing system. Such a 'command economy' is necessarily bureaucratic, inefficient, and regressive, and it could bring about temporary stagnation in the generation of *ik*, but it could keep many people alive for a considerable period in crisis conditions.

Economic Devastation

Since the nineteen-seventies, Economists have demanded the imposition of their concept of 'competition' – by decree – even in areas of natural monopoly, where the infrastructure can only safely and efficiently be administered by a single management and where the cost of duplicating or triplicating infrastructure is absurd waste.

In Britain, by 1980, the main utilities – water, gas, electricity, telecommunications, roads, and the railways – had been brought into state ownership under successive administrations; other services, notably telephones and television, had been developed under state and municipal ownership. The Conservatives were content to keep them in the public sector through the nineteen-sixties and seventies. The pace of investment in capacity and infrastructure, and the prices that were charged by state-owned utilities and industries, could be manipulated; so-called 'social tariffs' represent an attempt to ensure the affordability of utilities to vulnerable individuals, and the manipulation of wholesale pricing could create a subsidy to selected industrial customers, including the other nationalised industries. Research and development, and investment in new plant and infrastructure, could be phased to minimise the impact on them of fluctuations in the economic cycle. Sometimes, nationalised industries earned a surplus, sometimes they received state assistance, sometimes there was a planned long-term investment strategy. Some state enterprises, notably the Post Office, made net payments to the Treasury for centuries.

Some of the Economists who assert (contrary to all experience) that their theory of 'rational expectations' presents the most conducive intellectual context for maximising efficiency in every economic activity also argue that optimum efficiency in the privatised utilities that are natural monopolies can be achieved by functional 'separation'. In the cases of gas, water, railways, and electricity, a 'carrier' can be sold the franchise to manage the fixed infrastructure (the pipes and pumping stations, or the cables and substations) for delivering the commodity from the source supplier to the consumers' access points. The carrier is remunerated by retail distribution companies that provide billing services and administration (including connection to the carrier's network and the meters). Maximum prices are set by the regulator that supposedly cover the operating cost – 'opex' – for each of the separated functions and the capital expenditure – 'capex' – that is needed to repair, replace, and extend the 'wholesale' and 'retail' systems. A third set of firms may be licensed to maintain and establish 'upstream' sources of commodities (boreholes and reservoirs for water, electrical power stations, access to gas fields, etc.) and they sell their output to the carriers in regulated quantities at regulated prices.

The upstream suppliers, the carriers, and the retailers must each maintain their own reserves of unused capacity to meet peak demand, and all the companies must be able to meet the demand from customers who might 'switch' to them, as well as bearing advertising and promotional costs to keep their existing customers and to replace lost customers with new ones. There cannot be an exact match of capacity with demand in extraction, distribution, or retail through the seasons, and the more competitors there are at any point in the chain, the more pockets of excess capacity must exist, all funded by the customers. Competing firms inserted into at least three tiers of the market may each claim to achieve high levels of efficiency, as defined by the regulator, but this can only be delivered securely at a higher cost than would be incurred in running the whole system *with maximum effectiveness* as an integrated monopoly.

Regardless of whether water supply is a state monopoly or has competing private providers, with or without 'separation', population growth and the intensification of human economic activity have driven water tables deeper and made clean surface water resources scarcer in India, in the Sahel, in southeast England, in much of China and Australia, and at hundreds of other stress points around the globe. Climatic variation has exacerbated drought in several significant regions. Most British people have grown up thinking of water as a 'free good' that is provided by nature and accessed as a public service, but in reality, for many centuries quality-controlled safe water – if it has been available at all – has been sold. Potable water delivered to the tap is a quon, and almost everywhere, the cost of delivering it is increasing inexorably. Water that falls as rain and snow in parts of urban areas where it cannot sink naturally into the ground must either be harvested or subject to managed removal, often in combination with waste water and sewerage. No community can, for long, evade responding to the fact that acceptable standards of public health and community hygiene come at a significant cost that will increase with demographic trends, urbanisation, and climate change.

People's tastes shift synergistically with product development. New technology and innovation in the media and leisure sectors generate a constantly expanding array of potential consumer choices. The demand for the experiences that are provided in some segments of the leisure market increases from day to day, while in other sectors, demand declines as the brands' designs and technologies are perceived to be obsolescent. Brandowners are challenged to keep the development of their *ik*, and their promotional strategy, ahead of the changing pattern of demand, not least in acknowledgement of pressure on terrestrial resources and rising awareness of the possible benefits and massive costs of the green agenda.

For the past half-century, pharmaceutical companies have been pressed to release cut-price bulk supplies of *generic* versions of their patented drugs for use by state hospitals in the advanced countries. In the contrary direction, in recent years some spiv companies have bought the facilities and the rights to make some generic drugs and pushed up the price significantly in the absence of significant competition. In other cases, patent-holders are put under pressure to permit the *ik* on their drugs to be used by other firms and agencies, who can make a cut-price version for state agencies. This principle has been extended to induce pharmaceutical companies to supply their products to less-developed countries at significantly less than their preferred quonic market price.

Some governments have threatened to remove protection from producers' *ik* unless they make generic supplies of their drugs available on 'special terms', for the state health service or to deliver more benefit from their spending on international aid. Some marxist and marginalist Economists see such outcomes as a step towards their *nirvana* of 'marginal cost pricing'; that is, setting prices that allow no return for the creation and preservation of *ik* which must, therefore, make capitalist innovation unaffordable. If the proposition were to be generalised into a licence for emergent economies to pirate any foreign-registered *ik* that their rulers claimed was 'necessary', the proceeds from their exports of pirated produce would soon overflow the kleptocrats' Swiss bank accounts, while the funds available in the more mature economies to support pharmacological research would be reduced or might even cease.

One mechanism that has been adopted to address this dilemma is to develop variants of proven drugs specifically for manufacture and distribution in less-developed countries, particularly for endemic diseases that could become more common in the post-industrial countries as mass migration continues. It is doubtful if the concept can be extended beyond healthcare and the provision of simple information and communications technology in the near future. Such manipulation of prices of sensitive products cannot ever emerge from free competition among patent owners. It is inescapably the product of government influence and intervention.

Chapter Five

Productiveness and Productivity

Human Nature and Political Economy

Some highly regarded philosophers and political economists have speculated as to whether human life could be 'better' if people lived without coercive organisations or laws to protect property, as appeared to be the case with the indigenous peoples in Australia and the Kalahari Desert, when European explorers first 'discovered' them. The situation of such peoples was described – even idealised – as 'primitive communism', in which each person drew on nature to meet simple subsistence requirements. On deeper examination, anthropologists found that the hunter-gatherers had complex structures for resolving or preventing interpersonal and intergenerational conflict, for the selection of breeding partners, for excluding strangers from their clans, for personal ornament, for religious observance, and for the treatment of perceived illnesses (both mental and physical). It also became obvious that many such people willingly escaped from traditional social and economic structures as soon as there was the chance of securing a waged job that would give them access to quonic consumption. Given this facet of human nature, the existence of a government is consensually accepted on the grounds that *ik* – and thus quons, and the possession of quons – cannot exist without the law of property, which is a major component of the rule of law that only a state – a *polis* – can provide.

In all relatively affluent societies, consumers have shown an increasingly strong preference to purchase or hire experiences that provide the user with access to more attractive intellectual property, rather than simply acquiring more material things. This tendency was represented by the sophistication of drama, of theatre construction, and of games in classical Greece, and by advances in astronomy both in China and around the Mediterranean. But sophistication has also descended to extreme decadence, as in the phase of Roman society that was damned by St Augustine. The present incidence of obesity in the formerly industrial countries demonstrates that sophisticated and sensible preferences are not always followed, even among the most economically and socially advantaged populations in world history. After allowing for such glaring exceptions, the shift from marcom to quon consumption, and changing patterns of demand for quons, confirm a remarkable 'greening' of consumer choice. Yet the ubiquity of pornography on the internet, blighted by increasing extremity of child abuse, shows clearly the ambiguity of such resources.

The perception that capable consumers prefer to receive the 'necessities, comforts, and conveniences of life' in the form of what this text calls quons, rather than as marcoms, has a long history. By the year 1700, European political economists had agreed that three indispensable 'factors of production' were required to provide any marketed wares:

- ***capital,*** the information and equipment that are necessary to convert raw materials into the objects and/or experiences that people want to consume, and are willing to pay for, plus a cash float to enable the supplier to buy the necessary input materials machinery, labour, and licenses that must be deployed before any product can be sold,
- ***land,*** the source of the materials that are extracted from or cultivated on the earth in the forms of crops, timber, animals, minerals, and water,

- ***labour***, the deployment of the intellectual and physical capabilities of human beings to produce things and experiences that they and others need and desire. Newborn babies are incapable of performing any labour, and as a general rule sufficient time and resources need to be allocated to a developing human being so that they acquire the level of intellectual and physical development that is optimal for them to deliver the quality of work input that produces the best possible output.

In the political economy of that period, the emphasis was on the physical input of labour that was needed for production, relative to the output-per-head that was required to 'fuel' labourers (and keep them socially quiescent), by feeding, clothing, and housing them according to the norms of their era. Much less attention was given to the recognised fecundity of the human race in creating ideas that could be applied in material production, and in the promotion of products, and in entertainment and the arts. The political economists elaborated a 'labour theory of value', which assumed that physical labour was combined with acquired skill in preparing some humans to perform each specialist task, including general labour. Adam Smith accepted this and postulated that by extending the division of handicraft work into more and more narrowly specified tasks, each employed man or woman would become more skilled at the one specific function. Thus their employer would have to pay for less 'downtime' as workers no longer moved from one work station to another, thus their productivity would be optimised. Smith extended the theory to conclude that the productive capacity of an economy was limited by the extent to which the division of labour could be subdivided. Nothing more could be supplied in an economy beyond that which could be achieved by sub-division of tasks; thus the 'extent of the market' was set by the constraint on the aggregate productivity of handicraft labour. It was shown much earlier in this text that Sir Richard Arkwright and a host of other inventors of machinery had made nonsense of this proposition before Smith wrote it down.

Political economists and Smith agreed that any 'good' would only continue to be available if the price that it fetched in the marketplace was at least equal to the full cost that the capitalist had to advance to hire the workplace, buy the machines, buy the input materials, hire workers to make the units (which often included paying the employees a rate that covered the cost of buying and bringing the tools that they owned), and hire men, carts, and horses to transport his output to the point of sale. TR Malthus wrote that some products and services could be sold for much more money than was needed to repay the capitalist for his entire outlay because of the attractive appearance of the goods they offered for sale, and/or their novelty or other perceived special attributes.

The proportion of the price of any good that exceeded the material cost of its production was recognised as an unearned surplus, which Malthus confusingly called a 'rent', a term historically applied to revenue that was taken from farmers by landowners to pay for the use of the land. Malthus also applied the term 'rent' to a surplus of cash income over the expense that had been met by a capitalist in the cases of industry, trade, and transport. Tenant farmers who grew cash crops and farmed animals for their meat and milk were also capitalists, and if they had innovative ideas in production that could increase their yield beyond the norm per acre or make their produce look more attractive to customers, they too received a surplus. The rent that the more effective capitalist farmers retained was distinct from the rent that they had to pay to the landlord for access to the land. Landlords employed stewards and agents who adjusted the rents-for-land upwards in an attempt to capture a bigger share of the surplus that accrued to the tenant farmer's skill. Not all the tenant farmers on a large estate were in the forefront of innovation, so although they may all have occupied land of similar quality, the rental element in the prices they got for their crops varied, and landlords had to settle for access-to-land rents that were affordable to all the farmers.

Invention, Innovation, and Economic Development

The luckiest landlords became exceedingly rich when urban expansion enabled them to lease or sell their land for housing and for commercial and industrial use. Landlords used their increased incomes to rebuild or extend their mansions; they also bought sprung carriages and fine clothes, designer furniture and china, went more often to the theatre and to concerts, and commissioned family portraits. This emergent pattern of quonic demand created employment for many more skilled workmen and women – and for quonic service providers, lawyers, doctors, musicians, and other entertainers, artists, and sculptors – than could have been employed if the economy simply consumed and supplied subsistence goods.

Most significantly, spending on luxuries supported the further development of high technology, as when landlords, merchants, and the most successful tenant farmers bought watches and mantel clocks, and some of them installed public clocks on church towers and stable blocks. This demand for all types of timepieces paid for the development of more sophisticated clockwork, as some experts offered miniaturisation of watches and others provided more accurate clocks. Hence it was that the leading clockmakers could put their names on the face of the clocks that they produced in an early example of branding, which enabled them to increase the mark-up above the material cost of production that they could charge in their prices. Clocks and watches provided systems of gearing that were available to be adapted into the first modern textile machinery, and into pumps and winding engines for mines, and eventually on railway locomotives, including many devices on which the inventors had registered their ownership of the *ik* in the form of patents. Capitalist ironmasters developed new technology to make better steel springs and cogs for clocks and watches that could be adapted on a large scale as springs to make carriage rides more pleasant for the passengers. This opened the way for the next generation to construct sprung railway carriages and wagons and thereby open up a new era in communications and logistics in which the new techniques of signalling and precise timetabling and timekeeping were essential.

The build-up of technological capacity in the eighteenth century was funded largely by the cash flow that the rich spent on novelty quons. The profit that pioneer capitalists received from supplying high-tech luxuries to landlords enabled them to invest in new ventures that developed into the factory system. Thereafter, larger factories mass-produced marcoms for use by the increasing population of urban employees, and the profits from those factories enabled more capitalists to join the landlords as consumers of fashionable quons. Malthus recognised that the boom in registered inventiveness that had occurred in the eighteenth century facilitated the response that suppliers in the urban community made to the growing demand for quons, as they are defined in this text. Thus the essentials of modern consumerism were recognised, more than two hundred years ago.

Malthus' understanding of this point was largely dissipated in the mid-eighteen-twenties when the more forceful Ricardo (with his enthusiastic publicist, James Mill) was held by the literati to have triumphed in a gentlemanly debate with Malthus on the use of the term 'rent'. It is an interesting byway of history to note that both Malthus and Mill were employed by the greatest venture in imperialism in British history, the East India Company.

Ricardo's form of classical political economy was prevalent for the next half-century, and it suppressed Malthus' recognition of the surplus, or rent, that could properly go to the controller of the *ik* that is applied in any quon. *Ik* could be combined with outputs from farming, commerce, material industry, and the huge range of service activities and entertainments, all of which provided a flow of spending power which enhanced the lifestyle of an increasing proportion of the population. Ricardo's *Political Economy* was accepted as the definitive source in the subject in the UK until JS Mill produced an extended but closely derivative version of the same material in 1848.

The Economic Consequences of Karl Marx

Karl Marx, who was born almost two generations after Malthus and who was destined to become much more influential in the political sphere over the ensuing century than any other political economist until Keynes, followed Ricardo in assuming that the economy is the means by which the mass of the human species provides for its material needs. In developing his theory of 'Dialectical Materialism', Marx reckoned that as capitalist competition became more intense, luxuries could only be enjoyed by a tiny minority of exploiters who monopolised capital resources by appropriating the surplus value that emerged from economic activity. He stressed the truism that nothing could be produced without the contribution that could only be made by 'living labour'. A capitalist could own the most modern factory in the world, supplied with the best equipment and materials, but yet without the application of human labour to those other necessary inputs there would be no output, no sales, and no profit. Marx therefore declared that one factor of production – labour – is the unique essential input into the economy and the source of all value that is generated. He concluded that labour should therefore be the recipient of any surplus value that was produced in the economy.

Marx postulated that a fundamental 'contradiction' was inherent in capitalist production. He observed that machinery was constantly being improved, and once a new technology had been installed in a factory it could produce massively more output, especially of a basic commodity (such as cotton cloth or pig iron), at lower unit cost, than the precursor techniques had done. If any marcom producer failed to apply the surplus of circulating capital that his works generated to buy the newest technology when his competitors did, the competitors would soon be able to undercut his price, take his market share, and leave him bankrupt. Marx did not recognise *ik* in his presentation of the manufacture of commodities using commodities, as he argued that the process of 'intensification' would be generalised over the whole economy. It appears not to have occurred to him that he was modelling a situation where (in terms of this text) ever-more marcoms are produced, from ever more complex and costly quonic equipment. In each sector of commodity production, every competing producer must invest a higher proportion of his firm's income from each period in buying improved capital equipment with which to mass-produce more marcoms, at a lower unit cost, in the next period.

This meant that in successive periods, capitalists would have to spend more of their turnover on the higher-tech machinery, so proportionately less of the circulating capital would be available for workers' wages. Under increasing competitive pressure, capitalists – including capitalist farmers – would dispossess the landlords, so that capitalism could capture the (Ricardian) rent income to invest an even larger portion of the turnover of the economy into enhanced equipment with which to produce more of the basic commodities that provided the subsistence of the increasingly-impoverished masses. Innovation would increase productivity, and more workers would be made redundant by every enhancement of machinery. Lower skill levels would be required of most people who remained in employment, as the machines became more sophisticated, so employees would have to agree to serve for a longer working day, or they would lose their jobs to the growing number of unemployed people who would become increasingly desperate to get work for even less pay than the reduced hourly wages that people in jobs were having imposed on them. Consequently, per capita demand from the working class for the mass-produced commodities would decline, and as more of the least efficient factories became non-viable, their employees – and the capitalists who had owned them – would become unemployed.

Confident that his analysis foretold the future, Marx argued that a new cohort of popular leaders should cut short the era of encroaching misery. The more intelligent and experienced people among the workers and the unemployed – including ex-capitalists –had to mount a revolution that would reorganise society and the economy. In the replacement system, people would exist as members of a community, as 'communists', not as autonomous individuals who were driven to compete with each other to survive. They were to be rewarded for economic effort 'according to their *needs*', while they would provide inputs to the economy 'according to their *ability*'. The whole of society would be concerned optimally to invest in new machinery and facilities that their efforts generated, so custodianship of investable funds by capitalists would be unnecessary. Money and the ownership of property would be abolished and thus the legal structures that protect the fact of ownership would be redundant. Autonomous firms and charities would no longer have any purpose. There was to be no differentiation in esteem between the output from 'work by hand' and 'work by brain', so anybody who created a significant invention or novel or work of art would be remunerated 'according to their needs', like everybody else. Marx ignored the aspirational and institutional aspects of *ik*, which were becoming prominent as branding developed around him in nineteenth-century London.

By the year 1960, Marx's refusal to recognise the significance of *ik* had been imposed as orthodoxy on more than half the population of the world. The innate hypocrisy of the gigantic Leninist sham was demonstrated by the fact that in all the Stalinist/Maoist dictatorships, the 'leadership cadres' in the ruling communist parties participated personally in free-world consumerism, as the North Korean dictator still does, in contrast to the extreme privation that the people suffer. This was sometimes disclosed, as when Stalin was photographed smoking pipes that bore the trademark Dunhill dot, and Mao's fondness for Western cigarettes, drinks, films, and music was occasionally mentioned in the media. Under Stalin's successors, tacky pseudo-brands were copied from free-world originals and labelled (like the Slovak Tatramat washing machine), but the products lacked all the substantive attributes of quonic brands; they were part of a doomed charade that failed to delude the subject peoples that their 'socialist' system produced a 'Western' standard of living. There is now a nostalgic jevic market in a few of the communist pseudo-brands, most notably the appallingly polluting Trabant cars, which is probably the ultimate irony to have survived from the stagnation of the Brezhnev era.

More Political Realities

The intelligent majority of British and American trade union leaders have always recognised that their members choose to spend their freely-earned wages on branded tobacco, alcohol, betting shops, traditional foods and sweets, patent medicaments, and popular entertainment: goods that no marxist would regard as 'needs'. This explains why democratic trade unionism has never been captured by communists, despite repeated attempts, and why the covenant between the British unions and the Labour

Party became precarious under Gordon Brown's leadership even though the party had become most abjectly dependent on union funding. It was part of Tony Blair's amazing run of luck that he had not needed to respond directly to this facet of fundamental economic reality. He gave his nominal deputy, John Prescott, a free hand to sweet-talk the unions, just as he left the economy to the egocentric delusions of the Chancellor of the Exchequer, while Blair tore up his party's roots, with the approval of an ephemeral personal following. It was a major cause of Gordon Brown's tragedy that he equally failed to grasp this reality, having pursued a wholly state-funded career route to Downing Street by way of writing a biography of a Scots Marxist and a teaching post in higher education.

Recent academic microeconomics in the free world has studiously ignored the central perception about competent consumers that was postulated by Malthus, and was differently expressed in J-B Say's contemporaneous writing in Napoleonic France, to the effect that the economy has an internal capacity for growth that is not explained in the Smith-Ricardo presentation. Though primordially opposed to each other, Marxists and mainstream Economists are equally determined not to acknowledge that gaining access to more, more-advanced *ik* incorporated into quonic goods, experiences, and services in successive periods of lifetime is now the predominating economic preference of the human species. Since quons are defined in relation to the protected *ik* that inheres in them, they are not sold in the kind of competitive market that Economists require their students to regard as the norm.

In the real world, acquiring ownership of *ik*, or – better still – developing their own *ik* through in-house research and development, and protecting the integrity of the *ik* that they control, has consequently become the focal point of quon providers' business planning. Following Adam Smith, even today naive academic Economists supposedly dream of an 'equilibrium' being struck between supply and demand in the global market for an archetypal ephemeral good (aka widget) at the notional point where the (incalculable) marginal cost of that unit equals the (incalculable) sum of marginal revenue that the (unidentifiable) marginal buyer offers for it, thus achieving 'perfect competition'. Capital is presented as an infinitely-divisible fungible resource, 'doses' of which can be brought to bear in the appropriate quantum wherever the capitalists who control it perceive their maximum opportunity for profit from sales of price-competitive 'goods', ignoring the fact that most firms, most of the time, cannot afford to expand, dispose of, abandon, or replace plant in which their capital has been invested. Capital budgeting in large corporations is concerned with multi-million dollar aggregates; it is not feasible to allocate resources to microscopic measurement of marginal data in the costing of component marcoms.

The continental USA suffered no bomb damage during the Second World War, while massive federal government spending on war materials had been channelled through a robust capitalist system that invested heavily in plant. By contrast, in 1945, Europe's industrial and social infrastructure, including much in Britain, was very seriously decayed in consequence of intensive wartime use, following several pre-war years of underinvestment and inadequate maintenance, and in many places plant had been damaged or destroyed by enemy action. A historically high proportion of individuals' incomes and firms' profits was taken in taxation to provide an increasing flow of revenue to enable the state to achieve the promised level of spending on economic and social objectives, while continuing to service the increasing public debt.

Until the mid-nineteen-seventies, a large slice of government spending was allocated each year to developing British industry's capability to produce more advanced radar, aircraft, and warships, nuclear technology, and sophisticated communications systems, which were deemed to be necessary as part of the arms race against the USSR. Economists have evaded pointing out that the same level of investment in innovation has not been maintained since the privatisation of some state industry and the extinction of the rest.

In the years 1945-51, the Labour government in the UK spent more cash in each successive year to acquire, re-equip, and then support the nationalised industries where their party's paymasters in the trade unions were strongest. Conservative governments (1951-64) tried to control the rate of growth of the public sector, but they nevertheless focused increases in state spending on housing, defence, small increments to higher education, and support (including tax concessions) for high-technology industries such as aviation, chemicals, pharmaceuticals, electronics, and telecommunications. Through the fifties and the sixties, politicians played an 'auction game' at each election, when the party manifestos promised to deliver different packages of increments to the existing mass of state spending.

Investment to support industrial innovation and greater productiveness was diminishing as a proportion of national product. The prevalent ideology (which is called Economists' Keynesianism in this text) held that, taking each year's national income figures as a baseline, a higher level of aggregate demand should be achieved in the next year. A supposedly ideal condition of stable economic growth combined with 'full employment' (generally taken to mean that less than 7% of the guesstimated total workforce was recorded as unemployed) would be achieved if the right number and magnitude of transactions took place across the whole economy. If the government's statisticians and the National Institute of Economic and Social Research predicted that there would be a shortfall in aggregate demand in the forthcoming year, the state budget should make good the deficiency, by reducing taxes, and/or by increasing wages to state employees, or slackening controls on borrowing money, or by increasing state pensions and benefits. Where it was thought to be necessary, the 'supply-side' of the economy received direct investment, for example in expanding the capacity of the state-owned National Grid to distribute electricity. Also available to firms were grants to support the purchase of machinery and to fund research and development, and the banks were encouraged to increase business lending. When it was judged to be appropriate, the Bank of England expanded the money supply to ensure that there was enough cash and credit in the system for all the additional spending in the economy to be possible.

It quickly became apparent that such measures facilitated inflation of wages and prices, and led to increased imports of both finished quons and of marcoms for use as industrial inputs, as people and firms found themselves with more cash available to spend on purchases than the economy could supply at current prices from the existing plant and equipment. Firms that faced shortages of skilled labour offered higher wages to fill vacancies, while sellers increased the prices of fashionable quons towards the maximum that potential buyers could afford with their increasing incomes and rising capability to borrow. Then, after every stimulus to the economy, there followed a 'corrective' budget, with tax increases, a reduced rate of increase in government spending, and with credit expansion curtailed.

The Destructiveness of Misguided Governments

While it became obvious that rational capital planning by firms was repeatedly stymied by 'stop-go' macroeconomic policy, it was also glaringly apparent that neither Economists nor generalist civil servants had any concept of the significance of *ik* in positioning their country best to cope with the process of globalisation. On the contrary, especially after the Thatcher regime embraced Monetarism, civil servants were awarded brownie points for advising their ministers to eliminate expensive items from their departmental budgets. It was not in their job description to allocate work to government research units or to advocate procurements incorporating *ik* that could help to fund the growth of innovative indigenous firms.

As expenditure by the departments for health, education, and benefits increased, defence spending was restricted by axing projects, by closing plant (shipyards, ordnance works, etc.), and by abandoning development options in space science, aerospace, shipbuilding, weaponry, and advanced communications, all of which could have enabled British companies to continue the tradition of creating and capturing globally significant *ik* that could have had massive civilian applications. Medical and military equipment – even including uniforms – was bought from abroad, while UK taxpayers financed redundancy and early retirement packages that curtailed the working lives of textile workers, as of world-leading scientists and engineers. Similar false economies were made in government research spending that could have produced genuinely new discoveries, and developed spin-off *ik*, in government research stations and in the universities. Published statistics never showed a deduction from national wealth of the opportunity-cost of abandoning ordnance factories, coalmines, railway lines, and coal-fired power stations which still had massive future productive potential, thus the published national income data falsified the real state of affairs very significantly.

To bring cash into the Exchequer, under various schemes of privatisation, year after year, uncomprehending governments (drawn from all three major parties) sold assets that had cost taxpayers many billions of pounds more than was obtained from the sales. Nor was the money that was received from these sales used to fund the next generation of productive investment or to create a sovereign wealth fund; it was blown in short-term spending. No British government adequately assessed the potential for productiveness of the industries or the research centres that they sold. Nor did they make the simpler assessment of the contribution that could be earned from the current and potential holdings of *ik* within the entities that were privatised. No more attention was given to the potential house-price inflation that would occur when hundreds of thousands of council houses were transferred to their occupants' ownership at knock-down prices.

Even in the new millennium, defence installations, school sports fields, government buildings, and hospital sites were sold; some were asserted to be 'surplus to requirements', but others, incredibly, were sold for leaseback by the state. Future scholars will be incredulous that the disposals list included key utilities and basic industries: coal, steel, water, gas, railways, electricity, airlines, and airports, as well as firms with globally relevant *ik*: Rolls-Royce, BP, ICL, BT, Cable&Wireless, Westinghouse (a world leader in nuclear power generation and the construction of nuclear generation plant), massive holdings of real estate, and a range of scientific research establishments. The most conspicuous instance of all-party serial incompetence was the privatisation and subsequent anarchic regulation of the railways. Some sectors of business that were privatised have obviously thrived outside the public sector, but such a rush to sell businesses without sensible appreciation of their potential to generate circulating capital – especially if they had remained in UK ownership – was a disastrous failure of statecraft.

In preparation for privatisation, sections of state-owned entities that were not considered to be saleable were shut down, including research and development units that had generated significant *ik* and had the capability to generate more. Such closures precipitated the failure of innovative independent firms that had been suppliers of specialist equipment and materials to the defunct organisations. The rapid post-privatisation increases in the market's capital valuation of some firms that thrived in the private sector because they possessed significant *ik* did not caution successive governments from privatising further assets on similarly dissolute terms.

In general, the prices of quons and of specialist quonic services that were sold by privatised businesses increased year-on-year by more than the published 'rate of inflation', and their productiveness increased. The privatisation policy was condemned in its early stages by former (Tory) Prime Minister Harold Macmillan as the equivalent of 'selling the family silver', to enable a spendthrift government to reduce a few taxes and evade increasing others, with scant regard to the future of investment in the country's material economy. Macmillan's comments resonated positively with large sections of the electorate, but had no operational impact on Mrs Thatcher's government as they pressed on with the asset stripping.

When major areas of British industry and essential components of the economic infrastructure were privatised, the state abdicated responsibility for allocating capital to research and investment, which had been a significant characteristic of nationalised firms. Economists asserted that allocation of capital by the state was invariably inefficient, yet after privatisation, capital spending on gas, water, electricity, telecommunications, and railways was subjected to capricious 'economic regulation'. Ofcom, Ofgem, Ofwat, and their peers created a pattern of constraints on enterprise that was in no sense superior to what had happened under state ownership.

Decisions affecting essential capital investment became increasingly subject to evasion and delay, as was exemplified in the absence of an investment policy for power supplies that became painfully obvious under the 2010 coalition government and continued after the Conservatives won the 2015 election. In 2016, insensate Economists in Ofgem responded to a storm of complaints that customers of power companies were being ripped-off by trying harder to force the customers to behave like the imaginary customers in a marginalist model market. Ignoring clear statements from organisations representing small businesses, who say that the principals of firms simply do not have the time to jump through such hoops, the regulators are demanding that consumers must spend time and effort in assessing competing offers to provide billing services for electricity supplies. Whoever does the billing, power from the same source comes down the existing cables to the existing meter on the customer's premises.

To 'improve' the contrived 'competitive' situation, domestic customers who had not switched supplier in the past three years would have their names and addresses given to competing suppliers (whether they want that or not) so that they could be importuned, all at the customer's expense. Thus, the fascistic demands of the Economics profession have been stretched to intervene in the lives of people who simply do not want the hassle of behaving like guinea pigs to serve their pseudo-science. If Ofwat is allowed (or is ordered by the government) to proceed on the track towards forcing 'competition' on domestic water supplies, a similar situation would arise.

Meanwhile, neither the government nor the regulator has had the common sense to address the medium-term issue of electricity supply as coal-fired stations are scheduled for closure. The prospects of electrical power cuts recurring, and of standpipes rationing the domestic water supply, are stronger for the twenty-twenties than at any time since the period of post-Second World War reconstruction.

The Thatcher-Major-Blair-Brown-Cameron policy continuum did nothing of significance to support new indigenous *ik*-based manufacturing; only a shrinking dribble of state money was available for 'blue skies' research in the universities and in a few remaining state research establishments. The research capabilities of British universities continue to be recognised however, for example, in the distribution of EU funds where the UK won a disproportionately large share, though this was threatened within a month of the Brexit vote, despite the international ratings of the quality of higher education institutions. Japanese-owned motor firms redeployed a small proportion of the available skilled labour which eighties Britain possessed in abundance, and their works proved over the successive couple of decades that manufacturing could still be highly profitable in the UK. Those firms also deployed British scientists and engineers on 'next-generation' projects which amply returned on the investment made in them. Similar results accrued under Asian ownership to Jaguar-Land Rover, which underwent a miraculous turnaround.

Meanwhile, outside the control of the government, the confirmation of English as the undoubted global language was combined with significant private investment in the relevant *ik*, to consolidate Britain's global prominence in cinematography, animation, theatre, advertising, and financial services, including sophisticated betting. There is a significant risk that these sectors, which require little fixed plant, will decamp to more amenable jurisdictions if taxation or regulation is perceived to become too burdensome in Britain, or if the terms of Britain's exit from the EU are deeply unfavourable to those businesses. Foreign investors have been increasingly willing to buy up UK technology firms in early stages of their growth, thus alienating the future revenue flows that will be earned by their *ik*. Post-Brexit policy must take account of this increasing risk.

Inescapable Monopsony

After Brexit, Britain will have a new degree of independence. The government must review the situation that has been described above and draw from it essential lessons. Central among them is the fact that only the government can command the defence of the realm, so the government must be the sole commissioner of defensive equipment that can keep the nation safe in a very difficult world. At the end of the Second World War, the UK had several successful aircraft manufacturers whose output had been crucial in taking victory. During the war, some of them had moved into the design of jet-powered aircraft, and by 1950 there were several options offered to the government for both fighters and bombers that would be capable of defending the country in the new Cold War with the USSR, while the companies also produced the first passenger jets in the world.

Over the next 25 years, greatly helped by stop-go economic policy and successive rounds of spending cuts, governments and civil servants so badly bungled the development of the aero industry that it became terminally sick by 1980. Planes were designed for the state airlines and for the Air Force and Navy, then budgets were cut again, so some designs were abandoned while others were subject to cost limits that removed their effectiveness. One firm after another vanished, and now only BAE and Rolls Royce remain with sufficient design capability to be world-class, and their operability in future is in doubt if the government continues its programme of austerity. The UK is a contributor to joint NATO aircraft design and construction, and to the Airbus range, but has not sufficient capacity to design or build complete planes. The situation in naval procurement and for the army is even more dire; new aircraft carriers are to have US planes for which they were not originally designed, because no British alternative has been funded. By the time those planes are operational, the UK will have had no effective carrier force for more than a decade.

Since 1991, the former USSR went through a deep depression, exacerbated by botched privatisations and massive corruption, but now Putin's Russia is striding ahead in military and naval technology, and the USA is dependent on the Russians to put people on the International Space Station. China is becoming a superpower in military and naval resources, and, together with India, it is staking a claim to be a leader in the 'space race'. Britain, first with radar, first with jet engines, inventor of television and discoverer of antibiotics, has approached invisibility in the areas where the Russians and Chinese are conspicuously succeeding. Yet the areas of technology in which China appears to be so successful are relatively simple, and, by contrast, wonderful achievements by British firms indicate very clearly that an era of opportunity has dawned that will make any past industrial revolution seem utterly trivial.

Mostly in small companies, often spun-off from universities, innovations are being made that are truly world-changing. Developments in space science have already produced satellite communications systems and are on the threshold of commercial space travel (even though that will begin as jaunts for the super-rich). Partly funded by the government's research grants and partly by private-sector investment, massively significant discoveries are being made in pharmaceuticals over a massive spectrum of potential treatments. Britain is unconditionally a world leader in a range of nanotechnologies with a vast potential spectrum of applications. ARM leads the world's microchip industry and huge potential exists in microelectronics, while inventions continue to be announced in power generation and transmission, and in the technologies for storing electrical energy. Reference has already been made to the depressing propensity for British firms to be unsupported by the finance sector in developing many of these emergent concepts into viable quons, so, all too often, they have fallen into the hands of alien companies that were able to fund (and thus profit from) the innovation.

In looking at an imaginary competitive market at the point of sale as the focus of a firm's attention, Economics approaches the issue of innovation from completely the wrong angle. This text has emphasised, above all, that intellectual discovery objectified as protected *ik* is the most important aspect of the contemporary economy. Alongside the duty to protect the lives and liberty of its citizens, the modern state has the duty to protect the *ik* that has been generated by its firms and its individual citizens. By keeping that resource under the ownership of its nationals and of companies domiciled within its borders, the global gain that can be made from other nations' desire – and need – for access to that *ik* is immense. A drastically deindustrialised country can only compensate for a deficit on material trade by achieving a surplus on financial services and by franchises of *ik* around the world.

Thus faced by the reality of intense competition and constant innovation, the government itself must become the investor of first resort. It must make resources available to credible proposals from inventors and discoverers so that their ideas can be confirmed as *ik* and carried forward to the point where a viable innovation can be presented to its potential market. The absurdly named NICE (National Institute for Clinical Excellence) has done a very fair job in selecting treatments for implementation, despite the appalling consequences for thousands of individuals of the constriction of budgets which compels the health service to implement the hard choices that NICE has taken. It is a far from perfect example, but it does show that with good will and the best people being involved, such an agency can be established to select and prioritise funding for each field of advancing technology. The research councils have been making decisions on which projects to support for many decades, mostly in relation to the universities, and their record is generally good, though anyone who has served on such a body will inevitably regret some of the options that they were not able to fund.

'Monopsony' denotes a market with a single buyer, and the word was used in heading this section to emphasise that the state is the only effective possible source of funds for most of the research output that may generate *ik* of economic significance. It is an unavoidable role of government in the context of the global economy. Government austerity has greatly exacerbated Britain's balance of payments problem, has intensified the consequences of deindustrialisation, and has increased social deprivation and the alienation of the electorate from the political class. In the inter-war years, Keyns proposed spending that would both create new infrastructure and re-deploy skilled men in their former employers' mothballed factories and shipyards. The task now before the government is vastly more challenging, but is already confronted by a wealth of opportunity to develop the intellectual output that is pouring from the people in the country. Credit is cheap. Billions of pounds should be mobilised in the greatest national project in history. Failure to seize this opportunity could be terminal for the economy and for democracy.

The Monetarist Delusion

The cross-party political class accepts that more than 40% of GNP must continue to be put through the national budget for pay for health, education, benefits and pensions, overseas aid, law and order, payments to the EU (for the time being) and the other 'essential' spending categories. Labour party policies would dramatically increase that percentage, regardless of the state of the economy. Government income from taxation is never sufficient to match even a seriously-reduced expenditure budget, so the state's income continues to be supplemented by incidents of opportunistic asset stripping. In the noughties, the Treasury and the Bank of England maintained a flow of monetarist rhetoric despite their daily acquiescence with the inbuilt policy imperative that state spending must go on rising. So state borrowing necessarily remained stubbornly high, and total public sector indebtedness continued to increase. Only growth in new industry, which can demonstrate both productivity and productiveness (as is explained below) can so expand the economy that the flow of taxation will become sufficient to meet the well-recognised societal needs. It has already been asserted that successive governments' policies have been totally counter-productive, and this case will be expanded in the following paragraphs, bearing in mind the positive evolutionary strategy that was indicated in the previous section to be feasible and, indeed, essential.

Margaret Thatcher and a few devotees apparently really believed in the mid-nineteen-eighties that the economic system had been pulled through a mindset change, a delusion in which they were encouraged by misleading indicators, such as a protest letter to *The Times* from 364 mostly 'Keynesian' Economists. We can now see that the state machine emitted monetarist rhetoric while it steered the privatise-and-spend juggernaut on through the nineties.

For a final few years (2002-6), relative stability in global quon prices enabled more consumers to extend their range of consumption, assisted by the increasing trends for the marcomic components of quons to be sourced in lower-wage emergent economies. The material component of the most-desired quons declined (in some cases, almost to vanishing point) in the cases of computer games, streamed music, and social media, all of which occupied an increasing proportion of human leisure time. Superficially-strong economic growth continued, focussed in the finance sector, retailing, sports and leisure, media and entertainment, and other 'services'.

The general public's awareness of monetary churning in the private sector was focused on the spectacular increase in the disparity between property prices and the cost of building the properties, which gave landlords and owner-occupiers increasing notional 'equity' that supported their access to further debt. No increment to the material or intellectual wealth of the nation was derived from churning the ownership of existing property, though the minority of families who sold their houses in order to 'downsize' to less costly homes, or who sold properties that they had owned on a buy-to-let basis, kept their capital gains (minus tax, in the case of property that was not the vendor's home), but very little of that purchasing power was invested in material industry. The average house price in the UK increased to 215% of the 1997 level by 2007, while the prices of computing and communications equipment (byte-for-byte) and most ranges of imported non-luxury clothing declined dramatically.

During 2007, it became inescapably apparent that there was a significant stock of unsold new residential buildings, most conspicuously in the USA, Ireland, and Spain, so prices of such dwellings stagnated and then began to decline; then lenders became reluctant to fund the asking prices for any homes, with the effect that prices fell precipitously. The most significant early symptom of the implosion of house prices was apparent when US repossessions increased as more and more 'sub-prime' borrowers who had overstretched themselves on their mortgages became unable to maintain their debt servicing charges. This forced the wholesale financial markets to query the valuations that had been set on securitised bundles of property loans, and hence in the third quarter of 2007 a systemic crisis in mortgage lending spread to become a cause of concern throughout high finance in the USA and in Europe.

Consumer spending had expanded almost continuously in the UK, as in the USA, between 1993 and 2007, despite the fact that a million jobs were lost from British industry, including many from companies that had become unable adequately to develop or to defend their once-significant holdings of *ik*. This decline in the number of (mostly-productive) jobs was unimpeded by the Blair government's nugatory 'industry strategy' of 2002, and there was no significant expression of concern about the dereliction in the material economy from Members of Parliament or the Economics profession. During the ascendancy of Gordon Brown there was no appetite seriously to examine the structure of the economy. Older MPs and commentators occasionally recalled that the 1964 Wilson government had promised to deploy the 'white heat of technology', in executing a 'National Plan' that presented ideas for widespread implementation of 'cutting edge' technologies. No subsequent government has attempted to promulgate a new National Plan, even when the systemic failure of the economy – not just of 'the banking system' – became agonizingly apparent in 2008. The adoption of austerity by the coalition government of 2010 effectively finished the Liberal party and tipped the economy towards disaster.

Inhibiting Growth in Britain

The whole paraphernalia of economic regulation in the UK, as it was reconstructed in accordance with the IMF loan conditions that were imposed in 1977, was not conducive to the empowerment of businesses to be successful as investors in exploiting original *ik* in the context of a global economy. Then, in the noughties, in both Britain and the USA, arcane accounting standards derived from Economics and from the demands of the tax system were imposed on all firms. While they have been reasonably effective in enriching the partners in firms of accountants, these rules limit companies' accumulation of strategic reserves to react against threats to their *ik*. Brandowning businesses should sensibly maintain pockets of 'hidden' cash, and permit flows of 'inessential' expenditure that can be redeployed to meet opportunities and contingencies that require the immediate release of resources to exploit and defend the brand and the intellectual property that supports it. Such squirrelling-away of contingent funds was accepted by traditional accounting practice as being prudent, provided it was not carried too far.

However, an incoming management team that aims simply to extract cash from a business can cut out 'fat', by 'slimming down costs' and liquidating hidden reserves, and thereby increase short-term returns to the owners. Such tactics were welcomed by auditors who followed the noughties standards, and by the fashionable majority of analysts who approve of predatory mergers and acquisitions, and applaud asset-stripping by 'private equity' firms that increase the short-run release of cash at the expense of long-term investment. So-called 'active investors' are even more likely to search for cash to extract at the expense of long-term development of a company's *ik*; thus, when they grab seats on company boards, their intentions are directly contrary to the primary duty of a company director, which is constantly to enhance a sound medium-to-long-term strategy for the business and ensure that it is implemented.

The core 'old-EU' states have hitherto kept their own brands of coffee, motor vehicles, electrical household goods, banking, insurance, petrol, beer, soap and detergents, furnishings, and many other product ranges. These brands have retained predominance in their national markets, despite competition from imports from the global giants, because they have been protected by linguistic, cultural, regulatory, administrative, sentimental, and chauvinistic barriers, which are all maintained with the vociferous support of trade unions. Such institutions have hitherto been effectively oblivious to EU integration. The social protection of indigenous brands maintains the productiveness of the investment in the firms that own the brands, and the mark-up that maintains the quonic status of the products enables the productivity of employees to remain high. This simple fact explains why reported turnover per employee in Germany in the noughties was recorded as being 19% – and in France 22% – above that recorded for Britain.

The economic statisticians' estimate of productivity in the USA – the home of brands such as Coke, Boeing, McDonalds, and Jeep, which can command a premium within their prices and nevertheless remain competitive – was 39% higher than in Britain. The *ik* that is embedded in Microsoft, Google, Dell, IBM, Apple, and many other global leaders in ICT is remunerated at a domicile in the USA, as are those of the global American news and entertainment giants, the dominant publishers online and in print, and (after forced restructuring) those of the biggest banks.

Even more remarkable is the success of pure intellectual property, developed with no material product at all, as exemplified in Facebook and successfully represented by hundreds of popular games packages and applications.

The retention of profits from sales in the USA, plus repatriation to the USA of the cash that is derived from transfer pricing of the *ik* that is incorporated in quons sold all over the globe, enables American business to continue to apply the massive concentration of energy in research and development that has hitherto kept America at the head of the *ik*-reflective league of productiveness. The idiocy of British politicians railing at the entirely legitimate and legal repatriation to the US of the profits from sales by Google, Amazon, and Starbucks in the UK is compounded by ministers' anxiety to induce foreigners to buy existing assets in the UK and to fund new infrastructure, on which the investors expect, in future, to repatriate profits.

Here, the nineteenth-century political economists' concept of productiveness – as distinct from productivity – is of the greatest relevance. Productivity is just a number, a statistical outcome, the answer to the question 'how much does each labour-hour in each defined job return to the employer, for each labour-hour of wages that is paid to the labourers?' Labour in this sense includes supervisors, quality controllers, etc.

High productivity need not be at all productive for the economy. If a foreign-owned firm efficiently organises its UK workforce, so that each employee has high productivity in selling imported goods, this has a negative effect on the economy, because all the costs of bringing the goods to the point of sale are paid abroad, and the profit on the enterprise can also be taken out of the UK. The same applies to a foreign-owned gas or water company under the form of privatisation that was adopted in Britain. Agreement is reached with the regulator as to how much of the company's permitted revenue should be spent on developing new capacity, maintaining the existing plant and infrastructure, dealing with customers and paying staff; thereafter efficiency gains and windfall profits may be subject to UK taxation, but then the residue is available for the alien owners to take away. There is no net return that remains in the economy; the business shows no productiveness for the economy in which the activity has taken place.

Productiveness occurs where the productivity of the workforce, and the firm's efficiency in using its capital, together yield a surplus of revenue that can be used for new investment.

In the decades before the Thatcher calamity, the surplus earned by private sector firms was largely distributed to shareholders, who were free to decide how much of their dividend to consume and how much to reinvest in the economy. A great deal of shareholders' dividend income was reinvested in established firms, or was available for the development of new firms which developed *ik* for incorporation in new products. In the post-Thatcher era, these sources of investment capability have been drastically reduced.

Some Economists have recognised that the theory that they have inherited does not apply to most prices, and they have tried to construct a measure of the total factor productivity of a firm or of a business sector, adverting to a yet-to-be-explained '**s**-factor'. The real-world **s**-factor is the *ik* that is embedded in quons such as Burberry accessories and the accessibility of knowledge through Google. The productiveness of a successful brand is derived exclusively from immaterial factors, the creation and deployment of intellectual property (which is quite distinct from the concept of direct labour productivity), provides a monetised assessment of process efficiency in marcom providing in extractive industry, in manufacturing, or in logistics. This can indeed simply be expressed in labour-time per wage hour.

The UK remains the domicile of a number of significant global brands, though many are now foreign-owned; other once-familiar British brands vanished as American, continental European, and East Asian brands increased their global market share. The Cameron governments ludicrously endorsed alien acquisition of firms that controlled highly-valued *ik* as 'inward investment'. Alien owners maximise the productivity and the productiveness of any indigenous plant that they buy along with the brand, for as long as it is competitive with manufacturing facilities overseas, and from the moment of the acquisition they are free to transfer offshore the circulating capital that derives from the productiveness of their *ik*.

Exactly in line with their tradition, Economists continue to hold to the doctrine of 'comparative advantage', which is a major component in their armoury of rusty devices with which to counter protectionist and mercantilist notions. It is obvious that Saudi Arabia, with massive oil reserves and very low costs for extracting the oil, has an absolute advantage in respect of that commodity over Iceland, which has no known oil. But Iceland has massive opportunities to exploit the heat that the island has in abundance from the degree of volcanic activity that is the major feature of the island's geology, so both countries have relative, or comparative, advantages in their access to energy sources. In both cases, the exploitation of the energy depends on the *ik* that can be brought to bear in harnessing the energy to productive economic activity.

Hitherto, the world economy has generated a huge demand for oil and gas as the technologies that deploy petroleum have blossomed during an era when oil and gas have been abundantly accessible, though (as noted earlier) the action of OPEC in 1973 and subsequently has had a major impact on capital flows between nations. More recently, fears about global warming have combined with economic chauvinism in net oil importing countries to encourage the development and application of technologies that will largely emancipate them from the need to import any sources of energy, but they will, in very many cases, need to pay to use other countries' *ik* and often hire alien firms of contractors to construct the plant in which that *ik* will function. Though it was the first country in the world to build a nuclear power station (for the state-owned electricity board), Britain subsequently sold Westinghouse in the cause of naive dogmatism and recently descended into a political farce with France and China about the contract that the Cameron coalition government had entered into for the construction of an untested type of power station on wildly unfavourable financial terms.

The notion of comparative advantage was formulated in an era when the British climate was wholly unsuitable for growing cotton, while British territories in the Caribbean and the southern colonies on the North American mainland proved ideal for the purpose. Thus, British settlers drove enslaved Africans to grow cotton, and sent it to the UK for manufacturing by Arkwright and others who had developed the means cheaply to mass produce cotton cloth. The reasons why manufacturing could be undertaken successfully in the UK were derived from the abundance of capital and the mature state of the law in the UK, so that the innovators could be funded and their *ik* could be protected. Also, the Royal Navy guarded the seaways and provided the best marine maps in the world, while the East India Company provided a closed market in Asia for British exports of cotton cloth.

Some writers have tried to show that north-west England had natural advantages that were conducive to cotton manufacturing: a cool and damp climate which supposedly made it easier to work cotton thread without it splitting or snapping, and 'fast-flowing streams' supposedly to power the water-wheels that drove the first mills. A five-minute visit to any of the historic water-powered facilities in the country shows that the last thing the engineers who built them wanted was fast-flowing water; the common features are a large lodge to store water, a small channel to direct an adjustable but very limited flow of water to the wheel, and a tailrace down which the water flows to re-join the stream from which the water in the lodge was drawn. The tortuous nonsense about a climatic advantage for cotton manufacture in north-west Britain is an extreme example of an effort to develop an Economists' truism into something far more elevated than it is. The simple fact of the world is that no country can simultaneously be the best at every sort of manufacture and every sort of technology, nor can any state be sufficiently strong to colonise territories that contain all the minerals and all the climatic zones that yield commodities that cannot be produced at home.

Therefore, every country, even the USA, must concentrate on those things that it can do with the greatest advantage for their own people and for their future, by making appropriate and sufficient investments in material resource production and in securing facilities for inventors and innovators. Then it must trade with the rest of the world, optimising on its secure *ik*, its climatic and its mineralogical advantages, preferably on fair-trade terms, in order to enable its people to enjoy what cannot be produced at home. The history of post-privatisation Britain shows that references to free trade do not of themselves create a pattern of investment that optimises the deployment of the material and intellectual resources that the country possesses. Political will must be exercised intelligently and selectively, to achieve a broad balance of payments, because there is no benign 'invisible hand' automatically optimising any country's situation in the global economy.

Meanwhile, politicians who commit themselves to giving everybody a 'fair' living standard have continued to defy the 'Iron Law of Wages'. The Iron Law, a core proposition of political economy that has never been disproved, states that no national economy can survive in the medium-term if it allocates more physical resources to consumption than that economy produces (net of imports and exports of material products, financial services, and *ik*, which should balance over any short run of years), after allocating everything that is necessary to maintain public and social services, and all the investment that is necessary to ensure that the economy grows satisfactorily

Governments openly suspend the iron law in time of war, and in other emergencies, when decisions are taken to consume part of the nation's capital and to allow an external deficit to accumulate. Any such period of exception must be followed by a corrective emphasis on material investment, such as was pursued successfully in Federal Germany from 1948. If a country carries a deficit on its balance of payments and/or on the state budget, the interest payments that arise and the repayment of principal that will fall due on that borrowing can fairly be stigmatised as 'theft from future generations'. By increasing consumption and alienating the ownership of a large swathe of productive industry, the UK has defied the law in almost every year since Mrs Thatcher's cohorts began to disperse and to destroy the nationalised industries.

The unprecedented success of British financial services between the 'big bang' of 1986 and the crash of 2008 provided a welcome boost to the balance of payments, but was nowhere near to closing the gap created by the deficit on material trade. The huge success of the knowledge industries, the arts, and small high-tech manufacturing firms has also assisted to reduce the payments deficit, but has no capability to eradicate it. By their very nature, the sectors that depend on advanced *ik* and insider knowledge of their market are in a constant contest with almost equally capable competitors worldwide, so that the premium on their newest financial and software products can quickly be eroded by competition.

Human animals make massive material demands, and while the quality of life rises as individuals are able to access more and better *ik*, and individuals' material demands grow by less per year while their sophistication as consumers rises, the requirement for the material components of consumption continues to increase due to a rising population. No plan to resolve the ongoing, long-term crisis that faces the country can possibly succeed unless it is absolutely concordant with the iron law. It was noted earlier that in 2012 Britain's recorded 'investment' was only 13.5% of GDP, barely half the global average and vastly less than that in the emergent economies. Despite the positive net position of financial services and the knowledge industries, Britain's overall balance of payments with the rest of the world was strongly negative, and the deficit reached a new record – equivalent to over 5% of the national product – in 2015. George Osborne's rhetoric about boosting manufactured exports in a 'march of the makers' was shown to be vacuous. The effect of his tenure of high office was to cut public spending in an obviously vain attempt to eradicate the annual increase in the state debt of an economy whose controllers were oblivious to the need for productiveness.

Germany's unique position in Europe owes everything to the fact that its economic system continues to recognise the central importance of productiveness, while broadly conforming to the iron law. Emergent countries emerge faster the more closely their policies conform to the iron law, as Britain did when it served as the great exemplar of the heroic phase of industrialisation. Closely related to the iron law is the differentiation of *productive* from *unproductive* employment, which was stressed by political economists until their strictures were lost in the emergence of Economics. Labour is counted to be productive if a portion of the output from the job is destined to be invested in future production, as *ik*, as machinery and components, or in the form of materials ready to be processed in the next period. Unproductive labour is any form of employment (or any state of remunerated non-employment) that involves the use of energy and material resources, and makes no contribution to providing *ik*, energy, or materials to be deployed in the future.

A favourite topic of some mid-nineteenth century political economists was whether or not, and to what extent, schoolteachers were productive workers. Most political economists were strongly in favour of compulsory mass elementary education, so the question of whether it was materially useful to the future of the economy was highly relevant. The object of schooling is to prepare young people for a fruitful adult life. Some of the skills that some teachers support, such as numeracy, political economy, literacy, and knowledge of physical science, are obviously of use to people who will become producers of material goods and of marketable intellectual property. Other things that good teachers present to school children – such as an appreciation of art, music, and literature – will not help most of the pupils to become materially productive, though an important minority of the population will build on their cultural formation to produce inspirational works that may help future producers to be in a better frame of mind to work effectively, and some will create performances and works of art that generate tax revenue and export earnings for the country.

Thus, as a segment of the labour force, teachers were classed as being partially productive, which made them eligible to consume a share of the wages fund. Since 1950, many teachers have repudiated their pedagogic duty to inculcate essential life skills. They call their pupils 'students' and assert that the role of the 'class leader' is to observe and facilitate uninformed autodidacticism by immature people. Such teachers can be tragically well-intentioned, but they impart no useful knowledge or social skill and they frequently tolerate bullying and disorder among their victims, who leave 'education' to become perceived as 'unemployable'.

The problems of the post-industrial economies can be resolved only after their politicians and political economists understand the need broadly to recognise the crucial significance of productiveness, which is inextricably linked with the development and defence of ever-more-advanced *ik*. The bowdlerised 'neoKeynesian' idea that various Economists have pushed periodically since 1950, that a general encouragement of spending on consumption will cause the economy to expand, has resulted each time it has been tried in the UK in an increase in the creation of consumer credit, a surge of imports, the export of capital, and an inflation of credit.

The government has applied financial pressure to hundreds of thousands of individuals to make them pass from a category of 'unemployed' to a classification as 'employed', heedless of whether or not that gives them access to work of measureable productiveness. More and more of the situations that degenerate governments call 'employment' and 'apprenticeship' can only exist under state subsidy, and are not subject to any test of productiveness. Politicians' verbiage about job creation masks the depressing reality of giving handouts to paupers, who full well know that any 'jobs' or 'training' that they are compelled to undertake serve a political charade, which conduces hardly at all to the wellbeing of the individuals concerned, or of the national economy. This situation is unsustainable. The terms of the social contract between the state and its citizens must be reviewed, frankly, in the light of the facts that have been shown here. The credibility of the political class with those who must be consulted is extremely low, so a new political order may be needed to gain enough public support for a revision of the role of the state, based on practicalities and reality. Real statesmanship is demanded. Whether the supply can meet the demand is an open question.

Chapter Six
Consumers and Compromise

The original and the ultimate purpose of all organised economic activity is to provide the means of survival, and additional discretionary consumption, for human beings. The totality of the human race faces contextual problems that militate against economic success, the potential overbreeding of the species relative to total available productive resources, political, social, and religious obstacles to optimising the distribution of resources among human beings, climate change (regardless of the extent to which this may be a product of human activity), and the universally enervating impact of entropy are significant among them. The effectiveness of any economy's consumption of human intellectual effort, physical labour, of input materials and energy on farms, in mines, factories, offices, workshops, studios, transport, and logistics, can only be judged by the efficiency with which the process directly or indirectly serves the ultimate objective of promoting human wellbeing through consumption that enables people simultaneously to add to the material and intellectual resources that are available to the economy while they enjoy their own lifestyle.

In the traditional European social model, it is assumed that most adults are capable of generating access to consumer experiences by selling their labour 'by hand and brain', during an economically active phase of life that lasts for between twenty and seventy years, which may encompass several career changes and periods of non-productiveness when one is expanding the experience that enriches many peoples' lives. Some people earn their living by selling their quonic services, ideas, or products directly to the public in an open marketplace, but the majority of income-earners – even the highest earners – earn their livings under contracts of employment or consultancy. Consumer experiences include intellectual and psychological events such as are accessed in the concert hall, in church, on the internet, and from the very important sense of wellbeing that derives from a consciousness of having financial security, as well as from benign physical and mental experiences. Making unreciprocated *oblations* is also important to many people; this can take the form of building a temple or a chapel, or placing flowers at a shrine or at the scene of a killing, or sending fan mail, or just giving someone a supportive word. These actions involve the allocation of time and/or material resources and/or effort that are of psychological significance to those involved. Many people also give money, and their services, to charity.

The Allocation of Personal Incomes

In any money-using economy, a significant proportion of an individual's income is necessarily allocated for buying things and experiences to be consumed during the days until the next salary, pension, benefit, or fee payment is receivable. Over thousands of years, worldly wisdom dictated that a significant portion of an economically active individual's income should be used to store material goods, or to buy investment **ka**s, which could later be drawn upon to maintain the owner in the winter, in case of drought, in old age, and in other circumstances in which she or he may be unable to maintain their desired living standard without drawing on reserves.

In the short period between 1945 and 1986, most Britons were able to believe that the welfare state would protect them from any unwelcome contingency; only later did the probability that it was unaffordable in the long-term give rise to the reasonable accusation that the post-war generation of baby boomers were in effect robbing successive generations of potential wealth. But also, between 1960 and 2007, many earners were induced to succumb to a social and psychological revolution. This was presented to them as a simple matter of finance, a proposition from banks and other providers of personal financial services, which ran counter to long-run human experience. This is the notion that a consumer need not be confined within an expenditure budget that is limited by his or her earnings, or constrained by the need to 'save for a rainy day'. People who accepted the proposition felt that they could constantly increase their borrowing, rather than pay off one loan before entering into another one. Millions made an increasing proportion of their purchases on credit cards and equivalents. Many of them lost consciousness of a periodic pattern of receiving and spending a finite income. They settled the obligatory part of their monthly accounts, often by direct debit; thereafter they let the negative 'balances' – consolidated *ko*s – increase, and accepted the myth that this was a new and better way to enjoy the good life.

In the deeply-depressed nineteen-thirties, Keynes assumed that most of the new spending-power that a government could create in a period of depression would be used to bring back into use shut-down existing machinery and unemployed people who knew how to use it. Thereafter, their spending would help to draw others into employment to develop infrastructure such as improved roads, or to exploit new technologies. By contrast, especially after 1980, the increasing facility for individuals to borrow led to the surge in imports of consumer goods that has been noted earlier, which led the country into a deepening balance-of-payments deficit on manufactured goods. While part of the balance of payments deficit had to be settled by transferring credit (and some currency) to overseas creditors, much of the deficit was added to the nation's borrowing. The massively-increased availability of credit that remained within the UK economy was largely absorbed in house prices and in the new wholesale financial trades, so overt general retail price inflation, which had been so disastrous in the nineteen-seventies, was contained at a modest level.

Following the 2007-8 crunch, British society has been unable smoothly to develop a stable pattern in the management of personal finances, principally because an even deeper systemic problem that has wantonly been absorbed into the economy has become ever more apparent. In very recent years, the increase in the number of people who are classified as 'employed' (principally on low pay, for limited hours weekly, supplemented by 'working' tax credits) in the service sector has made it appear – to the naïve, which category apparently includes at least half the members of both houses of parliament – as if the historic problems of non-employment and visceral poverty can be eradicated. In terms of published official data, the employment and welfare policies of the two Cameron governments were a massive statistical success. But in terms of political economy, almost all that additional employment has delivered negative productiveness and has developed no *ik*. It has facilitated the importation of consumer quons and marcoms for processing into quons or for packaging as neoquons, at the cost of a massive export of capital. The external indebtedness of the UK has increased alongside the rise of personal debt, and many of the assets that foreigners now own in Britain are firms (including privatised utilities) on which British consumers depend. The owners have every right to expect tribute to be paid to them, by British consumers, for the indefinite future.

A commitment to 'end want' was adopted as state policy in Britain during the Second World War. The implementation of the promise, principally through the payment of cash benefits, defied the cautionary lessons of history, especially the propensity displayed by most humans to accept benefits without any sense of obligation to contribute to production. In seventeenth- and eighteenth-century Britain, as both a consequence of increasing population and as a stimulus to its continuance, farming largely became a cash-crop business. Technical change in agriculture and animal husbandry was facilitated by changes in land tenure that compelled many children of dispossessed peasants to leave their home villages and seek work in towns, where the abundance of cheap labour supported the emergence and growth of a huge range of trades, industries, and service activities.

To reduce social tension and prevent food riots as prices rose during the wars with revolutionary France, an Act of Parliament of 1795 spread the 'Speenhamland system' over the whole country. This regime of universal benefits ensured that every family received a guaranteed minimum cash income, indexed to the price of bread. A much older law, the Settlement Act, specified that people were only eligible to receive these 'relief' payments in their birthplace, or in another civil parish where the authorities allowed the individual to 'settle' officially. Legal resettlement was a common occurrence in London, where the demand for labour was voracious, but not in most other localities. After 1795, the income supplements enabled couples to breed, then to maintain their children while they remained in their home parishes, regardless of how many children they had and of whether or not the parents were engaged in productive labour. As a consequence of the rising cost of the Speenhamland system around 1800, an increasing slice of the incomes of landlords, merchants, manufacturers, and farmers was taken in successive years in a local property tax called 'rates', from which the benefits were paid. The money that was taken as rates could not be invested in the future growth of the ratepayers' businesses or spent on their own lifestyle, but the 'upper and middle classes' put up with that imposition as the price of keeping the 'lower orders' quiescent during the succession of wars.

By 1810, the Speenhamland beneficiaries had demonstrably become a very significant proportion of the population. They consumed mainly marcoms: home-cooked food, home-made clothes, utensils that were made and maintained in the home, and locally-made, handcrafted products. Thus, in the economy overall, quon purchases – though they were growing in number, at rising prices – represented a declining percentage of all consumption. The economy was potentially headed for stagnation as the disbursement of circulating capital in the form of unearned incomes became more blatant.

In his *Essay on the Principle of Population (1798)* TR Malthus postulated that human population has the capability of growing 'geometrically'; two parents can easily have four children who, with partners, can have 32 children, and so on generation by generation, for as long as they could all be fed. Most political economists agreed that productive resources can only be increased 'arithmetically' by adding individual work stations to the available capital stock, or by extending the margin of cultivated land incrementally by inputting a great deal of labour and investment. Malthus' principle was interpreted to imply that if Speenhamland benefits continued to be available to all comers, the poor would breed 'with utter recklessness' and the majority of the national product could ultimately be absorbed in unproductive consumption by the recipients of benefits. Rampant population growth would only be subject to a positive check when some pandemic brought about a massive death rate, or during a famine following a disastrous harvest failure, or when wars for control of resources killed many people.

The timescale against which the population would grow to crisis level might be extended if society lapsed into 'vice' – mass homosexuality and/or prostitution and concubinage – but the contraceptive impact of those preventive checks on population growth would only defer the date of the inevitable catastrophe. The post-1960 option to include convenient contraception and abortion on demand among one's lifestyle choices was not envisaged in the early nineteenth century, so the most accessible preventive checks that are available in the present day were not even imaginable then. The sixth edition of Malthus' *Essay* of 1826 was to be regarded as definitive, and it is credited with providing the basis for the idea of natural selection to be developed by both Darwin and Wallace, who presented the concept simultaneously in 1858.

It was not Malthus' intention in writing his *Essay* to repress aspiring young people or to denigrate the poor. To the contrary, he pointed out that a high standard of living could be enjoyed by the masses only if they kept their numbers small enough, and worked hard enough, to share the national product optimally. He emphasised that investment must be at a high enough rate for everyone to find a productive job and to share the fruits of their labour into the future, always allowing for the fact that some politically and socially necessary jobs were not materially productive, but were essential to maintain coherence in society. He had undertaken massive research on population trends and their relation to economic activity in the known world, and concluded that higher human welfare was achievable by combining restraints on population growth with rising quonic consumption, which would yield increasing rent that could partially be used to increase investment.

As was shown earlier, unlike Ricardo, his contemporary, Malthus contended that there were two flows of income that were received by human beings and by corporate entities which could be described as 'rent'. One was a payment to the people and institutions that had the good fortune to be the owners of land, for allowing access to that land for housing, urban business, farming, mining, and other productive activities to be conducted on it; the amount of that sort of rent on various plots of land varied with the productiveness of the soil or the mine and on the distance of the plot from population centres.

The second form of rent was the excess of income over the costs for physical preparation and transport of the components that arose from sales of what this text has identified as quons. This was a form of 'rent' that was claimed by holders of intellectual property in patents, copyright, brands, and trademarks, both in respect of material and keynic 'goods', but both nineteenth-century political economy and post-1890 Economics chose to ignore it.

Meanwhile, Malthus' thesis on population was accepted by the ruling classes, and gained so much scientific credibility that he was admitted to a Fellowship of the Royal Society, a degree of recognition that has properly been denied to modern Economists. Immediately following the great constitutional reform of 1832, both major parties in the House of Commons (for which the voter qualification was to be a ratepayer) approved the establishment of a Royal Commission – the highest form of public inquiry – whose report fully accepted the Malthusian analysis of the impact of the benefits system.

The draconically amended Poor Law of 1834 abolished universal cash benefits. Every adult was to be faced by a simple challenge, to exist independently on the basis of his or her own assets and earnings. The only alternative to keeping oneself and one's children was to surrender all the rights and liberties of a British subject – and any assets that the person might still possess – and accept the status of a benefit-dependent pauper who would be compelled to live in a workhouse, where living conditions for fit adults had to be 'less eligible' than those of a free man who was receiving the lowest subsistence wage that was on offer in the open economy. Although the act was not implemented in its full rigour throughout the country, the broad principle that it established did prevail.

The remaining 66 years of the nineteenth century witnessed a continuation of high population growth, unprecedented inventiveness, mass emigration to the colonies and the USA, high investment, massive improvements in the productivity and the productiveness of labour and of investment, and rising overall prosperity, as well as the Dickensian scenes of poverty and degradation that disclose the Victorian era as having been very far from idyllic. The overwhelming majority of the population – including all females – did not have parliamentary votes, so they could not overturn the New Poor Law at the next election. Instead, they accepted the responsibility to work to maintain themselves and their children.

To mitigate the harsh environment of developing capitalist exploitation of the workforce, parliament passed the Factory Acts, which regulated workplace conditions, including strong measures to ensure that the law was enforced. The state also facilitated the rise of trade unions by allowing them to exist in the legal framework of Friendly Societies (i.e., as mutual insurers with limited scope), and parliament eventually extended the right to vote to all male householders aged over 21. By the first decade of the twentieth century, life for most citizens was, at the least, more tolerable than in any earlier era and a commission was established to advise the government on means to mitigate the rigours of the Poor Law. By then, branded products such as the Daily Mail, Beecham's Pills, Pears soap and Cadbury's chocolate had become commonplace, and pubs, theatres, and music halls were affordable, at least occasionally, to almost all consumers.

In parallel with the workhouse system, individuals who were adjudged to be incapable of maintaining themselves autonomously due to disabilities, mental health problems, or personality disorders, were separated from the paupers and admitted to county asylums. The callous closure of these refuges late in the twentieth century led directly to the tragic and highly visible problems of homelessness, beggary, despair, malnutrition, and displays of violence and self-harm by inadequately supervised mentally ill individuals that have subsequently become features of British street life. It has also resulted in the criminalisation of tens of thousands of ill, addicted, and inadequate individuals, who are currently consigned to prison because their behaviour is not consistent with the right of the majority to live undisturbed by the nuisance that these people involuntarily cause. Such tragic cases have always existed, and though it had many drawbacks, the system of asylums cared for them, usually quite well, according to the criteria that prevailed from time to time.

Poor Law to Welfare State, and the New Pauperism

In the consciously more affluent society of the early twentieth century, a Royal Commission report of 1906 led to modifications of the 1834 Poor Law. That was followed by improvements in welfare that accompanied reflation and re-armament in the nineteen-thirties, but the residue of the workhouses remained until the mid-nineteen-forties. The Second World War was a period of austerity tempered by optimism, and the Labour Party won the general election in 1945 with the commitment to create a welfare state that was characterised without embarrassment as a 'New Jerusalem'. Behind the idealist rhetoric was a perception that cash payments to beneficiaries were less susceptible to critical scrutiny than was 'indoor relief' – residential provision – that required 24/7 attention to the needs (and, in many cases, the control) of each inmate.

The closure of large residential institutions started with transferring the remaining wards of former workhouses to local hospitals, under the Attlee government. It continued through the sell-off of the vacated asylums during the Thatcher era, the Blair-Brown disposal of community hospital sites, and the recently-announced cull of district hospitals. The subsequent desirability of many of the abandoned structures to developers has belied the negative image of the 'poor law bastilles' that is presented in soft-left social history.

The 1945 government introduced a new form of income supplements, reminiscent of Speenhamland but payable from general taxation, by giving a 'child allowance' to every mother of a second or subsequent child regardless of the employment status of the parents. In paying the allowance directly to mothers, the government intended to convey the message that this cash was explicitly for the care of the child, embedding a concept of the division of labour (and of responsibility) between the parents in a nuclear family. Tory ministers extended the scope of the allowance, and of other 'assistance' that was paid to families from national taxes, when they provided low-income supplements as a temporary means of supporting living standards while they were attempting to limit the rate of nominal increase of wages in their period of office from 1970 to 1974. Similar thinking was applied by the Thatcher-Major regime in the period from 1979 to 1997.

An explicit intention of the ministers who adopted these packages was to encourage people to find and to keep jobs, even if they were poorly paid and regardless of their material productiveness, because this would help to minimise the published number of the 'unemployed'. Creating jobs had been the principal basis for the popularity of both Adolf Hitler and Franklin Roosevelt before the Second World War, and it was considered axiomatic by politicians for several decades after the war that democratic institutions would be at risk if a statistical situation that could be damned as 'mass unemployment' should reoccur. When Edward Heath's Conservative government introduced their income supplement in 1971, it was intended to be a short-term measure, designed to reduce the threat of hyperinflation. As with other such expedients, once it had been introduced, there was never an 'appropriate time' to withdraw the subsidy, so the mass subsidisation of wages became institutionalised and it survives to this day within the package called universal credit. The underlying redistribution of resources was *from* using circulating capital to maintain national defence and investment in material production *to* the provision of heath, educational, and social services, and *into* a system of benefits that restored hereditary pauperism and built up deficits both on the domestic budget and in international trade.

The consolidation of that policy during the Thatcher years, while the supply side of the economy was devastated, is still not sufficiently appreciated in the United Kingdom. Throughout the period from 1945 to 1979, British governments believed in maintaining a 'mixed economy' in production as well as through the provision of nationalised health, education, and welfare services. Meanwhile, a major feature of the post-war reconstruction and extension of urban areas took the form of publicly-owned housing, administered by local authorities. Rural slums were also replaced by council homes. This meant that state-owned industries and utilities were developed alongside the private sector of trade and industry. Politicians of both ruling parties were open to persuasion by the trades unions and the employers' trade associations, usually acting in concert, to allocate significant funding to maintain a wide range of firms in existence even if they were temporarily unprofitable due to the vagaries of international commerce. Industries that were considered to be strategically significant received subsidies and credit guarantees on export sales, and were given government orders set at prices that were above international market minima. Many firms in the private sector were also offered grants for research and development and for new plant, and their produce was protected by tariffs against competing imports.

Besides effectively supporting wage levels, these policies facilitated the creation and development of indigenous *ik*, as when successive British governments had provided investment funds to develop television, telecoms, and nuclear power as publicly-owned operations, built the national grids in electricity and gas, and, together with France, developed Concorde. Much of the state's investment in industry was demonstrably productive. By 1970, a vast cohort of British scientists, skilled technicians, and support staff in transport, mining, utilities, media, and industry received incomes that were effectively guaranteed by the state. In most years, their wages were fully financed from their firms' corporate earnings.

In the very different ideological climate of the nineteen-eighties, after Mrs Thatcher came to power, the major nationalised industries were first slimmed down, with the employees' redundancy costs and the cost of demolishing the plant paid for by taxpayers, before the residue of the operation was privatised. As a concomitant of this process, a wide range of highly skilled private-sector businesses that had supplied state-owned and subsidised firms with capital equipment and support services (many of which held internationally recognised *ik*) became non-viable and were closed down. Equivalent replacement jobs were not available for many of the skilled employees who became redundant, and whole research teams who had worked in smokestack industry, in mining, in shipbuilding, and in their supply chains were dissolved. The Treasury sloughed-off the cost of supporting investment in the survival and development of industry, at an incalculably great cost to future national income. The destruction of capital in the forms of scrapped machinery and equipment, dissolved research and technical facilities, written-off or alienated *ik*, redundant researchers and involuntarily-retired craftsmen, was a massive defiance of common sense.

From the nineteen-twenties until 1990, the Leninist regimes in Eastern Europe mendaciously asserted that all their subjects had access to excellent educational, medical, and other welfare facilities 'from the cradle to the grave'. Consequently, non-communist governments – especially in Europe – responded to that challenge by promising to deliver superior universal health, educational, and social services, which were provided through state organisations that each developed massive institutional inertia. The sudden collapse of communism in 1988-91, and the subsequent fuller exposure of the lies on which the Soviet regime had relied, enabled democratic governments to review their policies.

But in the United Kingdom, the expansion of both the number of beneficiaries and the range and content of their benefits and tax credits continued. Thatcherite ruthlessness, which dominated industrial policy, was not carried over into the welfare sphere; hence, the 'hereditary paupers' multiplied, families who partially accepted and partially opted for existence on benefits in successive generations. Thus, the Conservatives spawned a bizarre throwback to the Speenhamland system. In most such cases, fortuitous unemployment in the first generation led to the next generation having no aspiration for education or employment, and thus a 'deprived' and/or 'problem' family was available to be added to the social statistics.

The anachronistic 'auction game' continued at each general election, in which the parties promised to put differing amounts more of taxpayers' money into the National Health Service bureaucracy, into failing schools and dysfunctional social services, year on year. 'Intellectuals' in the Labour party welcomed the bifurcation of industrial from welfare policy because the influence of the industrial trade unions on the party was weakened by the dramatic reduction in their membership and resources. This enabled a clique from the chattering classes to capture the leadership after the untimely death of John Smith. When they took power in 1997, Tony Blair's ministers and their special advisers accepted the Economists' dogma about the superiority of imaginary markets above state provision, but they did not try to cut back state welfare provision as such. They sought ways of placing responsibility for the delivery of health, educational, and welfare facilities outside the nominal boundaries of the public sector. They introduced pseudo-private-sector contracts for the provision of services, while hiring thousands more bureaucrats to run the ongoing public-sector services, and the scandalously high cost of some privately financed construction contracts adversely reshaped the cash flow of the schools and hospitals that were entrapped in such spivvery for decades into the future. The Blairites compounded their folly by continuing with privatisation of state assets.

The tax revenue that the UK received from North Sea oil came significantly on stream to coincide with the high tide of Thatcherism. Over the subsequent three decades, while Norway accumulated a massive sovereign wealth fund, British oil tax was largely channelled into income support, family supplements, payoff packages, allowances, and pensions for tens of thousands of skilled productive workers who 'retired early' involuntarily.

Thus the calamitous economic and social impact of Thatcherism was partially concealed by the mass distribution of a fortuitous bonus. Successive governments extended benefits to the consumers who had been evicted from the asylums, and to young people for whom traditional craft apprenticeship with its first-class on-the-job training no longer existed. Politicians' paranoid determination to avoid accusations of 'racism' meant that the benefits system also supported thousands of opportunistic immigrants who settled in formerly industrial towns where there was ample cheap housing and little risk of becoming conventionally employed, other than in the distribution of the additional imports of foodstuffs and marcoms that their communal tradition demanded. The benefit of North Sea oil has predominantly been dissipated in consumption, which individuals have allocated largely to buying imports. Consequently, Britain's massive cohort of hereditary paupers, many of whom were misdirected through fake apprenticeships and inapplicable degrees, makes the country less capable of paying its way in the world in the next twenty years than it would have been if the oil had remained untouched.

Nominal Jobs and Real Incomes

Since 2008, thousands of private sector firms (especially manufacturers and traders in marcoms) have found themselves unable to maintain the necessary level of investment in new quonic equipment, because of the demands that the tax-and-benefits system makes on their revenues. Many firms have been forced into liquidation by these pressures while their competitors in emergent countries did not have to face comparably large social charges. Margaret Thatcher's government was quite spectacularly reckless in replacing mass productive employment with mass benefits for the unemployed, while they also paid income supplements to hundreds of thousands of employed people. The alarming situation that already existed in 1997 was compounded by Tony Blair's contempt for history, as New Labour impelled Britain towards a Malthusian crisis by combining unrestricted immigration with failure to understand the importance of investment either through the development and protection of ***ik*** or the construction of plant that incorporated the latest designs for generating quons. When Gordon Brown became prime minister, the new Labour publicists boasted that 'we have created two and a half million new jobs since 1997'; that 'achievement' was indeed ascribable to the government, but it was very brittle. The great majority of the jobs were in retail and in personal services.

About half of the new jobs, including the majority of full-time jobs, were taken by European immigrants. Many of the jobs that were taken by native British were only afforded by the employer for a small number of hours' engagement per week at the minimum wage, on the assumption that the salary would be combined with a tax credit. Employment growth in retailing, care homes, hospitality and catering, entertainment, and contract cleaning – in large swathes of the public sector, as well as in the private sector – occurred in the decade before the 2008 crisis only because income support from the state was available, while many small employers engaged illegal immigrants at wages below the statutory minimum. Millions of parents convincingly said that they could only be available for limited weekly working hours if the state funded childcare, thus adding to the cost of the bizarre concoction. Meanwhile, pseudo-jobs were funded by 'into-work' and 'back-to-work' subsidies for targeted groups of non-employed individuals, many of whom were allocated to programmes of preparation performed by private-sector businesses at significant cost to the state, and with no clear criteria for the assessment of their success or failure. None of this massive expenditure or of the bureaucratic drag by which it was burdened took account of the crucial question of whether or not the activities would support material productiveness or the development of *ik*.

A further and deeper dimension to this issue has been advancing and has now reached the stage where it can be a major threat to society and to the political order. The media have widely reported on developments of artificial intelligence for two generations, and most people are now aware of self-driving vehicles, and of highly automated warehouses where their online purchases are processed. Such phenomena are still seen as exceptional, but it does not take an enthusiast (or a prophet of doom) to see that this phase of the implementation of technological development presages a fundamental change in productive relationships, in the demand for labour and in potential patterns of remuneration. Examples are already available of the potential for machines to replace people in performing complex diagnostic tasks as well as in postal sorting offices, and on farms where harvesters guided by satnav can clear the whole crop from hundreds of hectares with no person present. The sort of world envisaged in 1909 in EM Forster's novella *The Machine Stops* is not yet imminent, but the means towards a vastly more automated world are all around us. Combine this fact with the evidence that an ever-greater proportion of the world's wealth is held by a small caste of super-rich and it is possible to see a future where the rich dominate an integrated computer-controlled world economy that is run for their profit, while the state is reduced to the role of provider of discipline, bread, and circuses for the dependent mass of paupers.

The complex of taxes and benefits that enmesh the population ensures that most individuals do not comprehend their personal relationship to the economy. All human beings are necessarily and constantly consumers; they must, at the very least, eat, drink, and sleep to survive, and while they are asleep they are digesting food, processing drinks, and dreaming to rationalise their daytime experiences. The most basic material lifestyle can securely be maintained only if the economy is investing enough to ensure the continuity of the necessary production. But there is no significant public or parliamentary cognisance of the essential fact that sustaining more than ten million people on a combination of low-wage employment with benefits is a fragile temporary condition of the economy. The pretence of near-full employment cannot survive far into the 'third industrial revolution', which has already begun. The technological implementation of this change cannot be halted, the concomitant socio-political threats and potential benefits have not yet been addressed, and this issue cannot be left aside for future consideration.

Socio-Economic Stratification

In the very shaky context of the contemporary economy, the most powerful category of personal consumers are the savvy and competent individuals who derive enough income from earnings and investments to secure all their preferred consumer experiences as quons, to accumulate pension rights, and selectively to buy insurance protection against adverse risk possibilities that can threaten their lifestyle. This most privileged group includes directors and senior managers of large companies, the more successful financial services professionals, providers of quonic professional services such as specialist medicine, accountancy, engineering consultancy, architecture, and the law, creators of *ik* in science, technology, music, theatre, literature, film, TV, artworks, and other collectibles that begin their existence already classified as jevs. Other potentially high-earners implement the spun-off output of *ik* that emerges from corporate laboratories and universities, or are high earners in the huge businesses of software development, press, media, and entertainment, including sport. The category also includes the minority of the population who conserve significant inherited wealth.

Britain's state-provided services are used selectively by clever *grauniadistas*, who know how to seek out the state schools and the hospitals that are successful and avoid those that are failing. These well-informed egocentric consumers are more likely to more quickly realise when they are seriously ill and demand appropriate treatment, and they are much more capable of moving their homes according to school catchment areas, and of assessing their children's academic progress and talking to teachers about it. If they encounter an interruption to their income flow in mid-career they can, in most cases, maintain their lifestyle by selling *ka*s, by releasing some of the equity in their real estate (commonly called 'remortgaging'), through borrowing from a bank against security provided by jevic assets such as pictures, by early withdrawal of life assurance funds, or by drawing-down part of their pensions savings. Such short-term financing methods are usually preferred to selling durable quons which in most cases can only attract a fraction of the prices that their owners paid to acquire them, if they are offered in a forced sale.

Very sharply differentiated from the most capable consumers are millions of citizens whose only admitted income is benefits received from the government. It has been considered axiomatic in most of Western Europe for more than half a century that a sophisticated socio-economic system must provide a 'fair' standard of living for all those who do not generate income for themselves. Old age is generally accepted as a valid reason why many people cease to be able to earn a sufficient income. In some countries, a state retirement pension is available only to those whose 'personal' pensions are not sufficient to match a standard-of-living specification. In other countries, all people over the set age are given a means-tested pension, and in some countries pensions are granted to all the aged regardless of their other income sources and of whether or not they paid significant contributions to social funds earlier in life.

Still the largest contingent of human consumers in the mature economies are those who occupy the middle ranges of the socio-economic distribution pattern, who do not aspire to be super-rich; nor would they be comfortable to find themselves forced to become abject petitioners for basic state benefits. Through their adult lives, most such people in the past three generations could 'get by' on what they earned, net of taxes, and their resources were sometimes supplemented by borrowing, or by modest inheritances or windfall gains, or may have been reduced by unwelcome risk events. Nevertheless, in the post-industrial countries, tens of millions of parents' earned incomes have been eligible for subsidy from the state, which has dissolved the ancient obligation on parents by their labour to provide for their children and to forgo some discretionary consumption in order to buy the necessities that will secure the children's healthy future as adults.

In the UK, British citizens, and EU citizens who have held jobs (and thus been eligible to pay tax) for the specified period, can claim immediate access to state benefits in the event that their income flow from employment ceases because of redundancy or illness. They can claim the full rate of the benefit, provided that they have previously followed the acknowledged rules of the game, which are:

1. while you are employed, spend your earnings every month, together with all the allowances and credits that the state pays you; don't try to save in any form on which the state could base a detrimental means test if circumstances should arise that enable you to apply for a state benefit,

2. buy all the durable and ephemeral quons and neoquons that you can, when you can, including holidays and entertainments, for which you

borrow the maximum consumer credit that banks and credit card firms will allow you.

British people who are in work may receive tax credits, but they must still pay the regressive national insurance levy, plus VAT, excise duty, council tax, TV licenses, vehicle tax, congestion charge, and other local taxes, and the shade of Robert Malthus met George Orwell's ghost at the point where individuals were charged income tax on their tax credits.

Many tens of thousands of individuals (predominantly of south Asian origin) decline to be placed in any stratified tax bracket; they declare no earned income and have no intention to pay the employee rate of national insurance levy, while they participate in the 'vibrant cash economy' that was highly lauded by a former canon of Blackburn Cathedral. These groups demand all the benefits that they can extract from the tax and benefits whirligig, and from the health service, to which they make no contribution. The potentially productive function of a comprehensive health service, provided free at the point of access, is to restore the sick and injured to their workplaces and to care for the children who will be the workers in future decades. The obligation to pay earnings-related national insurance contributions, separate from income tax, to pay for the health service, pensions, and unemployment benefit was vitiated in the very early days of the welfare state when it became clear that the employees' and employers' contributions to the 'national insurance fund' would never be sufficient to meet the outgoings demanded from it. The media made great play with the fact that millions of people came forward with previously-unmet needs for false teeth and spectacles, and the weight of this demand alone set the new health service in deficit. The shortfall had to be met from the state budget, and the national insurance levy became, as it has remained, effectively a supplement to income tax.

While the economy slithered into the crunch in 2007-8, already almost five and a half million people in the age range 16-65 were officially reported to be wholly dependent on benefits, and eleven million people lived in households where no individual was in employment. Tens of thousands of idle young males were minimally remunerated to remain dysfunctional 'hoodies', and the number of teenage NEETs ('not in education, employment or training') increased every year. The emergence of this alienated underclass was a direct consequence of purblind economic policy, ably assisted by ideologically motivated subversion in the educational and social services. The lifestyle for the most obvious victims of these socio-economic failures was desperately restricted, conducive to petty criminality – especially in the distribution of drugs, and the acquisition of the cash with which to enter that market – and to the casual sex that propagated their sub-species.

The subsequent creation of hundreds of thousands of partly or wholly sham apprenticeships, alongside a much smaller number of authentic traineeships, has barely scratched the surface of this massive problem; motivating career prospects are not available for the ill-educated output from the failing schools. Few people give any credibility to Theresa May's hare-brained notion of allowing any comprehensive school, academy, or free school to become a pseudo grammar school, and the principal impact of her promulgation of the scheme is that a large part of the credit that she gained as an incoming prime minister has evanesced. The fatuity of over-expanding the university system (notably in the provision of cheaply-taught 'useless' degrees) is being recognised by more and more potential undergraduates. Perceptive young people (and their parents) become apprehensive about accumulating debts in excess of £50,000 in student fees and living costs before they face the pecuniary Himalaya of housing costs when they become employed.

This latter dilemma has led professional partnerships, financial services companies, IT businesses, and technologically-based manufacturing firms, and even some farmers and horticulturalists, to recognise the possibility of attracting young people who have attained good A-level results and what are perceived to be appropriate personalities to begin working in their organisations at eighteen. By providing training in-house accompanied by part-time access to the relevant professional qualification, and often including a degree scheme, these employers gain able and vigorous staff who do not fall into the louche lifestyle that debilitates many full-time undergraduates.

With notable exceptions, a significantly higher proportion of the sons and daughters of most of the ethnic minorities that have become established in the UK since 1960 now enter professionally oriented higher education than do socially classified C and D indigenous whites. Many children from coherent immigrant groups are consciously determined to achieve non-beneficiary lifestyles by their own efforts, not least those who have direct experience of societies overseas where benefit systems do not exist. The more percipient among them also recognise the medium-term unsustainability of reckless borrowing to fund mass income support and minimise their call on student loans funds by living in the parental home while studying.

By contrast, able-bodied, 'unwaged' native British beneficiaries demand the services of hospitals and schools for their children as a matter of right. Many of them use abusive and threatening language, expectorate, and resort to physical violence against civil servants, teachers, medical, and nursing staff. Minorities from other ethnicities have adopted these destructive behavioural patterns, along with the dependency lifestyle. The predisposition to irrational anger and the tendency to violence that some of these subsets of the population display – especially when fuelled by alcohol, cannabis, heroin, cocaine, or chemical cocktails – has exacerbated the age-old problems of intimidatory neighbourhood gangs, successive plagues of graffiti, 'no-go' areas, knifings, and random kicking attacks. There is no indication, however, that the chavs and hoodies, who have been so effectively denied adequate education, example, religion, aspiration, patriotism, and self-confidence, have displayed any susceptibility to being enlisted into a communist 'army', whose disciplinary requirements they would find intolerable, and whose ideology would be inaccessible to their understanding. The young people who have travelled on EU passports to join Islamist madrasas and jihadist groups are among the least susceptible to marxist indoctrination, and individually they have resisted (or turned away from) the prevalent yob anticulture before they found their lethal vocation.

In many emergent countries, a significant tranche of the population occupies a customary social status that determines, or attaches to, the individual's economic function. These include chieftainship, landholding, peasant farming, hunting, fishing, religious leadership, handicraft, or domestic service (which is often tantamount to slavery). These people's consumption of home-grown and home-made commodities has historically been supplemented by marcoms that are supplied by local craftsmen such as blacksmiths. Millions of people involuntarily occupy such a customary status by inheritance. In some legal systems, such people enjoy rights of land tenure, and/or access to woodlands and waterways, or have customary rights to ply a trade. Every year, tens of thousands of traditional roles are swept away in the process of urbanisation and through the industrialisation of forestry, agriculture, and fisheries.

Although it is very rarely recognised clearly, either by the victims or the perpetrators, forcible evictions of people from the sites that they have occupied under customary tenure deprives them of irreplaceable *ik*. This applies when smallholdings and farm buildings are bulldozed and the inhabitants are relocated. It also happens when workshops and homes where craftsmen marketed their own wares become non-viable when marcoms serving the same purpose are mass-produced. National income accounting does not include the negative impact of the huge loss of *ik* that is entailed in these processes, nor do economic planners take cognisance of the potential leverage that would be achieved if the people could deploy their inherited *ik* (especially customary rights) as security for borrowing that could fund their autonomous participation in economic development. These manifestations of the ignorance of the political class again display the bankruptcy of policies that are influenced by Economists.

The people who are deprived of their ancestral assets and livelihoods in the emergent economies must seek wage-paying employment in mining, quarrying, agriculture, materials processing, and transport, from which they derive the means to become market consumers. Their spending generates additional employment opportunity in bars, cafés, clubs, cinemas, shops, passenger transport, communications, police, personal services, medical services, education, and administration. Cash wages in emergent economies in marcom-producing plant and in service activities were of the order of 5% of a typical European nominal wage rate at median 2006 exchange rates, but that was sufficient to enable an individual to experience an acceptable lifestyle according to local criteria. Over the past decade, money-wages and real wages have increased significantly in China and in several other leading emergent economies, funding households to move into quonic consumption on a significant scale. The rapidly shifting balance of global economic power will now accelerate the changes to which this section has drawn attention.

Personal Finance and Economic Reality

Making the transition from a traditional status within an under-developed economy into autonomous consumerism within a market economy is intrinsically a stressful experience. To accommodate to such an environmental shift successfully, the individual must appreciate that the more significant she or he can become as a buyer of quons and of quonic services, and as an owner of keynic investments, the greater is the impact of that individual's decisions on the structure and dynamism of the economy of which he or she is a component. The individual must learn about taxation, regulation, and how to recognise responsible access to credit, and thus optimally become empowered to expand their turnover and thereby contribute to the growth of an economy.

For the overwhelming majority of individuals in every socio-economic classification all over the world, current quonic consumption – gratification derived from products and services that are fashionable, which embody protected *ik* – provides more certain satisfaction than does any right to receive deferred income (or any other contingent benefit) in the future. It requires great self-discipline and reasonable confidence in the stability of the economic order, combined with positive indicators of the individual's prospects for longevity, for that person *voluntarily* to forego up to twenty percent of possible consumption in every week all through a working life of around forty years to pay instalments into the fund for a pension that may never be drawn.

A desperately bad example has been set by the UK, where successive governments' policies since 1990 have massively reduced the potential purchasing power of personal pensions that are due to become payable over the next few decades. There is equally little incentive for an individual to allocate a further slice of income to buy contingent keyns, such as critical illness insurance and home contents insurance, that the buyer hopes never to call upon. While the monetarist delusion prevailed, millions of individuals in Europe and North America offset the immediate impact of their surrender of spending power to tax and to pension contributions by progressively increasing their consumer debt. The gambling instinct in humanity also plays a significant and subtle part in the human consumer's calculation of wealth optimisation. Millions of people hope to be able to meet future spending requirements – and to settle their debts – from windfall gains, though they have no practicable idea how this good fortune would be achieved.

The decision by the British government in 2014 (at the behest of George Osborne) to allow people to spend their accumulated 'pension-pot' on retirement, or even earlier, rather than buy an income-for-life will, in most cases, provide them with a few tens of thousands of pounds that will quickly be spent. A large proportion of the recipients of earned incomes accumulate debts that they may expect to resolve when they become eligible to liquidate their pension funds. Thus there is a huge danger that in 'freeing' pension-savers from the obligation to buy annuities, their personal pension resources will be exhausted prematurely. Thereafter, the number of long-living aged poor will add a massive burden to the government's spending on social care and housing benefits.

Western European governments have bought electoral support with massive handouts ever since the USA imposed 'democracy' following the defeat of indigenous fascism in 1944-5. For two generations thereafter, it was presumed that Europe was intrinsically so rich, and was possessed of such massive economic momentum, that there could never be a problem in maintaining the population at the standard of living to which it had become accustomed. It is still widely assumed that the economy will enable the vast majority of the citizens of the European Union who are now aged between 22 and 62 to get and to keep jobs that will in turn enable them to enjoy at least pre-2008 living standards. It is also still assumed that citizens will be supported comfortably as state beneficiaries in all the cases where their earned incomes do not match their families' assessed 'needs' until they reach the age at which they will receive a pension sufficient to fund a comfortable and varied lifestyle. Already-established patterns of employment make any such simplistic assumption unrealistic; some four million adult Britons, mostly male, now class themselves as 'self-employed', often with irregular and periodically-exiguous incomes from which they contribute minimally to taxation and national insurance that fund the hollowed-out residue of the welfare state.

European citizens in general are not being sufficiently prepared to face the fact that the parameters within which the government can function in future will have to be based upon the classical principles of political economy, expanded by recognition of the crucial role of *ik* in establishing each economy's strongest competitive advantages. Economies that are innovation-rich countries will most quickly implement artificial intelligence, which will remove the need for millions of jobs across all skill levels. The political rogues' trick of compelling people to take nominal jobs so that they can continue to be eligible for income supplements will cease to be sustainable. During the 2012 General Election in the United States, some cynics argued that there was already an inbuilt majority of state dependents who will always vote for the candidates who are thought most likely to retain or to increase the benefits that they claim, and that assumption remained common in 2016. While Donald Trump exploited concern about Hispanic immigration to the USA, the influx of desperate refugees (and of ruthless economic migrants) into Europe made voters there aware that unsustainable welfare expectations threaten to remove dynamism from the economy and to undermine civil institutions. Without a radical restructuring of the economy in most of the post-industrial countries there will be increasingly abject socio-economic alienation and inter-communal violence.

But this will not be the end. At the great turning points of history, as in classical drama, hubris is followed by nemesis with cataclysmic suddenness;

that is the way of the world. For the eurozone and the UK, and for the mature Commonwealth countries and the USA, the 'credit crunch' of 2007-8 and its immediate consequences will in retrospect be seen as the prelude to the traumatic re-education in high technology and simple economic reality that is yet to be experienced. The cosy and easily practicable solutions to social problems that were adopted between 1950 and 2000 have been kicked into history, and a much more challenging context has been created. In her statements as a candidate for the leadership of her party and as an incoming Prime Minister, Theresa May indicated some awareness of the yawning gap between the perspective from the Treasury and that from Hartlepool, but that impression was soon undermined by her schools policy. The education of the political class has not yet been begun.

Chapter Seven

Past and Future

Having spent several years investigating the question of how nations generate wealth, Adam Smith shared with many other writers the conclusion that no country does this particularly well. Regimes engage in competitive actions – including wars – that destroy rather than enhance the aggregate wealth of the nation, and they often allow interest groups to dictate policies that are disadvantageous to the majority of the subjects of the state.

So we noted that Smith looked for an alternative, and when he hit upon the idea of universal free trade as the context within which economic activity would be optimised by letting people follow their perceived self-interest, he was so pleased with his notion that he wrote as if this principle was comparable with the physical laws that Isaac Newton had adumbrated. The universality of gravity had become accepted throughout the scientific world, and Smith craved the same sort of intellectual hegemony for his principle. Unlike Newton, Smith could present no evidence that his supposed law conformed with nature when it was applied to the world around him; there were no experiments by which it could be tested and no examples that could be measured. The whole history of humanity before 1776 provided no example of free trade in operation, but Smith asserted that his totally-untested principle must be correct, because everything that had been tried was wrong. 250 years later, building upon a spectacular record of failure, Economists have become more dogmatic than ever about the supposed benefits of free markets, despite the evidence in favour of subtle regulation and fair trade.

We have seen how democratic politicians have paid lip-service to Smith's 'great principle', but in most countries, most of the time since Smith's publication, they have continued to act pragmatically, recognising that the general will of the population establishes consensual limits to the operation of self-interest, especially where it has been perceived to serve the interests of the few against the many. Throughout the nineteenth and twentieth centuries, and into the twenty-first, politicians have upcoming elections to win, and in between elections they have hyper-critical media to appease. A conspiracy of politicians, journalists, and economic statisticians propagated the myth that the management of the British economy in early 2016 was broadly successful, citing data that showed more people nominally in employment than ever before and 'economic growth' at about the highest level of any developed country. This was presented as convincing evidence that the UK was a successful socio-economic system within the European Union, and that changing this status could be ruinous.

Prime Minister Cameron and his close supporters were stunned to discover that the nation did not believe them. Yet several times in the preceding chapters it has been shown that the vast majority of the jobs that have been created in the UK over the past thirty years yield low productivity and nil (or negative) productiveness. This is because the overwhelming majority of these jobs are in services such as bar work, personal grooming, and retail shops, together with the logistical and administrative services that make the front-line delivery possible.

A large and increasing proportion of what service employees handle, like 'affordable' clothes, is imported, and many quonic goods and services are sold under global brands that are foreign-owned, so the profit that is generated by these sales is available to alien owners who decide whether to invest in more outlets in the UK or to take their profits elsewhere. There is a great deal of obfuscation around this simple fact, and ministers have simply accepted that one job is as good as another in collating the economic aggregates. It is argued that smart technologies will replace millions of jobs in the service sector within twenty years, and that the consequential collapse of the employment bubble will be catastrophic.

There has been a lack of rational leaders who have questioned whether it really can be in the national interest to allow an industrial sector, its employees, and its plant and their locality permanently to be deprived of income because some foreign firms are temporarily offering cheaper marcoms. The decision whether or not to protect an industry, and thus the region where it is located, depends on many factors. It was utterly unhelpful that Economists cowered behind the dogma of free competition and simply repeated the mantra that the market must reign supreme. They declared that any factory that couldn't compete successfully should die, regardless of the context.

In a recent example, during the period 2005-2016, more and more ordinary citizens across Europe read with concern press reports that the continent's capacity to supply itself with steel was increasingly under threat. The origins of the EU had come in the form of the coal and steel community that was set up in the aftermath of the Second World War, with the hope that as the war-torn steelmaking plant was restored or replaced and the flooded mines were pumped out and brought back into use, the available product would be shared optimally to assist in reconstruction of the continental economy. Thereafter, as economic recovery progressed, it was accepted that it would be sensible to prevent countries from over-expanding their capacity to produce steel, which could lead to a degree of competition that made everybody's investment unprofitable. Thus the European Union emerged from a desire to ensure sufficiency of supply of essential marcoms, within a protected environment.

For more than two centuries, iron and steel have been the most basic and universally necessary marcoms for trade and industry, indispensable in making defence equipment, nuclear power generators, all types of vehicles, ships, and aircraft, and thousands of other materially essential products. By 2010, as a crucial component of that nation's spectacular emergence as an industrial power, China's steel-making capacity had been expanded far beyond the current needs of Chinese industry, so the surplus was offered around the world at prices very much less than the post-industrial countries' cost of producing the same grades of steel. This phenomenon of countries 'dumping' their surplus production is not new, and both the EU (moderately) and the USA (severely) imposed tariffs to reduce the impact of this steel in competition with native production.

As the media explained the situation in 2014-16, steel production was the great example of how successive British governments had self-harmed the economy through Britain's very own energy policy. By being holier-than-thou over their policy to reduce carbon emissions, British governments had, by 2016, made energy virtually unaffordable to industries whose processes were energy-intensive, as is steel making. In addition to this burden, the UK steel industry was more heavily laden with taxes than were EU or US producers. The British government did not have the credibility (or sufficient support from other EU countries) to argue successfully for the EU-wide tariff against Chinese steel to be increased. So at the time of the referendum it looked as if the last major steel producer in the UK would be shut down. The fall in the exchange rate of the pound that followed the Brexit vote eased the problem, at least temporarily, by making British steel competitive again in world markets.

The crucial political question remains: 'marcoms, by definition, carry no *ik*, but the plant with which they are produced may be (in whole or in part) protected by patents; if a country is home to firms that possess the patents of the latest technology, and it also has a natural advantage in sourcing materials, the productiveness of its steel industry will be the highest possible. How far, therefore, is it sensible for the government in another country to prop up within its own territory a steel firm which does not have the same advantages? The answer must be pragmatic; long-term protection may be worthwhile if the removal of the country's one producer of a key marcom would result in other indigenous firms being subject to a risk of interruption of supply or extortion by the advantaged alien producer. Temporary protection may be adopted to protect the balance of payments in the short-term, or to enable firms to restructure their plant, if they can demonstrate a reasonable probability that the steel that they produce will thereafter be competitive with those from other global producers. All cases where marcom producers appear to become uncompetitive should carefully be reviewed, with acceptance of the probability that long-term competitive advantage should be recognised once any question of dumping has been eradicated. Where no strategic consideration applies, it is often an application of natural justice for a rich country to accept competitively priced marcoms from a poorer country so that there is a modest transfer of wealth from the importer to the exporter.

The dumping of surplus marcoms onto other countries has been common practice for centuries. The most enduring example is where a combination of the best available farming technology with ideal weather conditions produces a crop far in excess of the national need in that year. A prudent government buys and stores some of the surplus (or gives tax and other concession to private sector traders to stockpile) against years when the harvest may be insufficient, then allows the remaining surplus to be exported, sometimes with a bounty paid to the exporters. If those exports are allowed into their territory by a foreign government, it may charge a tariff on the import, partially to offset the loss to their balance of payments created by the external payment for the crop. Surpluses in years of especially good weather are a fortuitous occurrence, but many crops grow better in some regions than in others for century after century, because of the composition of the soil and/or the climate (as distinct from the weather). It is sensible for governments to distinguish between the two types of situation – short-term local glut and long-term natural advantage – and to treat them differently.

By the middle of the nineteenth century, politicians had generally come to accept the commonsense principle of 'reciprocity'; pairs or groups of countries could gain mutually by taking advantage of each other's natural advantages and strengths, with safeguards. This principle is particularly relevant in respect of crops and minerals which can be produced much more easily in some places than others, and which do not occur at all in other climatic and geological conditions.

Natural advantage in the production of crops and minerals is a definable and limited occurrence. Humans' capacity to develop technologies which require imported supplies has created situations where newly invented, patent-protected marcom-providing plant is so superior to any previous method of production that it is cheaper for the firm that has introduced the new plant to import the materials, process them, and deliver the marcom in export markets than for any competitor to deliver the product using the old technology. In a world where intellectual property is protected, competitors to the firm that introduced the new technology must seek to acquire the technology, and the reciprocating principles of fair trade require that they should pay a fair price for access to it. Both in the mercantilist era and under the mixed economy, governments would consider giving subsidies to investing businesses and protecting their output from competing imports, to give them time to secure the home market as they grappled to introduce a disruptive innovation. However, so long as disparities between the emergent and post-industrial economies' standards of living remain significant, the patent protection of plant is less of a decisive factor in the costing of marcoms than is the cost of labour per unit of output.

Selective protectionism – and not free trade – has been the preferred experience of most states throughout history. The immense recent success of China in building a modern infrastructure while developing massive industries, hundreds of millions of homes, a world-class military with access to space science, and rising living standards for the masses, has been achieved entirely in a mercantilist context of policies. Since 1990, the USA has renewed the industrial base with such diversity that US firms can again supply many of the marcoms that their economy requires, especially where new materials and new production techniques are applied, with an enhanced awareness that political protection is necessary for the development of native industries as technology evolves. It is simple common sense that strategically sensitive sectors that temporarily need protection, at least while they adjust to changing circumstances, should have that protection. A post-Brexit Britain that fails to shrug off the dogmatic core of Economics will have no prospect of building a secure economic future. The dire predictions of the 'Remainers' in the referendum campaign would be fulfilled, with compound interest, even if the UK is able to retain access to the European Economic Area.

The relevance of the statistics that were used to support the claim that the Cameron-Osborne economic policy was a 'success' has already been challenged in the earlier chapters. At least half of the jobs that have been created in the UK in this century display negative productiveness. Material resources are needed to provide the context in which each job is done, including consumable supplies and the material components of the operative's living standard, but the vast majority of jobs in the UK deliver no net surplus for reinvestment. Thus, as Theresa May appeared to understand on coming into office, the boasted 'achievement' of the Tory government is very close to a catastrophe. Applying a test of productiveness to each job in industry and commerce demonstrates whether, at the end of a period of time (usually measured as a year), there is a surplus of relevant fungible resources available, over and above the replacement of all the inputs that were necessary to achieve the output. If there is no surplus, or if the surplus is siphoned out of the economy by alien owners of businesses or by an imperial power, the activity is unproductive.

The British economy has been increasingly bereft of productiveness for at least 45 years. The productiveness of some benign activities, most obviously healthcare, is not susceptible to measurement because the human benefit of treatment is not calculable, but the productivity of healthcare facilities – the number of cases treated effectively in any given facility – is measureable, and is often measured. It is essential that all susceptible sectors of an economy display productiveness, because they must provide resources that are needed for the areas that are considered essential but which cannot be measured in that way. The nub of the British tragedy is that productiveness has been removed from most sectors of the economy where it should be recognised as the main criterion for success.

Managing Money

Assuring the availability and stability of the money supply is a primary function of the modern state. When money almost collapsed in 2008, everyone was reminded of the extreme fragility into which the system has been reduced by decades of inadequate performance by governments, central banks, and (quintessentially) by the other regulatory bodies that have been given notional partial responsibility for governance of the system of exchange. When the USA abandoned the gold exchange rate for the dollar in 1971, that removed the last residue of the gold standard against which currencies had been measured for many centuries. Over the subsequent years, Britain and the USA led the rest of the world in granting regulatory sanction to (and sometimes simply choosing not to notice) the emergence of classes of business that created a parallel universe of bets, euphemistically categorised as 'financial products' which existed in cyberspace. The great majority of them could not by any stretch of the imagination be said to facilitate trade in the material economy.

Clever operators in the cities of New York and London developed new forms of securitisation of real-world keynic assets (such as mortgages on homes) and new types of betting, much more aggressively than anywhere else, and their firms consequently took in business for the rest of the world. Through the nineteen-eighties and nineties, as British industry declined, so the finance sector stood out more and more significantly as an area in which Britain remained a world leader. The government netted a huge flow of taxation and licence fees on the financial betting businesses and in income tax on the extremely high earnings of many of the innovative sector's operatives.

During the nineteen-nineties, American financial services firms became concerned at the way in which novelties brought business (including US business) to their global competitors in London. By exerting huge pressure in Washington, the Wall Street lobbies were able to have US prudential regulation and legislation pared back enough to enable New York to compete more-or-less on even terms with London. In a quid pro quo deal that seemed trivial at the time, the Clinton Administration required the finance firms to support mortgage lending for house buyers whose incomes and past behaviour would not have met traditional criteria of reliability and ability to service their debts. Thereafter, for a few years, increasingly innovative means were found apparently to secure wholesale financing for the sub-prime mortgages. Besides exploiting the state-guaranteed housing financiers, Fannie Mae and Freddie Mac, to absorb much of the second-tier risk presented by that class of mortgage, the retail mortgage agencies were able to pass on significant potential losses to the wholesale market through securitisations that were subsequently melded by the wholesalers into 'complex products' sold on by both New York and London conglomerates. When default by tens of thousands of sub-prime mortgagees produced an aggregate amount of bad debt that threatened to sink Fannie Mae in 2006-7, it triggered a seizure in the wider markets into which securitised mortgage default risk had been released. Then it quickly became essential for the entire range of US finance businesses to be supported by the Federal Reserve system and federal government.

The most important device that was developed to resolve the immediate crisis was the massive creation of money by the Federal Reserve, acting as the central bank of the USA, under the odd designation 'QE' (Quantitative Easing). A significant proportion of the new money that entered the system through QE enabled the surviving majority of wholesale financial institutions to service most of their cyber obligations. QE was specifically not invented to support the material economy. If the increment to the money supply could be kept quarantined in the finance sector, restoring 'value' to most of the extant betting contracts and increasing the regulatory capital resources in the conglomerates' banking divisions (as required by the central banks), the risk of price and wage inflation in the real economy was minimised. But if the new money should 'escape' into the general money supply, an increase of **M** in the USA would most likely stimulate the expansion of **T** while bank regulators would try to prevent an excessive increase in **V**. If such a strategy should succeed the relatively small price impact of the monetary expansion (**P**) would be accepted by participants in the real US economy. By contrast, in the UK, the greatly increased money supply that resulted from the Bank of England's own QE was predominantly deployed to enable the market in financial products to stabilise. Coincidentally, Britain's QE facilitated a great increase in lending for house purchase, which led to a rise in house prices that was only briefly checked by 'project fear' at the time of the EU referendum.

It will greatly help to maintain price stability and social cohesion in Britain if the Bank of England and the government can eventually write off a significant component of QE, by cancelling state securities held by the bank, and by the bank recalling a countervailing quantum of the money that had been created to buy them. This would reduce the National Debt and enable the bank to use the rest of the QE-derived securities that they still held to form a distinct reserve with which to underwrite a properly structured, regulated, and reserved wholesale betting industry. Such a readjustment would enable London to consolidate the role that it developed willy-nilly between 1987 and 2007 as the most highly skilled market centre for financial futures, options, swaps, derivatives, etc. If Britain does not optimise this massive opportunity to develop a properly defined, globally accessible megabetting business – which the world palpably wants to have available – the time-lagged consequence of QE will be highly disruptive inflation of everyday prices. That would further deepen the tendencies to stagnation and depression that have prevailed for too long. The UK must risk-manage the after-effects of QE constructively and opportunistically, at the right time.

Reference was made earlier to Keynes's role in the Bretton Woods Conference, which was convened in 1944. The result of the conference was the establishment of a notional system of governance for the global monetary system, based on the International Monetary Fund (IMF). This was originally composed of the successful World War Two allies, but then the Soviet Union and its satellites left when the Cold War become defined. Thereafter, the IMF was effectively an economic wing of the NATO/SEATO complex of alliances, under which the 'capitalist' states sought to coordinate the management of their monetary systems.

Soon after the US dropped the gold-exchange standard in 1971, the IMF created a new 'reserve currency': SDRs, Special Drawing Rights. This made for a deeper confusion of roles; the IMF had become part policeman, part bank, part research institute, and part talking-shop. Over the decades, most of the emergent countries joined the club, and the former communist states and China (still nominally communist) re-joined after 1990. The importance of the fund's existence has remained beyond doubt; if it did not exist, something of the kind would have to be invented, though its practical effectiveness varies from case to case and from time to time.

Institutionally quite separate from the IMF, the Bank for International Settlements (BIS), was by origin a clearing-house where the main central banks could arrange settlements and lend money to each other, under the cloak of Swiss law. In the confidential context that could be maintained in Basle they were able to reach agreements that would have been much more difficult to develop in the relatively open sessions of the IMF board. Thus, after the 2008 crisis, it was the shadowy BIS that set guidelines for how much liquidity banks should hold as a proportion of their total capital and in relation to the amount that they lent to others. This ad hoc set of decisions by central bank governors is likely to be brought fully into force in all major economies before 2020, though the BIS has no direct democratic mandate, and its guidelines do not give adequate recognition to the wholesale betting business, which some governors have declared to be 'socially useless'.

It is central to the interests of the UK to identify, differentiate, and defend the megabetting business that can make a huge contribution to the country's economic salvation, yet successive governments have declined to articulate the crucial differentiation between this business and banking. The EU and the ECB – which are even more determined not to make the distinction – have nevertheless tried to make rules that apply traditional banking regulation, and the BIS banking reserve requirements, to wholesale betting, and then to impose a 'transaction tax' on each contract. As has been suggested earlier, more revenue would be gained, more appropriately, by imposing betting tax on such deals.

Politicians must agree upon a rational means of regulating banks and of separately governing the financial betting business, in the transcendent interests of humanity. Once that vision becomes practicable, the primary unmet need will be for a global monetary standard, and here the best hope is to develop Keynes's vision for the International Monetary Fund, *bancor*. Such a truly supranational means of exchange would provide an effective control over the external exchange rates for all the member states' currencies. With an upgraded constitution and a balance of voting power that in real time reflected the contemporary pattern of world economic strength, a reconstituted IMF could allocate the new reserve currency to each country (or monetary union), proportional to trade and national product, which would enable the currency zones to settle their net obligations to each other. The events of 2006-8 proved that money is too important to leave to the control of national governments, or of entities like the European Union; that is why the supranational gold standard survived for so long, and why it has advocates even today. Clarity about the operation of Fisher's Law, and in the balance of payments for each currency zone, can be optimised by using a twenty-first-century form of *bancor*, and until that is achieved, instability and gamesmanship will be inherent in the system of international trade and in every facet of monetary manipulation.

Globalism

The defence of *ik* and the management of revenue arising from its possession, in direct defiance of any principle of 'free trade', predominates in the evolving global trading nexus. It is in the reciprocal interests of states that they all protect the intellectual property that is domiciled in every other mutually-recognised country. In the nineteen-forties, corporations based in the USA consolidated their control of a high proportion of the world's leading brands, and seventy years on that country probably has an even greater predominance over the rest of the world in brands that incorporate income-generating, registered, patented, and/or copyright *ik*. These facts enabled the post-Cold-War superpower to sustain a massive medium-term deficit in its federal budget and on its trade in 'goods'. Fracking and the rise of middle class consumerism in China and India enabled the USA to shrug off most of the concern about the deficit that built up before the 2008 crash.

Over the period 1990-2004, the first phase of the new globalisation that followed the collapse of the Soviet empire and the reorientation of India and China saw accelerated deindustrialisation in much of the US industrial heartland. But even when American marcom production had largely collapsed due to fierce competition from the emergent countries, the ownership of brands and of intellectual property was not sold to foreign corporations, to any significant degree. US brandowners closed factories and laid off American employees as they sourced marcomic components from whatever were the cheapest competent sources of supply while manufacturing capability spread around the world. In many cases, the whole of the physical assembly of products carrying US brands took place outside the US, following the example of Japanese 'offshoring' in the nineteen-seventies. Similarly, American retailers increasingly sourced marcoms worldwide, while retaining their domestic customers in the US, where retail chains sold many of the imports as their own-brand neoquons.

By the start of the second decade of the twenty-first century, however, the rising living standard of an increasing proportion of the home population led Chinese firms to concentrate more on making components for their own indigenous brands that aimed to capture the growing home market for quons, diverting many of the ablest entrepreneurs from their former focus on marcom exports. The increasing cost of labour in making some marcomic components in China eventually made it viable for some firms to begin, to resume, or to expand their own marcom production on US territory. The American industrial renaissance can be expected to strengthen with the advent of smart technologies, and eventually there will be expanding markets for wholly US-manufactured quons – including US-made components – in China, India, and Brazil, as living standards rise there. The emergent countries that have financed their manufacturing sectors largely by exporting marcoms to the post-industrial world will increasingly become mixed economies in the dual sense of providing a quon-based lifestyle for an increasing proportion of their home population while having a sensibly pragmatic approach to the retention and development of significant public sector services in the fields of health, education, and essential utilities.

The majority of Americans continued to enjoy one of the highest living standards in the world in the years after the credit crunch. The exchange rate of the US dollar declined, helped by quantitative easing and in consequence of the accumulation of an ever-greater public debt. The negative signs for the future that these data predicate do not alter the fact that the recognised strength of the US economy ensures that securities issued by American banks, and US public sector debt, remain acceptable to be held as reserves by private and public institutions all over the world. The credibility of those assets depends on the continuing ability of American firms and US government research facilities to develop their *ik* ahead of overseas competitors. A huge risk to America's predominance in developing industrially-applicable *ik* will arise as the federal government makes further reductions in the space programme and in defence research.

The United States' economic hegemony, which has underpinned its dominant political position since 1943, can progressively be eroded in the coming decades as the major emergent economies develop their own military and space research and the spin-off technologies, while US, British, and EU governments continue with the policy of disengagement from investment in military and naval capability. But just for now, the US retains a very significant technological advantage, while China, as the most massive creditor of the US Treasury in history, has a vested interest in the sustainability of the US debt.

We have seen how, between the nineteen-sixties and nineties, the European Union forfeited sectors of production by eliminating an array of small specialist businesses when the large-scale smokestack industries for which the small firms had provided technical support and specialist inputs were 'rationalised'. Before the cull, large, ageing steelworks were conspicuous for a high output of pollutants and high maintenance costs. They were also paying tightly-unionised labour very high wages (by comparison with earlier periods and with other countries) to make marcoms that could, by 1990, be more cheaply produced by more modern plant – and in many cases by primitive workshops – in low-wage societies.

This industrial change was accompanied by a major cutback in the demand for coal and the consequential redundancy of miners. The modernisation of transport networks led to a great reduction in the workforce on the railways as most shunting of goods wagons was eliminated, single-manning of trains became common, and vastly fewer signalmen were required, while operations became quicker and more efficient. Less brutally implemented than in Britain, but with the same effect, the mass unions that had been able largely to dictate terms of employment lost most of that power, so while highly-skilled Europeans continued to have higher wages than Asians into the twenty-first century, an increasing proportion of employees (especially in the south and east of the Union) faced static or even declining real wages as their employers faced increasing global competition. Much of what Germans value as the *Mittelstand* – freestanding, innovative, entrepreneurial small and medium firms – was eradicated in other, less far-sighted countries.

As the number of people in subsidised pseudo-employment increased, so the number of people receiving partial benefits remained high. The consequential demand for cash to pass through government accounts led both to increased taxation (on everybody, but especially on the employed and on their employers), to burgeoning government debt, and to tensions within the eurozone as the northern members of the single currency tried to ensure that it did not become primarily a long-term transfer mechanism to move wealth from north to south.

The 2010 and 2015 British governments wallowed under the delusion that any flow of funds that could be called 'inward investment' must be 'a good thing'. They had no qualms about firms being sold to aliens together with their brands and their portfolios of *ik*. The new owners were usually happy to continue running obsolescent plant in the UK as long as the net profit that they could make from global sales of the brand was satisfactory. But as the plant became costlier to maintain, and the wages payable in the UK remained disproportionately high compared to pay rates in emergent countries, the only facilities that were necessarily retained in the UK were any final assembly units which validated the attachment of a 'made in England' or 'made in UK' label, where that was seen as a substantial marketing asset. Some high-tech and some localised products (such as Harris Tweed and Scotch whisky) continued wholly to be manufactured in the United Kingdom, but more and more of the material components of the British brands that were successful on the world market were no longer British-made, nor were the final goods assembled in the UK.

Nevertheless, a large proportion of foreign-owned but British-registered firms retained some research and development functions in the UK because of the combination of experience, expertise, and invention that was available to keep their *ik* refreshed and competitive. The most successful high-tech firm in Britain, ARM, produces processor chips that are installed in the overwhelming majority of mobile IT devices worldwide. In the earliest days of the Theresa May government, taking advantage of the decline in the exchange value of the pound that followed the Brexit decision, a Japanese bank bid successfully for control of ARM. The new government made a show of considering whether to try to intervene, then let the deal go ahead, before saying that they would carefully consider such deals in the future, well aware that ARM was very much a one-off. The new owners promised to keep the company HQ and the principal research facility at Cambridge, and speculated that the workforce could double. Similar undertakings had been given, and broken, during earlier takeovers and there was general cynicism about the honesty of the expressed intentions and about the government's will or capability to intervene in such cases.

Many smaller companies that had been capable of rapid growth were not sufficiently supported by bank loans or by venture capital within the UK, and so their frustrated owners sold their interest to aliens on terms that compensated them personally for surrendering significant potential future earnings. Foreign-owned firms that sold British-branded quons were not incentivised to relocate manufacturing to the UK. It was most advantageous for global brandowners to locate their next marcom production facility in whichever low-wage economy offered the highest probability of holding down costs for a sufficient run of years to ensure that the plant paid for itself. Business taxation, combined with the introduction of a raised minimum wage, disincentivised entrepreneurs in the UK, making it more likely that firms with highly-rated *ik* would be taken over by aliens. Thus the rump of UK-owned industry continued to shrink, despite the constant appearance of innovation and originality that has historically been Britain's great source of economic strength, and thus the downward spiral in the 'real' economy has been intensified.

The aggravating factors that so beset the United Kingdom have operated less powerfully on the nearby continent. Italy retained a whole raft of significant indigenously-owned firms which sold strongly branded quons made in Italian factories. The French politico-economic elite moved easily between the civil service and the finance sector, and they ensured (with little need for explicit direction by the government of the day) that key companies and essential basic technologies were kept in French ownership or sealed within euro-companies, if necessary with large-scale recapitalisation organised by the leading banks and insurers, which were themselves kept in French ownership by the same means. Major infrastructure including railways and electricity supply remained under state control and although alien investors (and would-be investors) in the private sector railed at the restrictive measures that preserved jobs at high wages for relatively short daily working hours, they could not crack the consensual France-first approach.

From its foundation, Federal Germany concentrated on gaining foreign exchange to support reconstruction by exporting quality-assured vehicles and electrical goods and then developing markets in advanced capital equipment in which their economy has held global leadership for three decades. Although huge burdens were adopted when East Germany was united with the West, and many plant closures followed, the German Democratic Republic had been the ninth industrial power in the world and the dowry that came with unification was not inconsiderable. The banking system was structured with a comprehensive pattern of localised, regional, and national banks which made funds available to individuals, to farmers, to small businesses, and to major corporations on a basis of close understanding of the uses to which any available funds would be put. This co-operation of the finance sector with the real economy gave the German model an immense advantage over several of the other states that joined the eurozone.

Leading firms in the emergent economies plan in the medium-term to sell branded quons around the world. Their governments do not want to impede those firms' accumulation of capital, or to choke off the growth of the home market for their emergent brands, by enabling the minority of relatively wealthy consumers to get too deeply into a habit of buying alien-branded quons. The exceptions to this principle are the franchised distribution of global brands of ephemeral quons, particularly software and access routes to the internet, fashion clothing and accessories, beauty/grooming products, news, information and social media, tobacco, drinks, and fast foods. These imports occur illicitly when they are banned, so most governments permit controlled quantities of these imports, monitor them carefully, and tax them as heavily as possible. Permitting such imports helps to keep the higher earners content to stay within the country, where they invest and provide innovative leadership. Larger-scale sales of foreign-brand quons may be permitted as national wealth rises, especially where the material components of the quons are assembled (and preferably sourced) and distributed by the local partner in a joint venture. Similar constraints apply to importing capital equipment and professional services; the medium-term net benefit of the import must be demonstrated before foreign exchange is released for the purchase.

During the past fifteen years in China and in India, and in a score of other advanced emergent economies, a quantum leap in marketed economic activity has been supported by the rapid and (with a few notable lapses) well-managed development of protected markets in indigenous wholesale and retail keyns. Foreign expertise is encouraged to set up 'representative offices' in most of these countries, to inform the development process, but aliens are not usually given traders' licenses on terms that would enable them to forestall or eclipse indigenous start-up providers of quons and services, including the management and issuance of keyns.

The ongoing rise of the stronger emergent economies will quickly enable their citizens to buy hundreds of billions of quons every year, whose makers will pay less and less tribute to American or European owners of *ik* as their own designs develop. Established international brands will come under much more intensive competition in their own home markets, especially from the emergent Asiatic and Latin American brands. New brands constantly improve their competitiveness by combining lowest-cost marcomic manufacturing with globally sourced *ik*, including the physical design of the final quonic product and of its packaging, and it would be very unwise to ignore key examples of global diversity like Australasians' transformation of the wine industry – even in France – or the phenomenal achievements of Australia, New Zealand, and South Africa in sports and medical science. It would also be foolish to ignore the possibility of European firms taking advantage of the continuing fecundity of entrepreneurial ability to create new facilities for producing marcoms as well as to develop new quons.

Economists talk and write grandiloquently about the 'benefits of free trade', but we have seen that this boils down to the same thing that was apparent in world business long before Adam Smith propounded his contrarian dogma. Rulers, whether the European autocrats of Smith's era or the variously-unenlightened democrats of today, come under irresistible pressure to exclude (or slap severe tariffs on) some imports of quons when they are stifling the development of an indigenous competitor to that class of quons. Similarly, trade unions and local government leaders petition for protection of marcom producers who become subject to 'unfair' competition. On the other hand, governments are constantly urged by marcom-makers whose firms are growing to remove all barriers to exportation, to enable their produce to be sold as cheaply as possible in other countries, thus allowing the firms to benefit from the economies of scale. The idealist concept of free trade will never be allowed actually to occur. Instead, there is a pick-and-mix system in which governments retain the option to adopt or to suspend aspects of multilateral reciprocal 'fair trade' agreements, while jealously supporting brandowners in the assertion of their intellectual assets globally.

Corporations that are based in the most rapidly emergent economies, and sovereign investment funds in countries that control globally significant supplies of oil, gas, and scarce minerals, will increasingly often be encouraged by their governments and their national monetary authorities to offer to buy the ownership of firms that control significant American and European brands, including buying control of keyn-trading corporations and their brands. We can expect to see US and European governments, and the UK, tightening their criteria for permitting alien takeovers of firms that possess significant *ik*, and it is increasingly likely that only firms whose *ik* is obsolescent will be sold to firms from competitor states. Japanese firms that 'offshored' a massive proportion of their manufacturing twenty and more years ago are now becoming concerned about their country's declining percentage share of the turnover from global trade; successive Japanese governments will press their financial institutions to fund major new technologies, as well as to exchange passive holdings of US securities for active control of a wider range of viable global brands.

Because they have to face elections every two years, members of the US House of Representatives are acutely aware of the need to convince their constituents that they will make enactments to enforce fair trade with other nations, especially when US employment is threatened by low-priced imports of marcoms. This results in temporary bans on, penal taxation of, or limitation of, certain imports, and to more permanent protectionist measures in some cases. Measures are also enacted to ensure that the USA retains its capacity to produce marcoms in some strategically-sensitive areas, even though the costs of doing so drive up their prices. Exporters from other continents must charge significantly higher prices for many categories of the products that they sell in the EU and in the USA than they charge in the rest of the world, to meet the requirements of importing countries' anti-dumping regulations. Specific controls on imports of cheap marcoms have also been applied in Australia, Canada, Japan, and the other advanced countries.

The most successful quons from emerging countries will soon be marketed globally as fully-fledged brands alongside the Korean brands that have become common in Europe, Australasia, and North America. The brandowners may eventually locate some of their future artificially-intelligent plant in the now-post-industrial countries; that would be genuine inward investment, especially as it would dramatically enhance productiveness in the recipient countries.

Products to which middle-income consumers and beneficiaries in post-industrial countries have become accustomed at neoquon prices will be improved and rebranded as quons, and focussed on the expanded affluent population of their native countries. Consequently, many of the old-world consumers whose neoquon purchases have helped the new-world producers to invest in creating the new brands will no longer be able to afford them. To maintain an approximation to their existing pattern of consumption, less affluent consumers in the post-industrial countries will be compelled to settle for the next wave of neoquons, some of which will be of inferior quality because of the lower technological level that will initially be achieved by the cohort of firms based in newly emergent economies from which retail stores in the post-industrial countries will source the marcoms that will be marketed as their own-brand neoquons. Alongside this development, indigenous brandowners will construct highly productive plant in which to undertake production of input marcoms, and of the final product, and so partially re-industrialise what is currently the post-industrial world.

A very significant shift in the distribution of the world's increasing wealth between states and economic communities is now well advanced. Driven by investment, the balance of power has very obviously been moving from the original OECD countries towards China, India, and the wide range of emergent economies that experience surges of development and market success, interspersed with setbacks which frequently result from changing conditions in their target markets, including the rate of increase of the demand for quons in their home markets. That trend can be reversed if the post-industrial countries can be first and best in implementing the next era of technology.

Diversity within Globalism

The economies that had become industrialised by 1960, most notably in Europe, with the USA, Canada, Australasia, and Japan, had each passed through a sequence of *Stages of Economic Growth*. WW Rostow, in his book of that title (published in 1960) renewed a well-established template for describing the interaction of technological with macro-economic progress, which had been developed early in the nineteenth century by List and was later adapted by Marx for his distinctive assessment of the origins and evolution of capitalism. The List-Rostow model showed how west European feudalism emerged from tribalism and slavery, then after several centuries of apparent stasis came the introduction of new farm techniques combined with a reorganisation of the relationship between landlords and farmers, a political and social process which took two centuries (in Britain, broadly from 1485 to 1688), which has hyperbolically been called the 'agricultural revolution'. This process was accompanied by a 'commercial revolution' from which banking and insurance emerged as significant sectors of the economies that developed inter-continental marine trade.

Those institutional innovations were followed by the so-called 'industrial revolution', which led to the mass production of marcoms under the control of capitalists who organised productive labour with the intention both of increasing their personal affluence and of accumulating circulating capital to invest in bigger, better, and more advanced production facilities. For the first century of this process (roughly 1630-1730), almost all manufacturing was by handicraft, so what changed was the extent of the legal recognition of *ik*, the financing and organisation of production, the sophistication of quons (both in design and in the techniques that were deployed) and the extension of the market both geographically and through the layers of the socio-economic structure.

Then followed the development of steam technology, from crude pumping engines for Dutch dyke-water and Cornish tin mines around 1700 to the first sophisticated railway, Liverpool-Manchester, in 1830. By then, steam power had been adapted to drive factory machinery and mass-produced output was despatched by rail and steamship around the globe. Rostow's account of this progression added a subsequent phase of mature industrial capitalism, under which brands became significant, with a consequent tendency towards monopoly capitalism which was confronted by antitrust laws that put a block on the excessive concentration of capital investment, though such laws did not challenge the exclusivity of *ik*.

This model broadly relates the path of progress that had been taken by the most-advanced economies that stood out in different sub-periods between 1500 and 1950. But there always were significant exceptions to Rostow's incremental developmental sequence. Feudalism was only introduced in Russia after it had been abandoned in the Dutch Republic and in the United Kingdom. The Netherlands pioneered the commercial revolution early in the sixteenth century, and the greatest examples of near-monopoly capitalism were in the USA after the Civil War. In the first half of the nineteenth century, European settlers who had personally been subject to feudalism accepted the continuance of slavery as part of their new American experience, and some of the most outrageous incidents of genocide to remove Native Americans from the expanding USA happened after the slaves had formally been emancipated.

The chain of progress that was chronicled by Rostow was alternately speeded and slowed by the occurrence of periods of rising inflation – booms – interspersed with recessions that had a tendency to collapse into depressions. Political economists recognised that developments in money supply, money management, monetary regulation, and legislation, such as company law and the protection of patents, affected the pace of economic development or regression under different regimes. But observers of the economy recognised that while governments could do much to influence the direction of the wealth-generating systems in their territories, there were many things that happened outside government control. Wars between foreign countries, discoveries of minerals, plant diseases, animal infections, technological advances, social factors, and variations in the psychology of business decision-takers all had significant impacts on economic progress.

Working-class consciousness emerged centuries before Karl Marx provided his rationale for it to adopt a contrarian stance against capitalism. Before Economics was conjured into existence, there was already a massive literature on 'trade cycles', and Economists were enthusiastically to develop several of the strands from that research in their new pseudo-science. It was a comforting thought that neither Economists nor politicians, and neither capitalists nor revolutionaries could prevent a natural process taking place whereby every thirty, fifty, or seventy years the global economy entered into a long-term trend for expansion or stagnation.

On the other hand, shorter cycles of price volatility (generally assumed to be four to seven years in length) were at least partially understood by clever speculators who could profit from timing their participating in market events. Gordon Brown, as Chancellor of the Exchequer for a decade from 1997, frequently related his policies to a mystic period called 'the cycle', which allowed him comfortably to hide behind uncertainty as to how long the cycle would take to reach the point when he could claim vindication of his decision-making. The overwhelming evidence that derives from the 2008 debacle – that the crash and everything arising from it was due to a failure of governance – has pushed aside any thought that massive contextual changes in the economy occur independently of human management. Only cosmic events such as a catastrophic collision of the Earth with an asteroid can exceed the adverse impact of incompetent and/or negligent governance on the human economy.

In the early twenty-first century, emergent economies commonly avoid 'stages' that were set out in the Rostow model. Development planners aspire nowadays to achieve the *simultaneous* emergence of mass marcom production (including crops and livestock), and brand recognition of indigenous quons alongside providing quonic services to affluent alien visitors, the development of keyn markets proportionally to the markets for goods and services, while facilitating a significant export of people. By these means, an emergent economy gains access to the global resources of *ik* that must be imported to enable local quon providers to emerge. Quonic services that are provided for foreigners range from conducting pharmaceutical trials, outsourcing IT services, working in brothels, and acting as guides on safari, to providing hospitals for 'health tourists' who undergo complex or ethically challenged procedures at a fraction of the price they would have to pay in their home countries. A private hospital will only attract international customers next year if it provides satisfactorily quonic levels of service to its current patients, so the treatment and the ambience for recuperation must be quality-controlled to the best international standards.

Motor racing and other spectacles have been promoted just as well in Malaysia as in France, and, in one notorious year, Grand Prix provision was much better in China than in Britain. While the Chinese built their Olympic stadiums, India became dominant in commercial cricket, and the success of the Bollywood film industry is legendary. Thus it was demonstrated before the end of the last millennium that international tourism, media, call centres, sport, and leisure can contribute significantly to the turnover that generates investment to fund economic development. Modernisation need not be spread over several successive human generations of mass industrial drudgery. Increasingly, individuals can be intellectually and psychologically prepared for participation in rapid change. With access to intercontinental media via the internet, they can fill gaps in their knowledge and understanding without risking the loss of face that has historically inhibited individuals from asking or answering direct questions of people close to them.

Some naïve commentators have confused the price impact of proportionately increasing consumption of quons in China with 'inflation'. The basket-of-goods that a middle-income employed Chinese person buys is increasing in price year-on-year for three main reasons: one is that a significant element of monetary inflation is systemic in a rapidly-growing economy, and China has generally managed this aspect confidently and competently (despite repeated Western predictions that it would fall apart in a crisis). The second is that some commodities are becoming dearer in the long-term, transcending short-term price fluctuations due to global economic factors, which China is trying to address by investing in primary production in other countries. Meanwhile, the third, and increasingly the biggest component in rising living costs, is that Chinese consumers are able each year to replace marcoms with quons, and to have wholly new quonic consumer experiences, one of the most significant of which is to occupy an urban apartment.

The biggest risk to stability in the development of China is generally recognised as the risk of a collapse of an unprecedented boom in property development that has been financed by increasingly-adventurous 'shadow banking'. The risk that some of the least-regulated lenders might collapse, or be found to be fraudulently managed, expands with the volume of total lending that the sector supports. So far, the Chinese banking authorities have been successful in managing their unprecedented task as the emphasis switches from the manufacture for export of marcoms to the marketing of quons in the domestic economy. This is a very subtle shift, and it is represented in macroeconomic data as a significant slowdown in the rate of economic growth, which belies the fact that a massive qualitative advance is progressing well.

Once more than five percent of the consumers in an emergent economy can afford to consume a mix of indigenous and globally branded quons, that cohort becomes dominant in shaping changes in the demand pattern for the entire economy. Taxes and import controls can continue to constrain the growth of demand for some imported brands, encouraging sales of emergent local quons. Around twenty percent of the population of China, of Brazil, of India, and of several other significant emergent countries, has now entered into a lifestyle that is becoming broadly comparable to that of their peers in the more advanced economies, and many millions more have a consumer experience that includes increasing access to locally franchised global quons and significant use of indigenous brands. Upwardly mobile consumers recognise the catalytic role of innovators in providing them with jobs and with opportunities for self-employment, and they perceive the counterproductivity of doctrinaire socialist opposition to the emergence of private affluence, provided that it works together with properly regulated banks in driving forward investment.

The government of China accepts the prospect of half a billion people consolidating their quon consumer status, of whom at least fifty million are the most affluent spenders, in the shortest possible timeframe, so that their country can move on from the residual legacy of the slave economy that the Mao regime imposed. Many millions of individuals throughout China have reinvented themselves in the roles of cash-crop market gardeners, as fish, poultry, or pork farmers, as restaurateurs, as traders, as components manufacturers, or as commodity processors, and their example is available for others to adopt. The farmers join skilled urban workers in expecting to consume quons, so the prices of agricultural commodities necessarily rise for that reason, ahead of global price movements, and in addition to meeting the costs of intensification of farming in terms of the demand for water, energy, fertilisers, and genetically modified or 'organically' certificated seeds. The flourishing of small businesses is a fundamental sign of economic health and dynamism. It was a feature of economic structures in Europe at least since the sixteenth century, but that is now under threat from taxation, the rise of regulation, and the unavailability of finance for investment; Asia generally has not yet fallen into that trap.

India is challenged to enable hundreds of millions of people consciously to shift themselves from traditional to consumer status and to provide a more effective economic infrastructure for the hundreds of millions who are already consuming quons, as well as to allow the sixty to seventy million top earners to secure their superior lifestyle and more confidently to accept entrepreneurial, technical, and managerial responsibility for the transformation process. Wilful traditional inertia has hitherto characterised much of the Indian population, as was repeatedly manifest in riots against development schemes, and it was a feature of much of the rhetoric that marked the celebration of sixty years of sovereignty in 2007. A large number of Indians from a range of ethnic and religious backgrounds have declared a clear preference to remain in their traditional rural and caste condition, declining to integrate dynamically with the global economy, which makes the economic management of their subcontinent an area of very special interest in the coming period. The legendary inefficiency of a bureaucracy that was inherited intact from the British Raj, then corrupted during the subsequent neocommunist regime, is also a huge barrier to efficient economic development throughout India.

Consumers in emergent countries will experience varying degrees of pressure to develop a fashionably green lifestyle. Holier-than-thou rhetoric from politicians who see themselves as 'first world statesmen' will continue to be received with contempt in less-developed countries, but the impact of desertification and of rising energy and commodity prices will provide persuasive arguments for conservation. Therefore, in all emergent economies, the typical individual's pattern of consumption will include less minerals, cereals, meat, energy, and water than an American consumed in the millennium year. Nevertheless, by 2030, better-off consumers in at least fifty now-emergent countries will have access to *ik* broadly equivalent to what their American peers will then enjoy, and they will benefit from access to a still-unimagined range of smart technologies. Typical consumers throughout the wealth spectrum in emergent economies will be conditioned to accept less of their 2030 consumption in the forms of physical materials, energy, and water than an average European consumer enjoyed in 2000, but they will enjoy access to more *ik* in communications and entertainment, and much better personal services than consumers in OECD countries have had in the recent past.

Demand supported by this evolving pattern of consumer preferences will enable firms in the rationally governed and (relatively) corruption-free emergent economies to develop indigenous brands and prepare them for global distribution, without the drain of capital that is lost in the post-industrial countries to high taxation that transfers funds from firms to state pensions, to family subsidies, and to social security payments. Over the past sixty years, emergent economies have also exported people to the other emergent economies and to the post-industrial countries. Such migration has sometimes been peaceful and consensual, but there had been several incidents before the present decade in which political catastrophe led to a sudden mass movement of people. This happened with the huge population of French settlers in Algeria, who fled to France along with hundreds of thousands of Algerians who feared what would be their fate in an independent state. Idi Amin expelled the Asian population of Uganda, most of whom settled effectively in Britain because they were already experienced as a trading expatriate community and they knew English. The flood of refugees from the devastating war in Syria in 2012 and the following years presented a new order of magnitude for such a flow of people, because there was no European host country with a specific sense of obligation to them. They may return to a pacified Syria over a couple of decades in the future, but it will not happen quickly, easily or cheaply, while a ragbag of self-styled 'refugees' from Afghanistan, Pakistan, Iran, and Iraq have forced their way into Europe in the wake of the Syrian exodus.

The departure of many of the better-educated and more ambitious individuals to take up careers in Europe intensifies the self-inflicted tragedy of post-colonial decay to which much of Africa has become prey. Many of these migrants have fled from kleptocratic governments which allow terrorists, gangsters, and warlords to prevent coherent economic development. The progressively more abject despoliation of large tracts of Africa by Africans has been tolerated by the global community for two generations, but now the continuing chaos in some countries is obviously driving out the population and obstructing access to sources of energy, crops, and minerals that are needed by the emergent powers.

Global corporations avoid investing in countries where the decaying colonial-era streets are unsafe, regulation is ineffectual, and the officials are blatantly corrupt. Where highly priced natural resources occur in an unstable country's territory whose exploitation is considered essential by a willing investor corporation, the facilities are almost invariably protected by imported security services. Thus, a new form of armed economic imperialism has emerged, which is seen in some oilfields and mining, quarrying, and agricultural areas. Many other potential sources of significant wealth are undeveloped – or have been abandoned – because of the absence of effective law and order, as well as the prohibitive cost of guarding and insuring the facilities and those who work there. For so long as both indigenous intellectuals and international *grauniadistas* continue to shield the reality of politicians' brutal incompetence behind a smokescreen of anti-colonialist hypocrisy, much of the African continent will show itself to be incapable of self-help or of optimising natives' benefit from assistance from outside.

Polynesians migrate to the Americas, to Australia, or to New Zealand, and people from Caribbean islands settle in North America and Europe. Millions of Latinos are reclaiming their collateral ancestors' lost territory, unnoticed for who they are by white and black US citizens who classify as 'Hispanic' millions of people whose genetic inheritance is predominantly Native American. The global migratory pressure is not yet bringing a significant flow of immigrants (other than from even less-successful former Soviet Republics) into Russia, and chauvinist Japan allows time-limited work permits for skilled individuals in the finance and media sectors, alongside a significant traffic in housemaids and sex workers; consequently, both those countries face a 'crisis' of diminishing population. Islamic countries whose governments have attempted to remain open to the mainstream of globalisation are increasingly under pressure from more militant exponents of the religion, and in territories where militant Islamists have succeeded in undermining public order – or have seized power overtly – interaction with non-Islamic trade and industry is at best uneasy and sometimes becomes impossible.

Before the 2016 referendum in the UK, French and British politicians carefully avoided acknowledging that their class granted citizenship or resident status to millions of assertively unassimilated immigrants from their former colonies, and for decades the chattering classes refused to recognise that any serious institutional problem existed. Even the widespread mutilation of girls' genitalia was ostentatiously ignored. The total number of unassimilated immigrants increased incrementally in consequence of the continuing import of spouses and of other relatives who reinforced several self-defined communities' linguistic, sartorial, and institutional alienation from the host population, which was fostered under the absurd dogma of 'multiculturalism'.

In Britain, hundreds of state-funded immigration lawyers demanded that the state should provide benefits – including free legal aid and priority housing – for new arrivals, some of whom were coached in the specious rhetoric of 'human rights' and briefed to declare that they would expect to be tortured if they returned to the countries of origin which many of them refused to disclose. This almost-cosy complacency was smashed by the mass immigration of 'Merkel's million' in 2015, such that by the beginning of 2016 the mood of Europeans, not only about recent mass immigration but also about the legacy of multiculturalism, hardened, and this trend is unlikely to be reversed as economic conditions become more precarious.

The migrant crisis and the rise of jihadism have also challenged the prevailing commitment to 'human rights', which were emphasised as an idealistic aspiration amid the horrors of the Nazi legacy. Subsequently, in several of the countries where the concept has been enshrined in law, lawyers developed a massive business that makes ultimately unsustainable demands against the state budget. Ever-widening interpretations of idealistically-drafted statutes have served as licences for lawyers to precipitate an exponential expansion of contested hearings and appeals that taxpayers have been compelled to fund. 'Human rights' are also the spurious basis for endless interventions and delays in the process of criminal justice under the UK's adversarial system of courts by which lawyers tie up police time and enable witnesses to be lost, or intimidated, or (by lapse of time) to become unreliable in their recollections. Tens of thousands of alien criminals have been released and not deported, so they can continue their disruptive activities without restraint.

Until control of the situation is recaptured from them (probably by terminating the adversarial system altogether) Britain's increasing over-supply of litigators will continue ruthlessly to develop their specious human rights business. The cost of the whole charade threatened to spiral out of control until the 2010 coalition government in the UK rationed the funds available for litigation. An increasing proportion of the indigenous population becomes open to racist right-wing propaganda which has drawn on these facts, and even mainstream politicians have begun to bid to retain votes by making concessions to those who are demanding an end to multiculturalism.

Global cross-border trade in fake pharmaceuticals and illegal drugs, in slaves, in armaments, and in related technology, has grown massively since 1990, and the human rights industry has fostered, rather than hindered, these sinister developments. The international black economy is now markedly more significant than it was in any earlier era. By their nature, these activities are not quantified in any country's official statistics, thus their role in accelerating globalisation and changing the pace and pattern of economic development through illicit flows of circulating capital cannot be assessed with any accuracy. Counter-terrorist and anti money laundering measures may slightly inhibit the further development of these crimes, but the rewards are so great, proportional to the alternative lifestyle opportunities that are open to the operatives, that evasions of state procedures will continue on an immense scale.

Some Critical Questions

Global brands can emerge from any country, under almost any regime. Leading brands like Fiat, Sony, and Boeing have proved their resilience, and ownership of brands can be bought and sold by corporations based in other countries, as Volkswagen owns the fully rehabilitated Skoda brand and Ford sold Jaguar and Land Rover to Tata. A Canadian corporation that owns a globally distributed brand of Scotch whisky can have its advertising designed in France and invoice its customers from a service centre in India. Scandinavian furniture designers locate their factories around the world in relation to the cost of transporting their products to the consumer, then they repatriate the returns on *ik* that form a significant component of the prices of their quons. Services and supplies can be bought wherever the brandowner can find the best combination of cost control and requisite quality of marcomic inputs to a final product, and the work can be switched to alternative suppliers at the end of every contract period.

Despite globalisation and the trend towards consolidation of major companies, niche and local brands will continue to thrive all over the world, often driven by dynamic people who could be on track to join the cohort of the super-rich. Some such firms are linked to the tourist trade, some serve the specific requirements of sects or cater for people with fads, disabilities, or hormonal imbalances, and many pander to wealthy minorities. Many highly-differentiated consumer groups can now find each other by internet and are thus freed from a need for geographical proximity in sharing access to less common consumer experiences. Several governments find this consumerist 'open world' threatening to their hegemony. A ruthlessly oppressive regime can very largely prevent any significant access to internet shopping by its subjects, but anywhere a neo-democratic rule of law prevails the demand of individuals to be able to allocate their own resources as they wish cannot be suppressed entirely.

Work by human beings in any economy should, in aggregate, display positive productiveness, and, over time, investment should be sufficient to ensure that the productivity of all labour is increasing, including that of health workers, police officers, and other essential contributors to welfare whose productiveness is not calculable in cash terms. In support of that objective, crucial economic questions that are only rarely (if ever) asked by governments, by firms, by consumers, or by the electorate, include the following:

- what proportion of the world's protected *ik* is domiciled in this country, in total, and by economic sector?
- where does this country stand in this league with other countries, absolutely and on a per capita basis?
- how *effectively* is *ik* that is claimed by this country's native firms and individuals protected by patent, copyright, brand, trademark, etc. In how much of the world is that protection enforced?
- what trends or shocks are likely to affect the effectiveness of the defence of that *ik*?
- what is the level of resilience of this country's domiciliary *ik* in the face of a major shift in demand away from the products or service categories to which that *ik* contributes?
- are firms and research institutes in this country investing enough in designing, testing, and protecting the next generation of *ik*? How is this assessed and evaluated?

- does this country's government adequately measure the productiveness of labour, in all sectors of the economy?
- does this country sufficiently promote the improvement of productiveness, through the tax system, through education, through the promotion and support of research, and through appropriate incentives for firms and individuals?
- are this country's tax and regulatory regimes optimally conducive to the generation, exploitation, and defence of robust *ik* by its citizens and residents? If not, what is being done, by whom, to improve the situation? How will their success be verified?
- what proportion of the world's *ka* trade is conducted in this country's currency?
- is the international *ka* trade that uses this country's currency genuinely profitable to this country (i.e., producing a net balance of payments surplus over a short run of years)?
- what proportion of the *ka* trade that is undertaken within and through institutions in this country is banking and what proportion is gambling contracts? Do the regulatory systems and tax regimes properly take account of, and enforce, this differentiation, and are their regulators fully aware of the total quantum of liabilities that is involved?
- what proportion of world *ka* trade – denominated in all currencies – uses contracts that are framed (and, if necessary, enforced, arbitrated, and/or litigated) in this country's legal and/or regulatory system?
- to what extent are the related legal services beneficial to the balance of payments?
- what proportion of the international *ka* trade that passes through this country do indigenous firms and individuals own? What proportion do organisations and individuals based in other countries own? In each case, what proportion is 'genuine' finance and what proportion is gambling?
- what net contribution does international finance make to this country's per capita income, and how does this compare with other countries?

- how strong and how speedy are the measures by which Ponzi borrowers are identified? How are lenders compelled to withdraw from any such position?
- what net contribution do properly-defined gambling activities make to this country's national income and to its balance of payments, including activities that have been characterised as 'hedging' or 'casino banking'? What additional or modified regulatory requirements are yet to be implemented, and to what timescale?
- what degree of risk to the stability of the currency and the financial institutions is derived from the country's exposure to 'genuine' international financial trade passing through its firms and institutions?
- what degree of risk to the stability of the currency and to the balance of payments is presented by international gambling contracts that are regulated and contractually due for settlement in this country?
- what proportion of the economy's quon sales is of brands owned by indigenous individuals and corporations?
- what proportion of the sourcing of the components used in assembling indigenous brands (*ik* and material inputs and labour) occurs within this country's territory, including coastal waters and directly-ruled overseas territories?
- what percentage of the cost of native quonic products is expended on imports of components (including materials and foreign-owned *ik*)?
- what is the potential of this economy to maintain or improve its position in manufacturing/assembling material and immaterial quons?
- what access to indigenous raw materials, or what climatic conditions, or other geographical factors give this country comparative advantage or disadvantage (vis-à-vis other economies) that can materially affect its situation within the global economy?

The above list excludes matters that are already covered adequately in published government statistics.

Crucial questions by which a political economist can better assess the resilience of demand in a country (or an economic community) include these:

- what proportion of the adult population autonomously generates household incomes that are deemed not to require any supplementation in doles, credits, or benefits?
- what proportion of this group is achieving productiveness in their work?
- what is the spread and distribution of per capita income within this group?
- what proportion of taxation do they bear?
- what proportion of this group is employed in the public sector?
- what proportion of public services do they receive?
- what proportion of saving do they contribute?
- how effectively are their savings directed into potentially productive investment?
- what proportion of today's highly-remunerated individuals could ultimately move through middle income status to existence as beneficiaries, over what timescales?
- what proportion of the adult population earns household incomes that provide a middle range lifestyle, which may attract some means-tested benefit?
- what proportion of this group are engaged in work that displays productiveness?
- what is the per capita expenditure stratification of this group?
- what proportion of taxation do they bear?
- what proportion of public services do they receive?
- what proportion of their incomes do they contribute to savings?
- how effectively are their savings directed into investment?
- what proportion of taxation do they receive as benefits?
- what proportion of this group is employed in the public sector?
- what is the stratification of state employees within this category, in terms of the proportion of their income that is received as tax credits, child allowances, etc.?

- what is the probability percentage of people from this category achieving high-earner status within one, three, and five years?
- what is the probability percentage of the middle income receivers descending, over what timescale, into benefit dependency?
- what proportion of the adult population is wholly dependent on benefits?
- what proportion of the population is predominantly dependent on benefits?
- what are the per capita income levels of any sub-categories that the state has designated within this cohort, and how do these compare with incomes received as median middle-range incomes?
- what is the rate of increase or decline of the beneficiary proportion of the population?
- what proportion of total taxation do the beneficiaries bear?
- what proportion of all taxation do beneficiaries receive as benefits? At what rate is this increasing or diminishing?
- what is the probability percentage of the elevation of persons from this category to unsupported earner status, over what timescale?
- what, if any, contribution does this category make (overtly and illicitly) to current production and to investment in the future capability of the economy?
- what, if any, statistically significant proportion of the population has traditional economic status (tribesmen, priests, etc.)?
- what is the aggregate size and the present impact of the existence of this subset of the population on the economy?
- what are the probabilities of any of these groups entering more fully into the market economy as producers, and how would that shift impact on existing projections and plans for the economy?
- what, if any, contribution do the various segments of this category make to investment in the future capability of the economy in their present condition?

The collation of these data would enable more effective and pragmatic economic planning to be undertaken, in line with our updated tenets of political economy. It must be accepted that many of the early results would be wide estimates. Only an affluent, predominantly productive economy can provide pensions, benefits, and tax credits for a significant proportion of its population in the future. The universal operation of Goodhart's Law means that if any one of the answers to the long list of questions that has been set out above is elevated to form the basis for a system of regulation or a template for economic management (including manipulation of the monetary system), it will cease itself to be acceptably accurate.

A 'saving grace' for some post-industrial economies is that, for the next decade, maybe two, the emergent economies will continue to need access for their exports to markets in post-industrial countries. They will also be keen to secure a medium-term income flow by buying firms and other assets in the post-industrial countries, including investment in new assets serving the major utilities. Thus they will be open to making genuine fair-trade arrangements with the post-industrial world, which will secure the *ik* that is registered in the counterparties. Until a sensible global monetary system can be established, it is likely that the emergent global brandowners will also continue to conduct their trade with other parts of the world – both commodity purchases and sales of marcoms and quons – in terms of the established reserve currencies for which the central banks in the post-industrial economies are responsible. So the Russian, Asian, and Latin American central banks will selectively support the dollar, the yen, the euro, and even sterling to facilitate their increasing influence on global trade, during an extended period in which the continuing availability of retail debt in the post-industrial countries will enable consumers to continue buying energy from Russia, Arabia and the Gulf, Africa, and Latin America.

Levin's Law states that bankers are so impenetrably purblind and arrogant that they will plunge headlong towards a new 'crisis' as soon as the last one has been resolved for them at the expense of the taxpayers, and after much distress to innocent individuals. After the next 'crunch' or 'crash', sovereign investment funds from the emergent economies will only participate in recapitalising Western banks if they then reckon that they still need them, and the terms of any participation will tip the scales of world economic power even further away from Wall Street and the City of London.

Conclusion

The massive human tragedy that followed the imposition of Marxist regimes in Europe and in much of Asia provided a depressing example of how idealist theory can become a curse upon humankind. Within a century (1917 to 1991), the Leninist application of Marxism failed, not least because it incorporated an irrational repudiation both of the natural instincts of human beings and the fact of the existence of ***ik***.

The full range of negative consequences of the much less brutal imposition of academic Economics on the 'free world' is only now becoming recognisable. This text has shown that normative Economics was adumbrated in the eighteen-sixties, partly as an attempt to transcend Marx's 'scientific materialism' by developing a form of 'economic science' that was derived from the pure stem of Adam Smith's dogma. Often called the 'marginalist' or 'Austrian' school of Economists, the founders simply set aside the principles of political economy as they were then taught and which had until then generally been accepted as well-evidenced axioms for statecraft.

The Economists imagined how the number of their chosen category of economic events – transactions – could be maximised by perfectly efficient imaginary firms trading with perfectly self-interested and fully-informed customers in a completely apolitical economic space. Marshall crystallised their model, which assumed that all participants in the imaginary economy would equally be empowered to acquire all relevant information that would enable them to take the rational decisions on which to determine economic events. That model has never resembled the world of human psychology, of political reality, or of material production and consumption. The Economists ignored the fact that free trade has never been implemented, they simply asserted that their model should be taken up in everyday life. One of the fattest cats of the Economics profession, who became governor of the Bank of England, has recently published a book in which (effectively) he recants, and declares much of Economics to be irrelevant to the real world.

Throughout the nineteenth century, the much-trumpeted free trade principle was set aside whenever 'trade followed the flag' and thus justified imperialism, which Adam Smith quite specifically abhorred. There was no prospect of genuine free trade being implemented for Britain until the Empire had been abandoned. Today, in direct conflict with pure Economic theory, the mass electorate in the advanced countries consistently supports policies that seek to control the allocation of wealth through society. Ever-changing regulations limit what products may lawfully be made, what level of taxation is imposed on different commodities and services, what ingredients may be used, where processes may take place, what emissions are permissible, and what steps must be taken to prevent environmental damage or detriment to human beings either as employees or as the general public. The identification, improvement, protection, and defence of intellectual property is central to the contemporary capitalist system, while Economics has virtually no cognisance of this fact. Capitalism continues to be weakened by its fudged monetary system, and by accounting standards that are based on counterfactual assertions about 'value', 'preference', 'equilibrium' prices, and 'efficient' markets, all of which are derived directly from Economics.

In the former USSR, the professors spout both Marxism and Marginalism while the capitalists and the fixers obey the laws of the jungle. In the countries where politics has been to a greater or lesser extent in thrall to Economics, living standards were reduced dramatically for millions of citizens in Greece, Cyprus, Spain, Portugal, and Ireland after 2008, and millions more were less seriously impacted in Italy. Figures released in July, 2016, by the Organisation for Economic Co-operation and Development showed that real wages in Greece and in the UK had declined by 10.4% since the pre-crunch period in 2007, while real wages increased in the USA by 6.4%, in France by 10.5%, and in Germany by 13.9%, with an average of 6.7% over all 35 member countries. The fact that the people of the United Kingdom – uniquely – shared the most intense misery with the Greeks came as a shock even to those who had put a negative interpretation on the policies of the Cameron governments.

Every year, the growth of the global economy is falling further behind the rate at which the advocates of man-made global warming demand the replacement of carbon-releasing technologies. The number of living humans is increasing, while modern communications have greatly expanded the economic aspirations of individuals. Billions of people exist in material and moral poverty, and hundreds of millions of them are ill because they cannot gain access to simple medicines, contraception, or basic clinical procedures. In global terms, Britons still have a very much better-than-average standard of living in what is billed as 'the world's fifth-largest economy', but that is no argument against efforts to restore real earnings to the 2007 level, and then to seek further improvement.

Recent climatic traumas and extreme weather events have emphasised the fact that there is a dynamic tension between the basic material demands of consumers (for water, air, energy, and food) and the limits of the world's capacity to provide them in a sustainable environment. It is feasible for a population whose fecundity is rationally controlled to enjoy a rising standard of living and to apply the necessary resources to counteract changing global conditions, provided that each legitimately governed state can continue to occupy its territory undisturbed. Individuals can be empowered to gain access to the fruits that arise from the constantly increasing *ik* that their species can generate. Understanding and acting on these simple Malthusian principles is the golden key for securing the future comfort and concord of humanity.

The unique power of the human intellect to invent solutions that constantly and incrementally enable the material economy to counteract the universal physical fact of entropy has been threatened in recent years, especially in Europe, by two destructive forces. The first was the attempt by some governments to respond to the recession caused by the crash of 2008 by imposing austerity, rather than providing and encouraging the right kinds of investment to secure economic growth. Then came the threat of mass immigration of people who have been schooled in violence, who are unsusceptible to European, Australian, or American social or ethical norms, and are contemptuous of the Christian heritage to which silly politicians appealed during 2015 when Europeans began to express justifiable concern about the influx. The threat of jihadi violence by any random individual among the incoming millions is real, and the need to address it is incompatible with successive governments' reckless succession of measures to strip resources from the police and from the military services.

Evidence of the extent to which Western forces have been debilitated was provided by a report, published in August 2016, that showed that in almost all areas, the Russian army is better equipped and armed that their UK equivalents, and by repeated media reports that a large proportion of the Royal Navy's ships lurk in port because there are not resources to maintain, staff, and equip them properly.

The most efficient British firms have continued to generate significant profit, much of which has been seized as taxation that was increasingly dissipated in unproductive consumption. The residue of the profit remains in the hands of the companies and many of them have hoarded it, paralysed by fear that any investment may fail in the prevailing economic circumstances. By contrast, start-up companies that develop new concepts addressed to new markets – even the many that could display evidence of success – have hesitated to seek loans to fund their growth because the company's owners were likely to be subjected to excessive burdens (even risking repossession of their homes) if the business should fail to service the loan. The development and security of new *ik* is the best investment that can be made, and it should be the focus of all efforts to revitalise the economy.

It is plainly in the interests of *ik* owners worldwide for their countries to adhere to fair-trade agreements, most-favoured-nation treaties, and agreements to recognise each others' *ik* and other reciprocating asset-protection measures that have misleadingly been categorised as 'free trade' arrangements. They are all essentially managed-trade deals that protect the micro-monopolies on which the protection of intellectual property depends. By enhancing the productiveness of a firm, *ik* is the primary generator of profit and thus of circulating capital. The productiveness of labour is highest where the employees are skilled, confident, and in good health, bodily and psychologically. The output of slave labour – including forced or fake jobs imposed upon the unemployed – is generally inferior in both quality and quantity to that from free labour, and this disparity increases the more *ik* is incorporated into the consumer offering and into the processes by which it is prepared.

One of the most-cited quotations from Keynes's *General Theory* is that, "Practical men, who believe themselves to be exempt from any intellectual influences, are usually the slaves of some defunct economist. Madmen in authority, who hear voices in the air, are distilling their frenzy from some academic scribbler of a few years back."

The quotation has frequently – and most unjustly – been turned against Keynes himself, as scribblers of the present era try to apportion the blame for the economic crisis that recently engulfed the post-industrial world. Keynes was in no way responsible for the crass Economists' Keynesianism that contributed so liberally to the fallacious direction in which the economy was driven during the first four decades after Keynes's untimely death. No previous or subsequent observer of the economy has written such well-honed tracts for the times, books, essays, and other pieces that exactly encapsulated the data that were of most relevance to the particular situation that existed at the time and indicated practical means whereby it could be improved. That was in total contrast to Adam Smith, who in isolation developed the ideology that has bedevilled Economics and thus the lives of millions of individuals whose governments have been enthralled by the pseudo-science that has been derived from the *Wealth of Nations*.

The attempt to force the economy to adopt an absurd concept of 'rational' market behaviour, as it has been presented in Economics, especially since 1990, has been ruinous. An alternative basis for understanding and managing economic life is patently needed. Some observers will think it strange that one should urge them to seek authoritative guidance from political economists (including Malthus, Say, Bastiat, Mill, and both Henry and Millicent Fawcett) most of whom were long-dead when Keynes wrote the *General Theory*. But much valid natural science derives from Archimedes, Pythagoras, Euclid, Laplace, and Newton, because their observations can be verified by the newest experimental and observational techniques. This brief text invites the reader to consider the long-ignored (but never disproved) principles of political economy, combined with a proper recognition of the role of *ik* in the economy. It can lead to a clear understanding of the massive problems that have been thrown up by the catastrophic mismanagement of the economic system that has been endemic in the democratic world since the demolition of the command economy that was required to manage the stresses of supplying the nation and the military in World War II.

In our 1971 book, *Can Britain Survive?*, the late Ken Watkins and I suggested that – even then – inflation, deindustrialisation, the deficit on public spending, diminishing productiveness, and declining belief in democracy itself would take many years to put right, if, indeed, a government could then have been formed that would have had the will to tackle the fundamental problems that were already apparent in the British economy. A decade later, Dr Watkins became an enthusiastic advocate of Thatcherism, while I watched with horror as industry was sacrificed to ideology and the British regions were driven from productiveness and modest prosperity to idleness and dependency. Half a century on, the United Kingdom's problem is massively more profound than it was in the dog-days of the mixed economy. But now, after the Brexit vote, there is at last an indication that some members of the political class recognise the need for a fundamental reappraisal of the context for economic policy, and a radical break from the dogmas that have proved so harmful.

At the very heart of Britain's economic failure lies the credibility given by generations of Economists to Adam Smith's assertion of the free trade principle, which was made truly dangerous in 1890, when Alfred Marshall produced his *Principles of Economics*. That seminal text set out to establish the new Economics as an exposition of how everyday business practice and consumers' actions should be understood in 'scientific' terms. It was mere speculation, but it *looked* like a science book, with simplistic equations and illustrations of parabolic curves. Academic Economists loved it; it enabled them and their graduates to pose as scientists. For almost a century and a half they have pushed this idea, of a norm to which reality should be made to conform. Unsurprisingly, every time it has been 'applied', the dogma has produced unfortunate results, in response to which Economists, like First World War generals, have demanded that the policy should be pursued with greater vigour at an increasing human cost.

No other country has been so heavily influenced by Economists for so long as the United Kingdom, and nowhere have they done more harm. Politicians and bureaucrats have known of no alternative to Economics, so they continued to submit to Economists' assertions that a sufficiently rigorous application of their theories could make the economy succeed, contrary to all the evidence. Since 2006, the British economy has ploughed into a trough, industrial output, real wages, productivity, productiveness, and material exports have not returned to 2005 levels. Increases in imports of consumer goods continue massively to exceed the rate at which material exports increase. Inflated by Quantitative Easing and still free to move with uncontrolled velocity, the available supply of liquidity is more than adequate for the financial sector to meet the opportunities that inventors and innovators can put to them, and no British minister needs to grovel before his Chinese equivalent to beg for investment in the UK.

The favoured policy has not worked. It can never work. So what can be done?

Any reader can work honestly through the list of questions posed earlier in this chapter, providing truthful answers – however embarrassing that may be – and assessing what can be done to improve the score that really exists in their economy today. At least, and at last, there is a significant measure of understanding in the British nation at large that *something must be done* that far transcends the barren objective of removing the deficit on the national accounts.

Far from cheeseparing, the government – regardless of party – should be borrowing heavily, taking advantage of low interest rates, to create infrastructure and facilities that will enable the innovative British community (including the talents of recent immigrant groups) to create jobs that are characterised by real productiveness. Of course, there will be waste and false starts, that is inevitable in any great public and private enterprise, but sensibly directed investment is hugely beneficial to the economy, and it can be even more powerful in creating a sense of optimism and dynamism in a nation that has hitherto been sinking through cynicism into bathos. Positive growth alone can return the balance of payments to surplus, bring the state budget into balance, and permanently maintain living standards for everybody.

By lowering the base rate of interest in the August 2016 package of measures, the Bank of England again showed the incomprehension of the needs of the economy that lurked in the Economics-trained members of the Monetary Policy Committee. Individual savers were hit once more with lower returns on their deposits, and the bonds which archaic actuarial requirements insist must be held by pension funds were to yield even less income, thus funds' deficits will have to increase (by at least £100 million) and potential future awards to pensioners became less. Companies faced by bigger pension fund deficits will be under pressure to divert income from investment to reducing the pensions deficit, and dividends will probably be reduced. Yet in the light of the public scandal concerning the retail chain BHS and its pension fund, politicians and the media created a strong flow of public opinion in favour of 'reform' of pensions supervision. If the outcome of this campaign is to compel firms to divert more resources into pensions funds and away from investment in business expansion and the implementation of new *ik*, this will be directly and hugely damaging to the economy at large.

The other focus of the bank's package of measures, to make funds available to the banks, in effect at zero interest, supposedly to be advanced as investment resources to real-world businesses, again shows the insensitivity of the Economists who advocate such packages. The banks carry no confidence with most entrepreneurs, who know that lenders impose conditions on firms that make innovators who borrow in the hope of growing their businesses virtually into debt-slaves. Vehicles other than the banks must be established to create a pattern of finance for industry and business that is free from the dead hand of the banks, which anyhow do not have staff who can co-operate with business as did the traditional bank managers back in the era of the mixed economy. This proposal is merely a recapitulation of schemes like Finance for Industry that were led by the Bank of England in the inter-war years to mobilise funds for business.

It is urgent that a new approach to material economic growth is taken, and only the government can initiate it. Faced by the prospect of nil or negative interest rates on deposits and near-zero rates on bonds, investing individuals and collective investors – especially pensions and insurance funds – should be enabled to buy new classes of bonds to be issued by a new range of investment trusts whose purpose will be to fund housing developments in all parts of the country, significant infrastructure projects outside London, and thousands of businesses whose plans display a grasp of current market realities and opportunities, especially those that incorporate the highest technology and fresh intellectual property within their aspiration.

The 2012 and 2016 Olympic Games triumphantly proved that British individuals can place the country at the head of the winners' league, provided there is rigorous selection of those individuals and enough money is allocated to their preparation. The great mass of people are happy to buy a lottery ticket – with the exiguous chance of a life-changing win – knowing that a significant slice of the ticket price goes to good causes, notably support for heritage causes and sport, including the preparation of Olympians. With careful thought and the appropriate marketing, a new class of lottery/investment funds for the selection of people (of all ages) who would place themselves in contention for recognition and support as innovators would attract hundreds of thousands of punters who would be willing to wait five years for a dividend.

The double-edged reality of the Brexit decision must be accepted. Britain must leave the EU, but must then have the closest possible trade agreement with the union that avoids submission to the future legislation of the parliament or to the litigated outcomes from the Luxemburg Court. European leaders have made it clear that a close relationship of the UK with the EU depends on continuance of the provision for the free movement of labour. It has been clear from all post-referendum analysis that immigration is a very major concern of the British, but it is also a growing worry to the EU as a whole, as has been confirmed in recent German elections. It should easily be possible to distinguish 'patrial' EU citizens from high-risk categories, such as the single men who form almost half of 'Merkel's million' 2015 migrants. Central European countries have been unequivocal in their refusal to have quotas of culturally alien opportunists forced upon them. Outside the political union but within the free trade area, Britain can assert the right to refuse to accept economic migrants from outside the union who may become naturalised in member countries on the understanding that they will then migrate to the UK. Migration has been declared to be a sticking-point; the negotiating position that is suggested here would not fully reassure the querulous majority of British voters (or the irreconcilable Remainers), but it could secure the sympathy of at least half of the member states of the EU who share the dilemma that is expressed by the British public.

The economic statistics of major countries over the past thirty years show that the countries that are most fully subject to Economists' dogma have the lowest growth, the lowest investment, and the lowest indices of the contentment of the nation. By contrast, nations that have pursued mercantilist policies have shown spectacular growth, investment, and citizen satisfaction, with China as the stellar example. An essentially mercantilist economic strategy can be endorsed as well by democratic consensus as by a dictatorship, and it will recognise the high desirability of entering into reciprocal fair-trade agreements. There is no necessary conflict between economic, social, and political progress, but we have seen all too clearly that government 'austerity' combined with asset-price inflation and the expansion of consumers' access to credit causes stagnation in the real economy. The vast majority of people in Britain are capable of grasping this point. Most Economics graduates do not teach the primitive dogma, nor do they refer to it routinely in their work as statisticians, historians, journalists, and consultants. These folk can gain intellectual liberty and enhanced earning power by escaping from the doctrine that they have never really believed; then they will be able to apply their knowledge and experience of the realities of life to contribute hugely to a dynamic strategy for growth.

Enthusiasts for new technologies assert that, even now, revolutionary changes in the capabilities of 'intelligent' machines are going into everyday applications that will imminently change the entire structure of the economy. They claim that tens of millions of jobs will disappear in the richer countries before 2025 with the coming of self-driving cars and delivery vehicles, including drones; leading to fully automated delivery of goods ordered online, and the general adoption of applications of smartphones that will gave fingertip control of everything in the home to the owner, wherever they may be. Little further in the future, they foresee both medical diagnosis and legal advice being delivered by applications more speedily – and more accurately – than by humans. The most optimistic of the enthusiasts foresee unlimited access to solar energy by 2030, providing power for desalination plant (among a host of other resources) and thus an end to global concern on water resources. Faced by a prospect of such comprehensive technological possibilities, the weaknesses of political systems will become ever more blatant.

Above all, the great task of politics in the coming decade is to extend a sense of empowerment to millions of people who have known, instinctively, deep-down, that they have been treated as stooges in a system where bureaucrats (themselves harassed by spending cuts and ridiculous performance targets) have attempted to implement half-baked and constantly-adjusted policies handed down by politicians, most of whom knew, instinctively and deep-down, that Economists' confident assertions and implausible predictions have never been vindicated by events.

Many of the most privileged people in British society have been outraged at the effrontery of the electorate in voting to leave the European Union. Against the millions whose lives have been stunted by the lasting impact of the 2008 crash stand the few hundred thousand who have most amply benefitted from the perverse socio-economic structure of contemporary Britain. This minority have assumed their superiority without themselves thinking very much, or at all radically, about the situation of the general population. They will attempt to have the Brexit vote reversed, but their power is broken, and intelligent Remainers recognise this as well as do diehard Leavers. This little book has shown how the political and social fabric of Britain has become threadbare. People with better brains, greater skills, and more useful knowledge than me will provide the intellectual resources from which a credible, optimistic pattern of economic policy can be forged.

Glossary

Bancor

JM Keynes's concept of a global reserve currency. The Latin noun *or* is the heraldic term for gold, and thus 'bancor' means bank-gold. Controlled by the IMF, bancor would replace gold as it was used to underpin the global currency system under the pre-1914 gold standard.

Brand

A legally recognised and protected corporate name, trade name, or product name which signifies the quality and service standards of one or more **quons**.

Chartalist

The term used by Keynes in his *Treatise on Money (1930)* to describe all assets that exist by the will of the state, or because they are recognised by the state, or because they are accepted or tolerated by the state (as happens with all contractual agreements that are eligible to be resolved by the state courts in the event of dispute). In terms of this text, a *keyn*.

Circulating capital

The portion of the receipts from sales of material and immaterial output during any period of account, often one year, that is allocable to increased wages, greater distributed profits, or new investment (after the firm has met all the costs of production, including maintenance of the plant, all the costs of maintaining and defending intellectual property, and all taxes and other impositions by the state and its agencies). Official statistics indicate that the British national stock of capital increased annually by 2.4% in the five years before the 2008 crash, and then rate of increase of capital declined to barely 1% per year in 2010-15, which did not compensate for inflation, so the nation's capital resources were being depleted while an increasing amount of business turnover was allocated to distributed profits and to wages.

Consumer's surplus

The potential spending power that remains to a consumer after making a purchase for which they pay less than the recommended retail price of their most-preferred brand among the range of quons that serves the purpose for which the purchase is made.

Cost centre

An organisational unit within a productive sequence that is resourced to perform a specified task (or group of related and/or sequential tasks).

Cyberkeyn ©

A financial instrument (**ka** ©) that exists only in cyberspace (an immaterial universe occupied by electronic data) that is the subject of an enforceable contract under a specified terrestrial juridical system.

Direct labour productivity

The estimated monetary valuation of the output that is attributable to an individual (or the average attributed output of a team) in extractive industry, manufacturing, logistics, or distribution.

Economic

To do with the provision, distribution, consumption, and ultimate disposal of material and immaterial outputs that serve the wishes and needs of the human race.

Economic agent

A natural person or a legally recognised corporate or collective entity that is capable of conducting business in the economy.

Economical

Sparing of resources.

Economics

A scientific or pseudo-scientific study of the economy, or of any phenomenon within it. In university and school syllabuses it applies most commonly to the pseudo-science set out in Alfred Marshall's *Principles of Economics, 1890*, and much developed subsequently, as is described in the text.

Economy

1. Carefulness in using material or monetary resources.
2. The system by which material and immaterial outputs are provided, distributed, consumed and ultimately disposed of.

Emergent economy

The economy of a state or community that has not yet achieved 'advanced' economic status, but where progress is credibly reported.

Ephemeral quon ©

A branded 'consumer good' or experience which is consumed in a short period, such as an entertainment experience, a drink, a session of legal advice, a meal, or a journey.

Estate

The total assets and liabilities belonging to a natural person or to a legal person.

Firm

A legal person, which may be a registered part of a group of companies or agencies, an operating division of a company, or the trading wing of a charity or association, that has been set up to perform specific economic functions.

Good

A 'widget', in 'neoclassical/Austrian/marginalist' Microeconomics. It approximates to a marcom ©.

Goodhart's Law

The idea that whenever any datum is taken as a key indicator of the state of an economy, it ceases to serve that purpose.

Grauniadista

A British citizen of the fashionable soft left, who is likely – if salaried – to have a job that was advertised in a certain loss-making publication.

Ik © (Intellectual keyn ©)

Any intellectual property that is definable and defensible at law as an asset.
(Pronounced as in 'trick' or 'quick')

Jev ©

A physical object whose price is what the most affluent competing buyer will pay for it at the time of sale, without reference to the cost of production of the asset. The category covers antiques, works of art and all other 'collectors' items' (Adjective, jevic).

ka © (Keynic asset ©)

An asset held by an economic agent, that was created as a debt by (or was lawfully imposed upon) another economic agent.
(Pronounced as in 'car').

Keyn ©

Any financial asset or liability, or item of intellectual property.

ko © (Keynic obligation ©)

A debt, the reciprocal of a **ka**.
(Pronounced ko as in 'cocoa')

Legal person

Any corporate, charitable, or state-controlled entity that has economic functionality and legal recognition (e.g., a 'corporation sole', a bishop in his working capacity).

Levin's Law

The proposition (by the columnist Bernard Levin) that bankers are intractably arrogant and stupid enough that they will start behaving so riskily as to initiate the processes that will end in the next crisis as soon as they have been rescued from the effects of the last one.

Liquidity

A term introduced in Keyns' *Treatise on Money*, broadly to indicate the total power to spend that can be made available to the participants in an economy, taking account of the ability of market experts to invent an ever wider range of credit instruments and to manipulate the velocity of circulation. Responding to criticism of the concept from Hayek, Keyns gently suggested that the Austrian (who had been imported to Britain to challenge him) had not understood it.

Macroeconomics

The study of the operation and management of whole economies.

Marcom ©

A raw material or a manufactured output which is sold as a physical product, in open competition with other items supplied to closely similar specification, with no brand that could convey to the purchaser any access to protected *ik*. Broadly the equivalent of a 'good' or a 'widget' in marginalist economics, or a Marxist 'commodity'.

Marque

A model or sub-brand within a brand.

Megabetting

Sophisticated gambling, usually undertaken by firms (but with some high net worth individuals participating), the category includes derivatives, spread bets, and most options and futures.

Microeconomics

An academic presentation of how Menger, Walras, and others who worked to create a new Economics in the period 1860-80 supposed that markets function. For the English-speaking world, the definitive text in this field was Marshall's *Principles of Economics* (1890).

Natural person

A human being.

Neoquon ©

A product or service that performs the same physical or psychological function as a quon, but is sold under the name and/or the warranty of a distributor (most commonly a retail store), at a price less than the normal retail price of an esteemed quon and without the cachet that attaches to a brand.

Opportunity-cost

The economic options that are surrendered when an economic agent commits a defined amount of spending power to a purchase, in preference to any potential alternative.

Patrial

A term that came into widespread use around the time when Britain joined the European Common Market to cover people of British origin who had been born and raised in another country, usually within the British Commonwealth. Most commonly, it covers those whose right to British citizenship derives from their grandparents. I suggest that it be extended to mean 'those who were born in the country, or whose parents or grandparents were citizens of the country' and it should apply to all the countries within the EU on the date before Britain leaves the union. Under the current Irish law, anyone with one (or more) Irish-born grandparent(s) may apply for citizenship. How many ancestors a person would need to count as a patrial EU citizen for the purposes of the proposed agreement would be determined in the light of circumstances at the time any negotiation is conducted.

Piracy (of intellectual property)

Illegal use of proprietary *ik*.

Political Economy

The name of the multifarious attempts to set out the rules which appear to point to success in the management of a regional, national, or wider community economy. The term was in use from about 1540 to the end of the nineteenth century, when pseudo-scientific Economics quickly became an academic orthodoxy. The principles of the subject were set out in the eighteen-seventies by Millicent Fawcett in a hugely popular textbook, *Political Economy for Beginners*. An online version of Mrs Fawcett's original text is accessible at the University of California Library.

Postindustrial

A term to describe an economy in which the proportion of the population engaged in manufacturing and extractive industry is less than 60% of the number of employees that were so engaged at the country's highest-ever level of such employment.

Productiveness

The contribution of an economic process to the generation of circulating capital. Unless an activity is productive in that its output can normally be sold for more than the full costs of production (including all the costs of servicing the intellectual property that is accessed during production, and all costs anent to maintaining the intellectual property that is implicit in the output) it is consuming capital unproductively and thus is not viable. The productiveness of a firm or facility can often be restored or increased by the purchase of new technology for the material delivery of components, or by creativity that leads to a patent, copyright, or other legal form of protection for new or enhanced intellectual property being established. The best-proven way to build up a healthy economy is by investing in scientific and other intellectual work that generates new and improved *ik*, combined with investment in appropriate plant and machinery, and in adapting and constructing buildings to house those activities. Refreshed or increased productiveness can also be achieved by investment in enhancing the fertility of farmland and fisheries. The necessary infrastructure includes relevant educational facilities at the highest international standards, a supportive system of taxation, the availability of sufficient finance, and a comprehensive, efficiently-run health service.

Productivity

The measurement of the efficiency of an industrial or commercial process in terms of cash spent per unit of output or of service, or in terms of the labour-hours deployed per unit of output. The effectiveness of any investment in enhancing the efficiency of a firm can be measured in terms of the productivity of the unit before and after the investment has been made. Comparisons of productivity between apparently similar countries and firms frequently provides evidence of how the productivity of a process can be enhanced.

Quon ©

A product or service, usually branded, that gives the consumer access to protected *ik* that is inherent in the material object(s) or the act of service that the purchaser or renter acquires. A quon offers significant consumer guarantees, and is priced at a level that enables the supplier to meet the costs of maintaining the brand's exclusivity and its reputation with its users. The price is sanctioned by the desirability of the brand to users.

(Quon is pronounced 'kwon' with a short 'o' as in 'none' or 'gone')

Real estate

See real property.

Real property

The ownership of a specified location on the Earth's surface. The current market price of any parcel of land depends on three sets of factors:

- first, the degree of security of the ownership (how firmly the proofs of ownership would stand up, if subjected to a legal challenge).
- second, what crops, structures, or other assets occupy the site, what is the perceived current market price of the ownership of the plot and the existing premises (and/or mineral right, crops, amenities, etc.).
- third, when land is leased, the rental depends on the period of the lease and on the degree of security that the tenant is granted, and on the perceived valuation of the assets in relation to the distribution of human activities, the quonic utility of the structures or other amenities that occupy the site, and on the lessee's potential to change the use beneficially during the lease period.

The potential alternative use of the land and/or of the structures on it may greatly increase or diminish the market price of a parcel of land, any significant change that it derives from secondary *ik* such as gaining (or failing to gain) permission to change use.

Rent

The term used in classical political economy (c1800 to 1870) to mean the 'surplus' that is received by a producer – and, in particular, an agricultural producer – over and above the material costs of production and the cost of capital (which is the rate of interest that would have to be paid to borrow the money necessary to acquire the plant and consumables, including the wages advanced to labour). While Ricardo ascribed this to the 'natural and indestructible powers of the soil', Malthus understood that another form of 'rent' was also derived from the control of what is described as *ik* in this text.

SECURITISATION

A security is any keyn that is regarded by investors as a trustworthy asset. The development of the verb 'to securitise' during the nineteen-eighties characterises the rise of classes of asset that were to be a central feature of the bubble that collapsed in 2008. Traditionally, bankers (and British Building Societies and their foreign equivalents) received deposits from their customers on which they paid interest, to incentivise the customers to leave their money on deposit. The firm could then lend the money to borrowers who were judged to be likely to meet the payments of interest and repayments specified in their contracts. In the case of a mortgage on a house or other property, the loan was usually very secure because the lender had a contractual right to repossess the property if the borrower failed to meet the terms of the contract. In the free-for-all that followed the 'big bang' in 1986, 'wholesale' financial intermediaries offered to buy customers' debts from the 'retail' banks and building societies.

The individual customers carried on paying their agreed debts to the retail financial institution with which the loan was agreed, which handed on an agreed proportion of the inward cash-flow to the owner of the security by which the payments on the debt were transferred. The bank or building society received the cash sum that the wholesaler paid for the book of business that they had sold, which they could lend again, then they could dispose of the resulting inward cash flow in another securitisation. By these means, the available lending power of retail institutions was massively increased and a new wholesale market was established. Consequently, and to a considerable degree, firms like mortgage lenders no longer needed – or even wanted – retail depositors.

SOLVENCY

The capacity of a corporate entity or an individual to meet all legitimate demands for settlement of debts and other obligations at the due times.

SURPLUS VALUE

Marx's interpretation of circulating capital under the capitalist system, where it is all appropriated by the capitalist class for fixed investment in preference to allocating a fair proportion to raising general standards of living.

Systemic risk

A risk that is sufficiently great that it can result in the reputational destruction or the insolvency of a corporate entity or a person.

Transaction

An event in which an asset is bought or hired.

Warranted marcom ©

A marcom that is sold with a retailer's (or a wholesaler's) guarantee or warranty; a **neoquon** ©.

The End.